M

FAUX TITRE

375

Etudes de langue et littérature françaises
publiées sous la direction de

Keith Busby, †M.J. Freeman,
Sjef Houppermans et Paul Pelckmans

Material Figures
Political Economy, Commercial Culture, and the Aesthetic Sensibility of Charles Baudelaire

Margueritte S. Murphy

AMSTERDAM - NEW YORK, NY 2012

Cover illustration: Industrial Exhibition. Goldware models. Design by H. Catenacci. *Musée des Familles,* September 1855. Bibliothèque nationale de France.

Cover design: Inge Baeten

The paper on which this book is printed meets the requirements of 'ISO 9706: 1994, Information and documentation - Paper for documents - Requirements for permanence'.

Le papier sur lequel le présent ouvrage est imprimé remplit les prescriptions de 'ISO 9706: 1994, Information et documentation - Papier pour documents - Prescriptions pour la permanence'.

ISBN: 978-90-420-3526-3
E-Book ISBN: 978-94-012-0801-7
© Editions Rodopi B.V., Amsterdam - New York, NY 2012
Printed in The Netherlands

For Brian, Philip and Celia

Table of Contents

Acknowledgements

Like most academic books, this work was a labor of love. Still I have incurred many debts and credit is due. Among those who have kindly offered suggestions after hearing or reading sections of this study, I acknowledge with deep gratitude my Bentley colleagues Ruth Spack, Louis Iandoli, Marc Stern, and George Ellenbogen; conversations with Samir Dayal and Mike Frank have profoundly enriched my understanding of all things cultural. Over the years I have presented portions of this work at numerous conferences, and I am grateful for the comments and dialogues that ensued; I want to acknowledge in particular Interdisciplinary Nineteenth-Century Studies and the American Comparative Literature Association for offering stimulating venues in which to present this work. The wealth of knowledge and insights of colleagues in the Pembroke Center Seminar on the Culture of the Market at Brown University in 1999-2000 helped shape my understanding and approach to the nexus of market and aesthetic culture; I am especially grateful to Elizabeth Weed and Ellen Rooney, who welcomed us and led us in this year-long discussion, and to Christy Burns with whom I have continued these conversations now for a dozen years.

I thank Bentley University for its generous support of this research in the form of more than one sabbatical leave and two summer grants for research at the Bibliothèque nationale de France and the Archives Nationales in Paris.

Portions of some chapters have appeared previously as essays: "Commodity aesthetics: The industrial exhibitions of Paris, 1834-1844, reviewed," *Journal of European Studies* 40.1 (March 2010); "Pure Art, Pure Desire: Changing Definitions of *l'art pour l'art* from Kant to Gautier," *Studies in Romanticism* 47 (Summer/Fall 2008); and "The Critic as Cosmopolite: Baudelaire's International Sensibility and the Transformation of Viewer Subjectivity" in *Art and Life in Aestheticism: De-Humanizing and Re-Humanizing Art, the Artist, and the Artistic Receptor*, ed. Kelly Comfort, Palgrave Macmillan, 2008. I am grateful for permission to reprint this work.

Finally, my debts to my family are immense – to Philip and Celia for their patience when my attention was focused on the nineteenth century instead of the present moment and for their good humor when tagging along with their parents on the highways and byways of academic research. My most profound debt is to Brian Cooper – for his unstinting intellectual and emotional support from the very inception of this project, for our many conversations about the economic and the aesthetic, and his insights, and for his generosity and patience in reading drafts of this work. It would not have been the same without him.

Introduction

It has been a commonplace that the idea of artistic and literary
autonomy is fundamental to modernism and its understanding of the
relationship between art and modernity. Not only literary criticism and
history, but Pierre Bourdieu's sociological theory to explain the creation and functioning of the sphere of art and literature as an autonomous field relies on a conventional view of art and literature in modernity as defined by an ideology of social autonomy. But such views,
not just belief in art's autonomy, but the oft-told history of the idea,
are being challenged. Jacques Rancière, identifying an "aesthetic regime of the arts" emerging in the late eighteenth and nineteenth century, observes a contradiction constitutive of that regime – that art's
status as "an *autonomous form of life*" set up a contradiction between
its presumed autonomy and "its identification with a moment in life's
process of self-formation," hence inhabiting a heterogeneous temporality that complicates the notion of modernity associated with autonomous art (*Politics of Aesthetics 26*). Fredric Jameson, in *A Singular
Modernity*, argues that the doctrine of autonomy was not embraced by
major literary and artistic modernists, whose experiments remained
within the realm of semi-representation, but is a post-hoc fabrication

of the generation of critics after WWII, particularly the influential Clement Greenberg. While looking at very different moments in the development of the modern aesthetic, Rancière and Jameson both point to not only the contradictions inherent in the notion of full artistic autonomy, but also to a more heterogeneous condition historically for art as both idea and product.

Thus the concept of aesthetic autonomy has been questioned not only as a practical matter, but as a consensus theory among artists and writers. While the separation and growth of the arts and sciences as disciplines would seem to offer an epistemological and academic buttress for the persistence of this concept, scholarship in recent years has repeatedly challenged this very separation. Further, economic and aesthetic discourses in everyday life in the nineteenth century themselves intertwine, undermining the thesis of art's autonomy and the separation of the aesthetic from the economic sphere in the era of disciplinary separation and consolidation.

At the end of his book on modernity, Jameson offers the challenge: "If we can still read Baudelaire today with the requisite intensity, or so this hidden premise seems to run, we also ought to be able to reconstruct the various other nonaesthetic modernities afoot in his period" (212). But, as relationships between aesthetic and nonaesthetic modernities are complex, slippery, and necessarily dependent on a sense of what constitutes the aesthetic, itself an unstable category, the more telling reconstruction may concern these very relationships. They are intertwined and mutually determining relationships: the aesthetic and the economic, for instance, often drew on the same networks of ideas and ideologies, while experiences of the material were shaped by new aesthetic sensibilities.

The approach taken in this book is one allied with the new economic criticism: it challenges the canonical understanding of the status of art and literature in modernity by examining the relationship between political economy and aesthetics, the focus on aesthetics in the marketplace and exhibition hall, and Baudelaire's own consciousness of the interconnection of the economic and the aesthetic on many levels in ways that shaped his own understanding of art and literature in a new material world. Rather than simply a disaffected artist, Baudelaire is a spectator desirous of both art and goods whose sensibilities cast light not only on his own poetic texts, but also on transformations in the tenor of everyday life and habits of perception.

In recent years, new understandings of the intersections between economic and literary discourses and disciplines have involved framing ideology as practice, and at the same time, practice as ideology, as well as new ways to approach literary representations of economic matters.[1] One practice that is readily read as ideology is rhetoric itself, but any assumption of the identity of the two can be misleading. For words and phrases allied with dominant ideologies may become so powerful and ubiquitous as to be used by all classes, to become free-floating in the culture, and thereby shift in signification. On the other hand, when we consider material practice as ideology, or the unstated meaning(s) of experience in the phenomenal world, the relationships and oppositions between camps and disciplines become all the more complex, layered, and disguised.

A central aim of this book is to examine such a complex field in the play between figures for the economic and the aesthetic – not in nineteenth-century Britain, the focus of so much of the new economic criticism, but in nineteenth-century France. For France, too, was a significant site for the confrontation and confluence of theories of aesthetic and economic value. Indeed, ideological debates in the first half of the nineteenth century raged more hotly in France: French political economy had the Revolution as a touchstone of what happens when supply falls short and bread is a scarce commodity. Yet part of the allure of the free market is its association with *liberté*, that revolutionary principle; *l'art pour l'art* theories circulated among philosophers, writers, and artists confronted with the real threat of censorship of artistic and literary works, while utopian thinkers with aesthetic and economic agendas deplored art's withdrawal from the realm of the social, and the lack of care for workers in a market economy. So while French political economy was taking shape as a discipline that would support free-market liberalism, *l'art pour l'art* advocates, for all that they were opposed to *les économistes*, touted artistic *laissez-faire* and the artist as an autonomous actor. Ironically this nexus of discourses and practices led not only to the notions of aesthetic autonomy that underlie much of twentieth-century literary thought and practice, but

---

[1] Here I draw on Catherine Gallagher's account; she finds, among the developments leading to the new economic criticism, "reformulations of the concept of ideology" such that it is "seen to be less a set of explicit beliefs than a set of practices, which we repeat even while protesting against them" (*Body Economic* 1).

also to the authority of economic discourse today. This book attempts to give a fuller picture of the ambivalence and battles in the formation of distinctions between art and the social and economic spheres in France, of cries for artistic autonomy countered by calls for engagement of the arts with industry or with social problems, of economic models that depend on the aesthetic sensibilities of economic actors as well as the self-identification of artists and writers with laborers and consumers. These commonalities between economic and aesthetic discourses suggest homologous responses to uncertainty, social discord, an ideology of individualism, and succor taken in a world of goods in a post-revolutionary era. There is also a dynamic of mutual inflection as economic discourse enters the public sphere, ripe for parody, but also used less cynically as grounds for theories of social organization. At the same time, economic discourse relies on a tradition of imagining mechanisms of social harmony, of tracing orderly models which confirm its validity.

Thus even as these discourses developed into separate disciplines, the interdependence of disciplines and the spheres they describe continued to structure experience. In the nineteenth century aesthetics and economics, the discourses of art and literature and of the market, in tandem generated notions of economic and social order, of the model of the self-individuating and desiring subject of modernity, and of her/his relationship to a new world of objects – of art and industry – engendering not only new practices, but new modes of perception, new ontologies that ultimately led to the discovery of modernity in the Baudelairean mold. Thus, not only is the idea of the autonomy of art in dispute in the nineteenth century, but, I argue, a figure as central to later constructions of its ideology as Baudelaire actually undercut its tenets repeatedly during his career: from an early aesthetic based in the homology of economic and aesthetic systems to a disdain for *l'art pour l'art* materialism to a later awareness of the role of the cultural and economic context in giving shape and meaning to art and literature, incorporated into his aesthetic of the bizarre and his urban poetics.

Baudelaire, of course, played a role in his own time as an influential, highly provocative, and yet visionary art critic and any account of theories of modernity must recognize his even stronger legacy as the first poet of modernity, a legacy that has been part and parcel of the very definition of literature and of modernism during the century following his death. A reconsideration of Baudelaire's sensibility in the context of these times and climates of thought also entails a challenge to his characterization as the avatar of autonomy, the disillusioned dandy, a role model of social disaffect for subsequent generations of artists and writers, as argued by Bourdieu, especially in *The Rules of Art*. In line with the approach heralded by Walter Benjamin of considering Baudelaire as reflecting and reacting to his economic and material era, I consider Baudelaire's modernity within the political economy, economic rhetoric, and commercial culture of his day, how the aesthetics that he strove to articulate throughout his writings on art were not based on a belief in art's autonomy, but grew from an awareness of art's new public face, the power of the practices of display, and the convergence between the pleasures of art and the pleasures of other objects. By the same token, his poetry bears the traces of its embeddedness in a changing socio-economic environment, in which desire and pleasure as well as trauma and shock (the focus of many recent books on Baudelaire) take front stage; his literary language, his metaphors and allegories would make this new material world more available or "real."

This book begins by exploring the concurrence in early nineteenth-century political economy and aesthetic writing in France of particular paradigms of thought and their discursive circulation that evidence an ongoing relationship of mutual influence between economics and discourse about the arts, despite growth in disciplinary distinctions. The key concepts of harmony or equilibrium and utility dominate debates in both fields: they reveal significant commonalities in structures of thought and shared inquiries and concerns about human desire, social order, and the possibility of reconciling the two. Further, both political economy, and art and aesthetics confront the dilemma of spirit and matter, of establishing theoretical bases for a moral order in an increasingly secular society while countenancing the drive toward the material that was also a rejection of the sensed sterility of some strains of Enlightenment idealism. As a result French political economy and aesthetics converge in theorizing the emergence of an individual and sensate subjectivity in the first half of the nineteenth century.

The rhetoric of utility serves as an example of this *sub rosa* convergence. In political economy, debates over value came to define utility in a way that contradicted the understanding of utility and the utilitarian in everyday parlance, especially that used as a sort of straw man in polemics in the arts. Such a trajectory is evident in the development of the notion of "utility" in Jean-Baptiste Say's exchanges with Ricardo and Malthus, and in the further theorization of consumer desire by the econo-engineer Jules Dupuit in the 1840s. Dupuit, anticipating neoclassical economics, defines utility as drawing on desire as well as need, and his theories aim at the measurement of this desire, built on a calculus of sacrifice that he assumes the individual consumer necessarily engages in. In this, Dupuit defines an aspect of a modern subjectivity similar to that emerging in the poetics of Théophile Gautier and Baudelaire, despite the anti-utilitarian polemics of post-Kantian aesthetic thought in France apparent in the lectures of Victor Cousin and in Gautier's famous preface to *Mademoiselle de Maupin*. In Dupuit's analysis, "utility" for the economic agent may be as irrational and capricious as the delectation desired by the artistic sensibility described by Gautier.

While political economy began to focus more on consumer choice as important to value, new institutions for generating and shaping public discourse about this new material culture emerged. The second chapter concerns such discourse by examining press coverage of the annual art Salons and of the periodic industrial exhibitions during the July Monarchy. Both the Salons and the industrial exhibitions constituted major public spectacles, attracting large crowds and broad coverage in newspapers and journals. Reviews of the industrial exhibitions frequently appeared in the same publications that covered the art Salons, and often in the same section of the publication – in the *feuilleton* space. Thus such reviews, drawing in part on the model of art criticism, generate an aesthetic of the commodity; as the public was taught to view these objects produced by industry with an aesthetic eye, so their value relied on principles that were not merely economic. This chapter looks at the contours of this aesthetic – how reviewers produced interest in these objects on display – and the larger discussion of the relationship between the arts and industry. Both kinds of exhibitions generated thought and discussion about the visual and material, even though one venue explicitly featured aesthetic values, and the other showcased industrial production. Coverage of these exhibitions also reveals both the dominance of progress as an organizing paradigm for the historical consciousness in the early nineteenth century, and ambivalence about this paradigm, a countervailing sense of cultural loss and decline.

The latter chapters of the book propose a reconsideration of Baudelaire's art criticism and poetry in light of these discursive strains and the growing commodity culture. Chapter three concerns Baudelaire's first important work of aesthetic theory, *Le Salon de 1846,* which takes up the question of needs and desires as relevant to the enjoyment of art. In the dedication, "Au Bourgeois," he represents the need for art, socially and individually, to make the case for its support by the *haute bourgeoisie.* He invokes the "utility" of art, but a utility defined in terms of pleasure – not utilitarian in the commonplace sense of only fulfilling basic needs, but rather in the sense of subjective "jouissance" and "volupté." In describing the fulfillment of this need as something earned, Baudelaire employs the language of investment and return, echoing the idiom of political economy and its denizens in the business world. But elsewhere in *Le Salon de 1846*, he formulates this "jouissance" as a delicious sadness, even a "douleur morale" evoked, for instance, by the contrast of colors, especially of red and green. Perhaps most striking is his description of such "douleur" in the pleasure of viewing erotic prints in a section tangential to the coverage of the Salon, but related to the interrogation of desire and need, an experience of viewing in which bourgeois time and space are destabilized and displaced.

Thus, while formulating a theory that would define aesthetic value as residing not in content, but in more abstract, formal qualities, thereby undermining any vestigial notions of art's sacral or didactic purpose, he frames an appeal for art's utilitarian function within bourgeois society: one of sensual satisfaction and specifically of the fullest or most efficient use of leisure time. As abstraction for Baudelaire is a realization of the materiality and emotional tenor of the components of art, like color, art as abstraction offers the viewer a sensual and emotional experience. This consciousness on Baudelaire's part, his willingness to mold his aesthetic theory into an appeal to the bourgeois spectator, reveals an important aspect of his aesthetic posture: his early efforts to engage a bourgeois audience and to negotiate a position for artists and a function for art within the everyday praxis of bourgeois society, a function, that is, beyond the simple commodity status of the individual work. It is an argument that also invokes aesthetic harmony as a generator of social and individual equilibrium, thereby linking art to the well-being of the social body.

The public's reception and understanding of art continued to be a concern for Baudelaire. The next chapter addresses the development of particular threads in his art criticism after 1848 related to broader social, cultural, and economic questions: the evolution of his attitudes concerning taste, especially the transformation of the notion of the universal into a cosmopolitan ideal; his strong critique of the ideology of "progress" associated with nationalism; and finally the emergence of an exotic domestic in the aesthetic of the bizarre. Looking at both his positive program for a universal art as well as his disparagement of certain *idées fixes* of his day, we find a more complicated picture than the profile of Baudelaire as an *l'art pour l'art* aesthete would imply.

In the wake of 1848, Baudelaire allied himself with a more socially conscious art, an allegiance now often viewed as an aberration. His preface to Pierre Dupont's volume of workers' songs in 1851 is perhaps the most strident articulation of this position: he criticizes *l'art pour l'art* as ultimately sterile, having excluded "la morale, et souvent la passion." But in 1855, a major event of both high and popular culture, the first French *Exposition universelle*, affected Baudelaire's thinking about the aesthetic, by giving him rich, visual evidence of the relativity of beauty and of the narrowness of the Western ideal based in classical models. While most critics, including Gautier, approached the works in the Beaux-Arts part of the exhibition as representations of the national character of the participating states, measured against the standard of French art, which they assumed to be world-dominant, Baudelaire theorized a cosmopolitan aesthetic, engendered through productive contact with foreign cultures, and a transformed subjectivity in the viewer sympathetic to such art. Using a Chinese "product" (thereby blurring distinctions between productions of art and industry) as an example, he expands his notion of relative beauty in an explicit attack on Eurocentric aesthetic attitudes and proposes a perceptual approach to these foreign objects that entails not only a revolution in aesthetic assumptions, but a full transformation of viewer subjectivity. This new aesthetic lays the groundwork for the idea of modernity articulated more fully in *Le Peintre de la vie moderne,* both in the sections on Constantin Guys's illustrations of the Crimean War in which exotic subjects and intercultural contact are portrayed and in the everyday aesthetic of the "bizarre" of the streets of Paris. Thus Baudelaire maintains an awareness of the social and contextual that links his "socialist" aesthetic to his later theories of the bizarre as the beautiful as a culturally relative notion.

As has been long acknowledged, an aesthetic drawn from his art criticism informs his poetry profoundly, but in this Baudelaire strives for a fully sensual aesthetic, which drives him toward the material and draws him into the dilemma of spirit and matter in a new key. The sensate represents aesthetic vitality for him, but also a problematic materialism. The sphere of the visual and material early on is informed by art and its display whereas in his last works, such as *Le Spleen de Paris*, urban display, or the scenes of everyday life in the French capital, embody the material and mediate between the aesthetic and the social in an economy of disproportion between rich (or bourgeois) and poor. Famously Baudelaire constructs the aesthetic of modernity through this urban consciousness informed nonetheless by the practice of viewing works of art and theorizing that viewing.

The final two chapters focus on the interplay of the aesthetic, the social, and the material in Baudelaire's verse and prose poetry. Here I draw on Rancière's understanding of the productivity embodied in word and figure in the nineteenth century, a making-real, through art and literature that Baudelaire's aspirations and career exemplify. Chapter five concerns *Les Fleurs du mal* and Baudelaire's drive towards an ever more sensate yet transcendent poetic experience. From early in his career, painting – the phenomenal realm of color and visual images – serves as a model for this creative endeavor, while sculpture is less congenial given its association with a neoclassical aesthetic; my discussion begins with poems that explore these alternatives to give a sense of the profile of creativity that inspired him, and those he rejected. Yet in many poems in *Les Fleurs du Mal* his desire to incorporate the sensate into his verse results in the use and abuse of objects of desire, especially evident in his tropes for women and their body parts, resulting at the least in a partial reification of these women. Baudelaire's misogyny, however, redounds on himself, as the *non-moi* becomes entangled with the *moi*. This crisis of subjectivity erupts in his portrayal of both human relationships and the relationship of the human subject with the inorganic, which illuminates the consumer desire theorized by political economists. In his poetry figurative language creates objects of desire and despair; metaphor makes the abstract material. Yet such striving is tempered by an awareness of the baseness of the merely material, of the emptiness of the sensate bereft of spiritual or moral heft.

The last chapter treats Baudelaire's *Petits poèmes en prose* or *Le Spleen de Paris* as his fullest exploration of the relationship between the human and material realms, and his sharpest indictment of viewing that does not *see*. This collection is forward-looking: the first important work in a new genre, the prose poem, and a fragmented a chronicle of "modern life." Baudelaire represents here the failure of social exchange and equilibrium among classes, mediated by a failure of things as tokens of social exchange. Such social dysfunction contrasts the growing draw and significance of "things" for the self-fashioning poet of modernity; having lost belief in the socio-economic harmonies of *Le Salon de 1846*, he nonetheless continues his interrogation of the desiring self. He finds some promise for both class mediation and a creative engagement with things in the realm of toys in an unsentimental portrayal of children's play as the freest form of creativity.

The approach of this book, then, is both discursive and materialist. An investigation of the interrelationships between aesthetics and political economy concerns questions of discipline formation and the construction of knowledge during that era; the outcomes of those interrelationships are still potent in the discourses of economics and art today. Further, such discourses had a broader impact, shaping everyday knowledge and practices. They surface, for instance, in the public understanding of exhibitions, of both art and industry, as evidenced in newspaper and magazine reviews; they circulate as tropes, half-truths, and types, and enter into the construction of needs and desires. In other words, such discourses both arise from and are transformed by material experience, or experience of the material. Benjamin's materialist approach is a model in his exegesis of Baudelaire's motifs as emblematic of the turn to modernity and his noticing of transformations in everyday life that remake the consciousness of the century into phantasmagoria and nightmare. This vein of Benjamin's critical materialism also informs the new attention to the power of "things" to represent or to resist representation, the interest in "thing theory" that Bill Brown has spearheaded. The fast-growing consumer markets coupled with the advent of a display regime with the construction of the arcades, the periodic industrial exhibitions from 1798 onwards, the annual Salons and their coverage in the press heightened the fascination with "things" in nineteenth-century France. The hold that "things" have on the public's imagination becomes evident in the coverage of the industrial, then universal exhibitions. Such a fascination infects Baudelaire's poetry and prose: his critical prose as he seeks to define an aesthetic that captures the sensate thrill produced by the most potent art; his poetry in its material figures of desire and imaginary of satiation.

Bourdieu's sociological theory to explain the creation and functioning of the sphere of art and literature as an autonomous field, as articulated in *The Rules of Art: Genesis and Structure of the Literary Field* and other writings, is also relevant to understanding Baudelaire's critical prose. Although Bourdieu's analysis relies on a conventional view of art and literature in modernity as defined by an ideology of social autonomy, his explanation of how this principle came to dominate the fields of art and literature, and how the arts' autonomy is sustained through a symbolic economy that pays off in the long term sheds light on the relationships between work or text and context that explicitly shuns a direct, reflecting (to use Bourdieu's own term) relationship. Rancière astutely critiques Bourdieu's approach for a "disavowed or hidden Platonism" which is "structural" for sociology; it assumes that the "ethos" of a station defines the "ethos" of what that individual knows, that, for instance, the worker cannot enjoy or "think" an aesthetic experience that is disconnected from what his hands produce ("Aesthetic Dimension" 16). Yet Bourdieu's structure is useful for understanding public productions that must play a part in the symbolic economy; it helps us describe and analyze the positioning of writers and artists within their field of production, to capture their potential trajectories as artists given the camps and polemics of the day, both among writers and artists, and within the broader discursive realms in society. This theoretical framework helps us see more clearly the thrust and resonance of choices made by writers and artists, why they felt compelled to engage the field in certain terms and how their works were experienced by their contemporaries. Baudelaire himself engaged in strategic positioning within the field of literary production, reacting to the polemics of the day and changes in the field; the signature ironies in his writing are testimony to the complicated and sometimes mercurial positions that he takes within the broader debates of his time. At the same time, Bourdieu's representation of Baudelaire's work and position within this field is reductive in that it is too beholden to the figure that he came to represent for the next generation of artists, and in the dominant twentieth-century reading of modernity.

Rancière attacks theories of aesthetic modernism, offering instead a less monolithic account of the changes in the status of the literary and of art in the nineteenth century. Interested in the ties between writing and democracy, he describes a "distribution of the sensible" ("le partage du sensible") within which literary language since Romanticism has a special function: he contends that the Romantic age did not deem language autotelic, but "actually plunged language into the materiality of the traits by which the historical and social world becomes visible to itself, be it in the form of the silent language of things or the coded language of images" (*Politics of Aesthetics* 36). (I take up this formulation at greater length in chapter five.) Rancière's larger concern is to demonstrate how what he calls the "aesthetic regime" made fact-based and fiction-based logics or discourses interdependent, even giving priority to fiction as producing the means of writing and comprehending history. The reviews and publicity surrounding the industrial exhibitions offer evidence of how romantic figures inform the everyday reading of the world, the imagining of experiential heights.

Further, if we look at Baudelaire's critical enterprise in his writings on visual art – his ongoing interrogation of existing aesthetic systems and his own fashioning of a new aesthetic – we find such a striving after materiality through language, a desire to capture and reproduce the impact of visual art in language, and a resistance against an aesthetic that moves beauty away from the human. In a way, Baudelaire exemplifies the "emancipated spectator," to borrow a term from Rancière: he describes and advocates a mode of viewing that is active, creative in its manipulation of the visual experience, and even transformative. Reception is an action at times more fully creative than many attempts to produce or create, a lament and theme in many of Baudelaire's poems, including those on ennui, a problem of stagnation which is ironically the inspiration of some of his most powerful works. In *Les Fleurs du Mal* and in *Le Spleen de Paris*, language makes visible the traits of the historical and social world in a romantic or post-romantic age, a world that emerges in the "silent language of things" (to echo Rancière) – in the streets, cafés, and garrets of Paris, but also across the very material body of his lover, where desire for her materializes as goods to be enjoyed and consumed. Through his desire to forge a poetics that would realize a modern world in all its beauties and horrors, Baudelaire also helps us understand the constructions that shaped the experience of the spectator of art and consumer goods, an experience of absorption in the fictions of nineteenth-century display spaces.

I

Equilibrium and Utility: Measures of Desire

utility . . . that difficult word
– David Ricardo, in a letter to Jean-Baptiste Say, 18 August 1815

The birth of aesthetics and political economy out of a single area of inquiry, moral philosophy, has received much attention in recent years. No longer is it a truism that the aesthetic is the anti-economic. As John Guillory shows in *Cultural Capital: The Problem of Literary Canon Formation*, "a consideration of the texts, pretexts, and contexts of Adam Smith and Kant reveals an original indistinction of aesthetics and political economy *as discourses.*" The two fields arose out of a single area of inquiry, moral philosophy, but were "separated at birth" (302-3). A reappraisal of the relationship between aesthetics and political economy in the eighteenth and nineteenth century has been part of the "seemingly tidal wave of scholarship investigating the relations among literature, culture, and economics," to quote Mark Osteen and Martha Woodmansee from their comprehensive overview of the "new economic criticism."[1]

But much of this scholarship has focused on Great Britain, while less attention has been paid to what happens in France, the birthplace of *l'art pour l'art*, but also a site of development for the new discipline of political economy, influenced by the work of Smith, yet indebted to eighteenth-century French physiocrats. The relationship

---

[1] Important work in this area includes Patrick Brantlinger, *Fictions of State: Culture and Credit in Britain, 1694-1994*, Mary Poovey, *A History of the Modern Fact: Problems of Knowledge in the Sciences of Wealth and Society* and *Genres of the Credit Economy: Mediating Value in Eighteenth- and Nineteenth-Century Britain*, Regenia Gagnier, *The Insatiability of Human Wants: Economics and Aesthetics in Market Society*, Philip Connell, *Romanticism, Economics and the Question of "Culture"*, Gordon Bigelow, *Fiction, Famine, and the Rise of Economics in Victorian Britain and Ireland*, and Catherine Gallagher, *The Body Economic: Life, Death, and Sensation in Political Economy and the Victorian Novel*, to name only a few.

between these two emerging fields in France is special in a number of ways and warrants attention. First of all, it goes without saying that the history of the period during which aesthetics and political economy emerged as separate areas of knowledge – the late eighteenth and early nineteenth century – was especially fraught with personal and political trauma for the French and anxiety about the nature and stability of France as a social and political entity. The experience, then memory of the French Revolution, the Terror, the ascendancy of Napoléon Bonaparte, the Napoleonic Wars, the Restoration and its demise in the Revolution of 1830, inaugurating the July Monarchy and finally its overthrow in 1848, lent all discourse a particular ideological edge, an awareness of its significance and of consequences that might be only too concrete (official censorship is only the most obvious of unwelcome responses).[2] As Richard Terdiman has argued, saturation by discourse distinguishes the modern period (*Discourse/ Counter-Discourse* 43) and in France tensions between dominant and subversive discourses were strong and "bore particularly complex disguises" (*Discourse/Counter-Discourse* 67-68). Secondly, while the British led the French in manufacturing and industrialization, the culture of the market in France was well-established and expanding with the early building of the arcades, the periodic industrial exhibitions from 1798 on, and the reputation of France, particularly Paris, as a fashion and luxury goods center. Finally, the expansion of the public sphere through the proliferation of newspapers and magazines, the central role of the press in the political and cultural life of the capital, and the strength of the public sphere of art, fostered and sustained by the annual Salons held in the Louvre, with broad attendance and wide coverage in the press, all encouraged circulation of aesthetic and economic ideas.

Thus the political, social, material, and affective climate in France during these decades was special, and so the impact of ideas in political economy, imported from Great Britain, and of new aesthetic values and models, imported from Germany, necessarily underwent particular transmutations. This chapter focuses on two notions with

---

[2] As one example of a concrete and explicit constraint imposed on the specific discourses examined in this chapter, in 1803 under Napoléon, the entire field of political economy was attacked when the Class of Moral and Political Sciences was suppressed with the less political Académie des Belles Lettres put in its place at the Institut de France (Ingrao and Israel 58).

widespread currency in the early decades of the nineteenth century central to the development of political economy and of aesthetics: equilibrium and utility. The first is often asserted or assumed for the working of markets, and is rarely contested, but it harks back to eighteenth-century conceptions of social harmony modeled on order in the work of art as well as concepts of natural order derived from the physical and biological sciences. The second is a contested, albeit fundamental notion within French political economy, while a far less theorized understanding of utility is central to the negation at the core of aesthetics' own self-definition. In other words, the discourse of aesthetics assigns a stability to "utility" in order to mark its own difference yet such stability is absent within the opposing discipline of political economy. By the 1840's, the econo-engineer, Jules Dupuit, in seeking to discover a means of measuring utility, redefines it in a way that dovetails with conceptions of subjective desire emerging in the late Romantic discourse of writers like Théophile Gautier and Charles Baudelaire.

These words, "equilibrium" and "utility," are "keywords" in Raymond Williams' sense: "significant, binding words in certain activities and their interpretation; . . . significant, indicative words in certain forms of thought. Certain uses bound together certain ways of seeing culture and society, not least in these two most general words. Certain other uses seemed to me to open up issues and problems, in the same general area, of which we all needed to be very much more conscious" (15).[3] Within disciplines, especially those in the process of consolidating thought and establishing foundational principles, such keywords perform a "binding" function by providing a common vocabulary, yet they may as easily open up disciplinary fissures. Their very definition may be put in question as the object of knowledge named by the keyword is rethought and disputed. Such was the case with

---

[3] Williams does take up the fate of "utility" under his entry, "Utilitarian." He notes the nineteenth-century division of the "longstanding practice of using things to make other things" into "art" and "utility" (328). As for the ultimate fate of the word within economics, he laments "the theoretical and practical specialization of *utility* to the terms of capitalist production, and especially by the translation of 'the greatest happiness of the greatest number' into the terms of the organized *market* (in its increasingly abstract C19 [nineteenth-century] sense), which was taken to be the mechanism for regulating this ultimate purpose. *Utility*, once a critical concept, became, in this context, at once ratifying and demeaning, and other terms had to be found to assert the principle of most people's happiness" (329).

"utility" in economic discourse in the first part of the nineteenth century.

While such keywords figure critically in specialist vocabularies, they are often widely used in quotidian discourses in ways that diverge markedly from the specialist meaning(s). In everyday use they are charged; they echo central societal concerns and conflicts, while marking repeatedly instantiations of such concerns. How they are used often reveals the politics, values, and class allegiances of the speaker or writer. Undoubtedly many significant and charged keywords circulated in post-revolutionary France, including the famous triad *liberté, égalité, et fraternité*. I focus on these particular terms – on equilibrium (and harmony) and on utility – because they are crucial to debates within both political economy and aesthetics with trajectories that illustrate the processes of discipline formation in the first half of the nineteenth century, and because, in their inflection within disciplinary debates, we can detect the pressure of extradisciplinary forces. Susan Buck-Morss reminds us:

> The discovery of the economy was also its invention. As Foucault told us (and neo-Kantians long before him), every new science creates its object. The great marvel is that once a scientific object is "discovered" (invented), it takes on agency. The economy is now seen to act in the world; it causes events, creates effects. (439-40)

It is also worth remembering that the "world" pushes back; that is, events and nonspecialist discourses, debates and patterns of usage in the public sphere also shape the discipline as it develops. The same is true for the aesthetic if we consider the spread of awareness of aesthetic principles through public lectures (for instance, Victor Cousin's "eclectic" philosophy and the tenet of the good, the true, and the beautiful) and the diffusion of these tenets to other spheres: the political, social, moral, and commercial. This dialectic is crucial to understanding more fully disciplinary development in the first half of the nineteenth century as the modern sense of the economy and of art were being "invented." Within the new discipline of political economy Smith's work carries an authority in France, allowing nineteenth-century economists to refute their forebears, the Physiocrats, and to redefine the central terms of the debate. But, as we shall see, when these initial terms constitute a near impasse for subsequent thinkers, the discipline, by defining, for instance, "utility" in contradistinction to everyday usage, and by drawing on examples from everyday life is being shaped, in effect, by extradisciplinary discourses and perceptions.

It is tempting, given much current concern that all cultural phenomena are now framed in terms of the economic, to discover the origin of this trend in the early nineteenth century, but on closer examination, we find that aesthetics and economics continued to mutually inflect one another well into the nineteenth century. Indeed, one might make the case that aesthetics did a better job of walling off economic discourse than the reverse, that the discourse of economics, in attempting to sketch and theorize the economy as perfectly functioning machine, relies on an underlying aesthetic. Yet it is also undeniable that the great challenge to art in terms of its own self-definition is the valuation imposed from outside by the market. But beyond tensions between the aesthetic and the economic, explicit or latent, is the broader resonance of these discourses for a society in the midst of, and for many, fearful of radical change. They work as palliatives, as prescriptions for stability, and as promises for a more beautiful and more comfortable future.

Equilibrium

The idea of equilibrium as a key explanatory device for the ideal functioning of society was well established already in eighteenth-century France, buttressed by analogies drawn from the physical and biological sciences. As Bruna Ingrao and Giorgio Israel show in *The Invisible Hand: Economic Equilibrium in the History of Science*, Newtonian physics served as a model for theories of social harmony in the French Enlightenment rejection of Cartesian paradigms. Montesquieu's *Esprit des Lois* employs an analogy with statics to conceptualize a social equilibrium which would guarantee political freedom in a social body composed of different forces and interests (38-39). The Physiocrats sought to express the laws governing human behavior in mathematical form; Quesnay's *Tableau économique* was "the first attempt to provide both a general and a quantitatively precise representation of the flows of production and exchange in an economic system" influenced by Quesnay's knowledge of the circulation of the blood (44-45). Turgot compared the functioning of markets to fluid dynamics, influencing the great British economists, explicitly referring to "equilibrium" in his "Letter to Hume" (46) and both Turgot and Condorcet considered problems of disequilibrium (Rothschild 76-77). Smith never mentions "equilibrium" explicitly, but his notion of "natural price" towards which the prices of all commodities gravitate relies on an equilibrium mechanism (Milgate 105-6). Smith's theory, of course, grew out of eighteenth-century British moral philosophy which had confronted the "problem of describing the order, harmony, or proportion" of civil society, and chose to represent this order as analogous to the "order, proportion, or harmony of a work of art, or any object of beauty, ... an order of the sensible rather than the intelligible," as Guillory explains (305). Thus, in the eighteenth century, the aesthetic and the scientific were already yoked in empirically-based models of social order.

According to Ingrao and Israel, it was the work of Nicolas-François Canard which included "the first explicit formulation of the concept of economic equilibrium . . ., together with a dynamic treatment of the same" (67). In 1799, the Class of Moral and Political Sciences of the Institut de France posed the following essay question: "Is it true that in an agricultural country every kind of tax is ultimately borne by the landowner, and, if so, do indirect taxes also fall upon him with an increased burden?" (Ingrao and Israel 67). Canard's work, published in 1801 as *Principes d'Economie politique*, won the prize. In it he argues that an equilibrium mechanism inevitably spreads out and equalizes any tax burden, a refutation of the Physiocratic doctrine that landowners alone should be taxed. The compass of the work is much broader than the tax question, however. Canard employs analogies throughout from both the circulatory system and statics to describe economic processes and finds an equilibrium mechanism in nearly every aspect of economic life that he analyzes.

Following Smith, Canard asserts that labor, not land, is the source of wealth, and he divides labor into three branches, and thereby, three sources of income: landed income ("rente foncière"), industrial income ("rente industrielle"), and income on moveable property ("rente mobilière"), that is, resulting from commerce or interest (11-12).[4] He describes the relationship among these three sources of income as an equilibrium, maintained through competition (14). Canard sees the same equilibrium as a factor in personal decision-making: for instance, competitive forces will steer fathers when choosing a trade for

---

[4] See, too, Ingrao and Israel 68.

their sons. And Canard insists on the importance of the principle of equilibrium to political economy: "c'est à ce principe que se ramènent toutes les questions de cette science importante" (15).

Canard discerns a like equilibrium between income and consumption, drawing an analogy to the relationship of arteries and veins in the blood system (20). In conceptualizing the determination of price, he turns to statics for an analogy: "Cette équation, que j'appellerai *équation des déterminations*, exprime l'égalité *des momens de deux forces opposées*, qui se font équilibre. C'est le principe de l'équilibre de ces deux forces que se rapporte toute la théorie de l'économie politique, comme c'est au principe de l'équilibre du levier, que se rapporte toute la statique" (30-31). Relations among sovereign states, too, are equilibrated, both through trade and in terms of national strength and population: "Tous les états réagissent les uns contre les autres, avec un effort qui les tient respectivement en équilibre: c'est cette réaction continuelle qui constitue un état et en forme un être politique" (125). In other words, a nation's own definition, indeed, its very existence, depends on a competitive tension with other states.

Canard's faith in beneficial and necessary equilibration is great. But equilibrium has its limits. For instance, human progress is due to surplus labor by the economic subject for if the desire for immediate "jouissance" were always in equilibrium with work, the state of things would always remain the same (another Smithian notion) (87).[5] Thus work outweighs actual enjoyment, and surplus labor feeds the economy as the economic subject becomes a sort of Goethean striver. And there is the problem of the time of equilibration. In answering the question posed by the Class of Moral and Political Sciences, Canard

---

[5] Christopher Herbert in *Culture and Anomie: Ethnographic Imagination in the Nineteenth Century* points out that in Smith's *The Wealth of Nations* "this compulsion acts to maintain a 'natural' state of equilibrium, rushing capital, for instance, into any enterprise where profit margins are abnormally high, and through competition, adjusting these margins so as to restore prices to their natural 'center of repose and continuance.'" Certainly this adjustment is a feature of Canard's Smith-influenced system as well. Herbert goes on to comment on the "significant ambiguities" surrounding "Smith's identification of unrestrained expansion and progress with repose and equilibrium," including the futility of the economic actor in desiring relative advantage (100-101). Smith, of course, envisions a general progress in well-being where self-interested economic actors inadvertently aid others, as Herbert acknowledges. By the same token, a whole generation aspiring to be new Napoleons by definition cannot succeed, although the culture as a whole may benefit from their literary and artistic furor, or new levels of productivity.

explains how the burden of any tax is distributed throughout the economy. But he does see that, with new taxes, there is necessarily a period of adjustment with consequent unemployment and poverty in some sectors. As a result, he is opposed to new taxes, rather than to taxation in general. To describe this process of adjustment, he borrows a term from mechanics: friction ("frottement"). During the period of "friction," the tax is "disastrous": mixing mechanics with circulatory systems – the friction damages most the outer, weakest branches of the circulatory system – he explains that those who were earning just enough to survive in "la branche imposée, et qui ne peuvent plus s'attache à une autre branche, se voient retrancher une partie de la nourriture nécessaire à leur existence, et périssent de besoin et de misère" (182). But, since those who die will not be replaced in the same proportion, the tax will eventually be incorporated into a new equilibrium.

Yet this is a version of the "short run/long run" problem that persisted in economic thought well beyond the advent of neoclassicism into the twentieth-century work of W. Beveridge and J.M. Keynes as William Dixon and David Wilson explain: "the short-run situation, informing how people are disposed to act, effectively determines the long run" (86).

Only by circumscribing problems of disequilibrium temporally and discounting their enduring effect is Canard able to sketch a model of social harmony where the opposing interests are not only reconciled, but opposition provides a healthful tension in economic life and international relations. And the desirability of such models was intense in post-revolutionary France. As Evelyn Forget notes, concerning Jean-Baptiste Say's fear of disequilibrium trade as a prescription for social disorder, "on the day that the Bastille fell, the price of bread was at its highest level for sixty years" (138). The idea of market equilibrium seemed to offer a blueprint for social stability and was virtually canonical in political economy from the beginning of the nineteenth century onwards.[6] Furthermore, as political economy sought to establish itself as a science, tropes borrowed from physics and biology served to validate this status.

---

[6] Forget argues that Say did not accept Smith's belief in a broadly-defined "spontaneous order," but does endorse the idea of a self-ordering mechanism in the marketplace ("Jean-Baptiste Say and Spontaneous Order").

While the word "equilibrium" may appear rarely in aesthetic discourse, models for harmonizing difference were everywhere. Indeed, one "classic" characterization of the shift from classic to romantic is of a shift from static models of harmony to dynamic ones, which are constantly subsuming difference. In the aftermath of the French Revolution and the Napoleonic wars, the desire of liberals to achieve social harmony without sacrificing individual freedoms drove aesthetic as well as political and economic thought. So, while the most obvious effect of economic discourse on aesthetic debate is Art's utter rejection of it, under the rallying cry of *l'art pour l'art,* homologies between Romantic conceptions of aesthetic harmony– aesthetics based on the dynamic reconciliation of contraries – and the social harmony of early equilibrium theory suggest both an implied aesthetic in political economy and a potential template for social harmony within Romantic theories of art. Both certainly were fueled by an ongoing fear of social and political instability. Meanwhile, the discourse of *liberté,* a legacy of the Revolution, powerfully influenced and connected in contradictory configurations economic, political, and artistic thought.

Victor Cousin's lectures are a useful starting point in mapping public discourse about art given his role as a popularizer of Kantian philosophy and his public stature. In his 1817-1818 lectures on the beautiful we find a typically Romantic "harmony of contraries" formulation. Cousin invokes this aesthetic when he argues poetry's superior position among the arts, since poetry is most expressive of thought. This is curious since verbal art constitutes the medium in which discord or *dissent* might be most clearly articulated. Yet such discord becomes a part of the apparatus of concord:

> La parole humaine, idéalisé par la poésie, a la profondeur et l'éclat de la note musicale, mais elle est lumineuse autant que pathétique; elle parle à l'esprit comme au cœur; elle est en cela inimitable et inaccessible qu'elle réunit en elle tous les extrêmes et tous les contraires, dans une harmonie qui redouble leur effet réciproque, et où tour à tour comparaissent et se développent toutes les images, tous les sentiments, toutes les idées, toutes les facultés humaines, tous les replis de l'âme, toutes les faces des choses, tous les mondes réels et tous les mondes intelligibles! (203)

While vaunting poetry's superiority to music which it resembles in its affect, Cousin trumps poetry's appeal to the intellect with its music. Harmony of extremes, of contraries, of difference : thus this aesthetic subsumes not only "terrible" and "irregular" beauties (156) to distinguish it from the symmetrical, ordered harmonies of neoclassicism, but also subsumes just about everything else imaginable within an architecture of formal harmony. In fact, subsumption of just about everything characterizes the school of modern philosophy that Cousin promotes: eclecticism, which takes only the "true" from past schools in a "spirit of conciliation" (13).

Another perhaps even more famous and influential articulation of the "harmony of contraries" aesthetic appears in Victor Hugo's preface to *Cromwell* of 1827. Here Hugo gave currency to the notion of the "grotesque" which serves as contrast to the beautiful, but the presence of the two in "l'harmonie des contraires" marks the work as partaking of the dual character of Christianity: body and soul; humanity and divinity. Such dualities characterize the modern era for Hugo. Castigating the classical ideal of beauty as limited, system-driven, and ultimately conventional, Hugo defends the "harmony of contraries" aesthetic on the grounds of realism. This aesthetic also includes formal contraries, as Hugo promotes "le drame romantique" as both comedy and tragedy, hence an instance of the "mélange des genres" (416-25 passim). Hugo, more so than Cousin, articulates a creed for the Romantic generation, and like Cousin, sees his aesthetic as a liberation from neoclassical strictures; much of the "Préface" is an assault on two of the three unities of classical theatre within a broader call for freedom for art, a revolution against the rules and systems of the previous century.

Why not simply call for realism, for the representation of the grotesque without appealing to the overarching harmony that would balance it against its opposite? Is harmony a last legacy of classical values? Perhaps, but it also has utopian overtones, that opposition may be transformed into a fuller synthesis. Hugo generates a string of opposing terms: ugly/beautiful; deformed/graceful; grotesque/sublime; evil/good; dark/light (416).[7] He even touches on the relationship between rich and poor in his invocation of Christian charity, characteristic of the modern era as opposed to antiquity:

> le cœur de l'homme, jusqu'alors engourdi par des cultes purement hiérarchiques et sacerdotaux, pouvait-il ne pas s'éveiller et sentir germer en lui quelque faculté

---

[7] Hugo speaks of "le beau antique" and "le sublime modern"; thus the grotesque serves as a foil for the sublime rather than the beautiful in the modern era.

inattendue, au souffle d'une religion humaine parce qu'elle est divine, d'une religion qui fait de la prière du pauvre la richesse du riche, d'une religion d'égalité, de liberté, de charité?" (414-15).

With the rich dependent on the poor in that their salvation depends on works of charity, this Christian equilibrium is rhetorically linked to a democratic order and hallowed principles of the French Revolution. Thus, "harmony" serves as a formal principle of mediation between these opposing qualities, values, and groups, an aesthetic solution to moral and social discord.

Utopian models of social harmony abound in the 1830's and 1840's. Followers of Henri Saint-Simon and Charles Fourier promoted systems that promised to harmonize individual interests with the general social good.[8] Romantic socialists during the July Monarchy like Pierre Leroux, Simon Ganneau, Abbé Alphonse-Louis Constant, and Louis-Jean Baptiste de Tourreil used the figure of the androgyne to represent the unity of opposites that their utopian visions of social harmony promised (Andrews). In the 1840's, the aspiration towards and the idiom of social, natural, and cosmic harmony were shared by former Saint-Simonians like Leroux and Jean Reynaud, Christian Socialists like Felicité de Lamennais, romantic novelists like Hugo, George Sand, and Eugène Sue, the historians Jules Michelet and Edgar Quinet, and the poet Béranger (Mitzman 663). Some thinkers specifically critiqued the harmonizing mechanisms of political economy while preserving the ideal of social harmony. In his influential *Système des contradictions économiques, ou, Philosophie de la misère* (1846), Pierre-Joseph Proudhon attacked political economy for its support of the status quo in its equilibria; these "economic contradictions," he charged, require untenable trade-offs: "the increase of misery in the present state of society is parallel and equal to the increase of wealth – which completely annuls the merits of political economy" (72). Proudhon advocates a different harmonizing mechanism in his model for the critical analysis of competing schools of thought, specifically aiming to harmonize the opposition between political economy and socialism of the day through a dialectic:

---

[8] Fourier wanted a "social order so conceived that the gratification of individual desire always served to promote the common good" (Beecher 239-40). See, too, Lynn Sharp, esp. 353-55.

it is, I say, a fact of science that every antagonism, whether in Nature or in ideas, is resolvable in a more general fact or in a complex formula, which harmonizes the opposing factors by absorbing them, so to speak in each other. Can we not, then, men of common sense, while awaiting the solution which the future will undoubtedly bring forth, prepare ourselves for this great transition by an analysis of the struggling powers, as well as their positive and negative qualities? (51)[9]

In 1848, in response to critiques like Proudhon's and in the press of the revolutionary moment, Frédéric Bastiat, the political economist and economic journalist, seized upon "harmony" to explain both the underlying mechanism and promise of an unfettered economy.[10] Bastiat's unfinished magnum opus, *Economic Harmonies*, purports to reveal providential and natural "harmonies" in the system of capitalism that would lead to brotherhood, community, and the general improvement of the lot and character of humanity if the market is allowed free rein (313). His use of the word, "harmony," derives from the long history in political economy of framing the workings of the economy as a finely-tuned mechanism, as described earlier in this chapter.[11] But his employment of the term is also meant to refute "socialists'" views of human society that see "men's interests" as

---

[9] See Mary B. Allen on the difference between Proudhon's dialectic as a social solution based on contract and Marx's:

> The social collectivity is thus a real union of differences, maintaining and balancing their contradiction, and not an artificial fusion in which differences are absorbed and disappear. This is the application of Proudhon's doctrine of 'equilibrium' as opposed to the Hegelian and Marxian doctrine of 'synthesis.' In politics the equilibrium is furnished by the contract, which is an explicit agreement between individuals, freely entered into and poles apart from the implicit collective contract, of which government becomes the pinnacle and agency of enforcement. (4-5)

[10] His dedicatory preface, "To the Youth of France," makes explicit reference to "our present ills of systematic obstructionism, parliamentary bickering, street insurrections, revolutions, crises, factions, wild notions, demands advanced by all men to govern under all possible forms, new systems, as dangerous as they are absurd, which teach the people to look to the government for everything" (xxxvi).
[11] Jörg Guido Hülsmann points more specifically to the influence of Charles Dunoyer and other French economists "who blended Quesnay's harmony doctrine with a new doctrine of class antagonism, namely, the antagonism of the political class and the industrial class," seeing this characterization of class conflict as a difference from Ricardo, Saint-Simon, and Marx who found antagonisms in the free market, rather than confined to the political sphere (56, n. 4).

"fundamentally antagonistic" and hence warranting government intervention or other forms of social structuring (xxiv).

First of all, Bastiat sees all economic principles as evidence of a vast divinely ordained mechanism, and thus harmonious on a theological basis. In this regard, his argument harks back to eighteenth-century providentialism, but also responds to the religious overtones of Christian socialism of his own time. Like many political economists, he frequently uses analogies from physics and biology to explain the naturalness of the system he is merely describing. How does this system work? For instance, the relationship between human-kind and nature is harmonious since human ingenuity learns to harness natural resources, and these technological improvements tend towards ever-increasing wellbeing for individuals:

> Here, then, is the harmonious law that can be expressed thus:
> Through labor the action of man is combined with the action of Nature.
> From this co-operation utility results.
> Each individual takes from the general store of utility in proportion to the services that he renders—in the last analysis, then in proportion to the utility he himself represents. (170)

What is unusual about this characterization is that what some would see as disruption of the harmony of nature – industrialization and its new technologies – Bastiat sees as the making available of nature's "gratuitous utility" to mitigate the "onerous utility" created through human labor. Through new technologies such as the steam engine and through the division of labor, commodities far greater than those that any single individual could create are put within reach of a growing segment of the populace.

His system, like Smith's, relies on self-interest as a motive force, and thus "property," the reward of striving, is crucial to the system and is in fact simply the embodiment of "services" rendered by the individual. On the question of "property," an especially controversial issue of the time, he is most adamant in his arguments against both political economists and socialists. He takes to task political economists for laying the ground for socialists' attacks by confusing utility – which includes the products and processes generated by Nature – with value, a measure of human services, according to his definition. Property, then, is the legacy of services previously rendered – enclosing, draining, improving the land, and so on (253). Competition constitutes a harmony as it makes commodities more affordable and spurs innovation. All in all, Bastiat's vision relies on an "invisible-hand" mechanism and ongoing technological progress which will increasingly diminish class differences as more and more individuals are able to purchase what they need and desire. His system also rewards foresight and prudence, and has a self-correcting mechanism: "Man's principal social tendencies are harmonious in that, as every error leads to disillusionment and every vice to punishment, the discords tend constantly to disappear" (29). But this is by no means a Malthusian check; a growing system of exchange abetted by the concentration of population means greater utility with less effort (78), and he speculates that new agricultural technologies in conjunction with self-limiting families, given human foresight, will mitigate problems of overpopulation.

It is worth noting differences between Bastiat's "harmonies" and the idea of market equilibrium. His concept is clearly vaster, yet the underlying equilibrating mechanism is not new, and differs little from that described by Canard. Nonetheless, while Canard's model was dynamic, it did not rely so heavily on technological progress and improvement in the standard of living as proof of its validity and divine origin. And despite Bastiat's repeated rebuttal of utopian social schemes, his rhetoric has its own utopian ring as he foresees social progress in a *laissez-faire* economy in the form of a more educated, wealthier, and less divided population. In this respect, as Hülsmann explains, Bastiat's "harmonies" contrast the later Walrasian models of market equilibrium that predict maximum social utility when an equilibrium price is reached: "Bastiat did not claim that laissez-faire was bound to produce a state of perfection. His contention was that, where private property is respected, a natural order comes into existence in which individual interests are not antagonistic but mutually supportive. Society then constantly progresses, even though it might never be perfect at any point of time" (59).

What is clear is that in 1848 there was no broad agreement between political economists and socialists, or even among socialists, of what "harmony" meant as a structuring principle for society, or of what a "harmonious" society would look like. Instead the definition of social "harmony" was itself a contested point. Undoubtedly this lack of consensus derived in part from the class conflicts that had grown during the July Monarchy, and so the theoretical parameters of social harmony and their implementation had direct consequences for workers and entrepreneurs. How does a society choose among visions? As Buck-Morss points out, Adam Smith's political economy offers "no perspective – that of God or king or Reason – from which the whole productive social body can be viewed" (446); Bastiat's insistence on the providential plan behind the principles of political economy in its very stridency is evidence of this general sense of a lack of shared perspective on the social apparatus. The desire for harmony, however, was acute, as shown by the ubiquity of the word in many different keys and the impassioned tone of its various proponents. The belief in the possibility of achieving social "harmony" may well fit Žižek's characterization of ideology, drawing on Marx cum Lacan:

> Ideology is not a dreamlike illusion that we build to escape insupportable reality; in its basic dimension it is a fantasy-construction which serves as a support for our "reality" itself: an "illusion" which structures our effective, real social relations and thereby masks some insupportable, real, impossible kernel (conceptualized by Ernesto Laclau and Chantal Mouffe as "antagonism": a traumatic social division which cannot be symbolized). The function of ideology is not to offer us a point of escape from our reality but to offer us the social reality itself as an escape from some traumatic, real kernel. (*Sublime Object of Ideology* 45)

That is, such theories assumed that social harmony was achievable and relied on nonviolent measures – through the market or through social engineering – to reach such states. Such belief was bolstered by the sense that aspects of the harmonious state were already working and could be observed – for Bastiat, market mechanisms as described above, the benefits of the division of labor, and so on. Bastiat's insistence on the naturalness of the free market or the present economic order in an unhindered state is evidence of his seeing this order as "reality," indeed, a sense of discovering what *is*. The kernel of trauma, of course, was that the first Revolution and its Terror were repeatable, and would be repeated, that "pastness," or the security of being beyond the state of revolution, was an illusion. Bastiat buries this trauma by insisting that socialist theories of antagonism among classes are themselves illusions; seen correctly, or in the ether of an entirely free market, class interests are harmonious.

Utility

While a model of harmony founded on oppositions may be common to political economy and aesthetics, "utility" presumably marks the point of divergence and mutual self-definition through negation. But in nineteenth-century economics, the definition of "utility" and its role in the creation of wealth and value was a subject of ongoing debate. Indeed, its redefinitions within the "value" debate to a great extent chart the turn from a productionist to a consumerist economics. Not surprisingly, the roots of this debate lie in the eighteenth-century. Many moral philosophers viewed utility as an aspect of beauty; Hume's and Smith's contributions are particularly crucial since utility as an aesthetic order arguably undergirds central mechanisms of Smith's political economy. In other words, the "beauty" or "elegance" of such mechanisms helps confirm their "truth," preparing the ground for a tacit aesthetic in political economy that works to give many of its core principles validity. Such an aesthetic also entails aporias – for instance, the problem of aggregating private tastes into public welfare – that would come to haunt the discipline of economics in the nineteenth century and beyond.

For Hume in *A Treatise of Human Nature*, utility is beauty in that it produces pleasure in the observer through the observer's sympathetic identification with others:

> where any object has a tendency to produce pleasure in its possessor, it is always regarded as beautiful; as every object, that has a tendency to produce pain, is disagreeable and deform'd. Thus the conveniency of a house, the fertility of a field, the strength of a horse, the capacity, security, and swift-sailing of a vessel, form the principal beauty of these several objects. Here the object, which is denominated beautiful, pleases only by its tendency to produce a certain effect. That effect is the pleasure or advantage of some other person. Now the pleasure of a stranger, for whom we have no friendship, pleases us only by sympathy. To this principle, therefore, is owing the beauty, which we find in every thing that is useful. How considerable a part this is of beauty will easily appear upon reflection Wherever an object has a tendency to produce pleasure in the possessor, or in other words, is the proper *cause* of pleasure, it is sure to please the spectator, by a delicate sympathy with the possessor. Most of the works of art are esteem'd beautiful, in proportion to their fitness for the use of man, and even many of the productions of nature derive their beauty from that source. Handsome and beautiful, on most occasions, is not an absolute but a relative

quality, and pleases us by nothing but its tendency to produce an end that is agreeable. (368-69)[12]

First, it is worth noting that aesthetic judgment here is subjective and interpersonal. It is mediated through the pleasure of the other, notably the possessor of the object (implying that property rights or, at least, ownership exists prior to the aesthetic sensation). The usefulness or "conveniency" of the object likewise involves a judgment by one subject based in the sensation of pleasure projected to another through signs of pleasure; thus judgments of beauty rely on judgments of utility in an interpersonal dynamic. Not only is the perception of beauty in this case dependent on that of use, but beauty also has utility in that it produces the sensation of pleasure and serves as the vehicle of sympathy for the stranger in whom this pleasure originates.

This passage develops notions presented in an earlier section of the Treatise, "Of beauty and deformity." Here, while stipulating that beauty is "nothing but a form, which produces pleasure" (196), Hume proposes that the "idea" of the utility of this form is the cause of "a great part" of its beauty: "The order and convenience of a palace are no less essential to its beauty, than its mere figure and appearance" (195). Kant will later take up the example of the palace to demonstrate that such delight in utility mars the purity of aesthetic judgment by introducing interest.[13] Yet the "interest" in the object in Hume is not self-interest; rather it is part of a mechanism for the ongoing construction of civil society. Howard Caygill describes how Hume's "field of mutual reflection" is a means of explaining the relation between individual and general sympathy through the generation of a form from "the infinity of past and present reflections" producing "artificial" virtues such as justice from individual instances of sympathy (73-74). This mechanism is lost in Kant's aesthetics, as he moves away from

---

[12] See also 195-96.

[13] Paul Guyer demonstrates that Kant does allow for an "adherent beauty" that takes into account utility, or what a thing is supposed to be. This judgment is still distinguished from the pure aesthetic judgment (446). On the other hand, Rancière discerns an egalitarian aspect to aesthetic judgment: "Ignoring to whom the palace actually belongs, the vanity of the nobles, and the sweat of the people incorporated in the palace are the conditions of aesthetic judgment. This ignorance is by no means the illusion that conceals the reality of possession and inequality. Rather, it is the means for building a new sensible world, which is a world of equality within the world of possession and inequality" ("Aesthetic Dimension" 8).

British empiricism and theories of civil society. Since Kant judges the sentiment of the agreeable to be distinct from and inferior to the aesthetic sentiment, he precludes such interest from aesthetic judgment, eliminating sympathy and this aesthetic mechanism for social cohesion.[14] But it is also worth noting that for Hume it is a perceived quality of usefulness in the object, rather than the attainment of its purpose, or end, that causes the aesthetic pleasure, again, emphasizing the role of subjective judgment. Hume makes this quite clear: "where any object, in all its parts, is fitted to attain any agreeable end, it naturally gives us pleasure and is esteem'd beautiful, even tho' some external circumstances be wanting to render it altogether effectual" (373).[15] So, while Hume's aesthetic may be grounded in a beautiful fiction of sympathetic reflection, he does theorize an empirical social base to aesthetics that takes into account the subjectivity of judgment.

Smith, in *The Theory of Moral Sentiments*, accepts the "utility is beauty" thesis: "that utility is one of the principal sources of beauty has been observed by every body, who has considered with any attention what constitutes the nature of beauty" (179). But he draws attention to the duality implied in Hume's distinction between fitness and actual use, developing what he sees as his original contribution to the question:

> But that this fitness, this happy contrivance of any production of art, should often be more valued, than the very end for which it was intended; and that the exact adjustment of the means for attaining any conveniency or pleasure, should frequently be more regarded, than that very conveniency or pleasure, in the attainment of which their whole merit would seem to consist, has not, so far as I know, been yet taken notice of by any body. (179-80)

---

[14] Caygill's reading of Kant's *The Critique of Judgement* as the negation of two traditions, that of British theories of taste, including Smith and Hume, linked to theories of civil society, and of German rationalist aesthetics, linked to theories of the police-state (Wolff, Baumgarten), supports this point: "Both accounts of judgement were considerably overdetermined by differing perspectives on political and religious culture, so when Kant negates them he is also negating the political and cultural freight which they carry" (297).

[15] Caygill helpfully distinguishes between individual instances of sympathy and "a reflected utility or 'form of utility' which is reexperienced by the individual as sympathy, a feeling for the whole." (73). He goes on to point out that it is this "field of mutual reflection" that produces pleasure in the fine arts as a "sublimated utility" in Hume (74).

In other words, "fitness" for convenience or pleasure produces a greater pleasure than the convenience or intended pleasure itself. Smith uses as an example the aficionado of watches who sells a slow watch for "a couple of guineas" and "purchases another at fifty," not because he is "more scrupulously punctual than other men," but because he admires "the perfection of the machine" (180). So this plea-sure – actually a reflection, anticipation, or memory of convenience or pleasure, whose reflection begets sympathy – becomes a delight in order, in the adaptation of means to ends. Significantly, the order of society is also a source of pleasure, so "the tendency of virtue to promote, and of vice to disturb the order of society . . . reflects a very great beauty upon the one, and a very great deformity upon the other" (316). And so the mirroring process increases exponentially: virtue is beautiful since the order it "promotes" reflects back on it. That is, the means (virtuous action) are deemed beautiful through a reflection of its ends (social order), while these ends constitute an order already made beautiful through reflection of its own end, presumably the happiness of all.

Smith sees this admiration of the well-adapted means over the actual end as a deception and an illusion, which the imagery of mul-tiple reflections implies. And Smith is equivocal about this illusion.[16] On the one hand, he paints the picture of the man who under the illu-sion of the greater "conveniency" of the trappings of wealth, spends his life pursuing them until "in the languor of disease and the wear-iness of old age" he sees that these "immense fabrics" are burdensome and add little to the satisfaction of basic human needs (181-83). On the other hand, this illusion motivates people to produce more than they need, creating the wealth of nations; in explaining the working of illusion, Smith employs the famous trope of the "invisible hand":

---

[16] Frederick Rosen argues that here Smith shows that the "problem of distributive justice" itself is an illusion, "although the reality he invoked against it was also based ultimately on an illusion concerning utility and the ghostly spectre of an 'invisible hand'" (70). Rosen recognizes the paradox of utility pursued as an illusion, yet instrumental to the building of wealth and civilization, but concludes Smith was not proposing "absolute principles" on which to base his moral theory, but simply describing how we came to such beliefs (73). Rosen notes that in the second chapter of Part IV of *The Theory of Moral Sentiments*, Smith critiques Hume's contention that utility provides the foundation to morality (74).

And it is well that nature imposes upon us in this manner. It is this deception which rouses and keeps in continual motion the industry of mankind. It is this which first promoted them to cultivate the ground, to build houses, to found cities and commonwealths, and to invent and improve all the sciences and arts, which ennoble and embellish human life; which have entirely changed the whole face of the globe, have turned the rude forests of nature into agreeable and fertile plains, and made the trackless and barren ocean a new fund of subsistence, and the great high road of communication to the different nations of the earth. The earth by these labours of mankind has been obliged to redouble her natural fertility, and to maintain a greater multitude of inhabitants. It is to no purpose, that the proud and unfeeling landlord views his extensive fields, and without a thought for the wants of his brethren, in imagination consumes himself the whole harvest that grows upon them. . . . The rich only select from the heap what is most precious and agreeable. They consume little more than the poor, and in spite of their natural selfishness and rapacity, though they mean only their own conveniency, though the sole end which they propose from the labours of all the thousands whom they employ, be the gratification of their own vain and in-satiable desires, they divide with the poor the produce of all their improvements. They are led by an invisible hand to make nearly the same distribution of the necessaries of life, which would have been made, had the earth been divided into equal portions among all its inhabitants, and thus without intending it, without knowing it, advance the interest of the society, and afford means to the multiplication of the species. (183-85)

The "invisible hand" of this oft-cited passage will come to represent the mechanism by which self-interested economic actors benefit others indirectly and unintentionally.[17] Smith is highly ironic here, of course, for the rich and those who aspire to be rich are under an illu-sion, while "the beggar, who suns himself by the side of the highway, possesses that security which kings are fighting for" (185). The role of the imagination is crucial: insatiable desires promote general welfare better than the satisfaction of limited needs. This position is consistent

---

[17] In summarizing the transition from theories of taste to political economy, Caygill argues that while Smith relies on Hume's theory of the formation of taste, which eschewed providential explanations, he reintroduces providential design with the trope of the "invisible hand." Rothschild, however, reads the "invisible hand" itself as ironic. Situating Smith's use of the trope within other prominent textual instances with which he was familiar, such as the "bloody and invisible hand" of *Macbeth* and a back-stabbing "invisible hand" in Ovid's *Metamorphoses*, she finds that an unironic understanding of the trope is at odds with other tendencies in Smith's thought: "the disregard it implied for the futility of individual lives, the reverence it implied for all-wise theorists, and the conflict it suggested with his own description of the political pursuit of self-interest" (which he condemned) (136). Rothschild sees Smith as much closer to Hume in avoiding reliance on providence as an authority for order than some of his rhetoric would suggest. See Caygill 44-4, 85-102; Rothschild 116-56.

with Smith's classification of the passions elsewhere in *The Theory of Moral Sentiments* where he argues that passions that originate in the imagination are more durable than those that originate in the body (29).

As Smith goes on to describe "constitutions of government" as "beautiful and orderly," so one might well suppose that the spectator who sees the providential self-ordering mechanism of the economy would also judge it a thing of beauty, and admire it for its order more than for its ends. Thus the concept of a self-ordering mechanism in an unfettered economy is validated in part by its beauty. It is worth noting that the sympathy involved in the creation and perception of beauty has its limitations in the wider social sphere. That is, while Smith posits a presumably universal subject who enjoys the pleasure of possession vicariously, and thus sees beauty, the rich in his account have little regard for those outside their class. Smith explicitly addresses the irony of loving the system better than those it would benefit: "From a certain love of art and contrivance, we sometimes seem to value the means more than the end, and to be eager to promote the happiness of our fellow-creatures, rather from a view to perfect and improve a certain beautiful and orderly system, than from any immediate sense or feeling of what they either suffer or enjoy" (185). That is, the beauty that theoretically we learn to sense through sympathy is more powerful a motivation to public service than sympathy itself. And, as Herbert points out, this irony reflects back on the maker of systems, the philosopher himself, and implies that any system is finally a product of its maker's imagination (81, 105).

Caygill notes that Smith's "definition of beauty as the pleasure of perceiving the fitness or proportion of a means to an end apart from any consideration of the end" is "a phenomenon Kant later described as *Zweckmässigkeit ohne Zweck*" (85). That Smith is taking a first step towards dividing utility as *end* from beauty is certainly true, but for Smith the *Zweckmässigkeit* is still defined by the object's particular *Zweck*; it is its mirror image. But Smith has introduced a version of disinterest: while the object's "fitness" potentially benefits someone, admiration of its convenience involves forgetting this immediate end with a consequent loss of sympathy. Thus the aporia of observations of indifference within a theory based in sympathy haunts *The Theory of Moral Sentiments* and, in a different form, all of political economy. In *The Wealth of Nations*, beauty no longer has an explicit intersubjective role in validating virtuous action, yet in a way the aesthetic sense simply becomes tacit in the commercial orders that Smith traces, the beauties of a system in which market price "gravitates" towards "natural price" or in which free trade among nations works to every participating country's benefit through the counterbalances of supply and demand. And the idea in *The Theory of Moral Sentiments* that for the economic subject, the imagination and the pleasure of contemplating beauty as order are motivations both to produce and to consume provides the philosophical underpinnings for the conjectural history of human progress leading to the present commercial age, elaborated in *The Wealth of Nations*. While the "invisible hand" seems to imply the reign of self-interest over sympathy, Emma Rothschild points out that Smith's "principal examples of self-interested behavior, in *The Wealth of Nations*, include manufacturers in incorporated towns, parish worthies, dukes of Cornwall, medieval kings, proud ministers, established clergy, and university teachers" (125). But he has "faith" "in the mildness and thoughtfulness of most individual men and women," "that they will usually not pursue their interests in grossly oppressive ways, and that they will usually wish to live in a society in which other people are not grossly oppressed or deprived." Rothschild adds: "This, and little more, is the foundations of the system of economic freedom. It is a pious hope, as well as a shortcoming of liberal economic thought" (156).

Whatever the fate of virtue and sympathy, explicit reference to utility as beauty disappears from Smith's discourse in *The Wealth of Nations*[18]. But Smith implicitly distinguishes utility from beauty or utility from ornament in considering the water and diamonds paradox, which he uses to illustrate the distinction between use value and exchange value in *The Wealth of Nations*:

> The word VALUE, it is to be observed, has two different meanings, and sometimes expresses the utility of some particular object, and sometimes the power of purchasing other goods which the possession of that object conveys.

---

[18] Neil de Marchi, however, gives an example the eruption of the aesthetic in *The Wealth of Nations*. He points out that Smith makes a significant exception to his opposition to government intervention and favors in supporting "[p]remiums given by the publick to artists and manufacturers who excel in their particular occupations" which encourage "extraordinary dexterity and ingenuity"(de Marchi quoting Smith) . De Marchi sees this exception as driven by Smith's admiration of "fitness," the aestheticized utility of *The Theory of Moral Sentiments* (30).

> The one may be called "value in use;" the other, "value in exchange." The things which have the greatest value in use have frequently little or no value in exchange; and on the contrary, those which have the greatest value in exchange have frequently little or no value in use. Nothing is more useful than water: but it will purchase scarce any thing; scarce any thing can be had in exchange for it. A diamond, on the contrary, has scarce any value in use; but a very great quantity of other goods may frequently be had in exchange for it. (31-32)

His choice of words for utility as value – "value in use" – implies a direct, not reflected means-ends relationship, so "fitness," the beauty of utility, seems to have vanished. If we consider the example of the watch-loving man, given in *The Theory of Moral Sentiments*, this shift in meaning becomes clear: the man who would pay fifty guineas for the watch with the perfect mechanism gets no better practical use from it, according to Smith, than he would from the slightly slow watch that he sells for "a couple of guineas." The utility that he admires as perfect functioning is not the utility of "value in use." One might say that this aestheticized utility contributes to value in exchange. It is this now latent utility that will resurface in nineteenth-century debates over the definition and measurement of utility in political economy. Here I would contest one point made by Guillory. He argues that "[t]he failure to construct a theory of the harmonious relation between a continuum of production and a continuum of consumption marks the point of the irrevocable disengagement of political economy from aesthetic questions, and thus its emergence as a separate discourse" (316). But, while the explicitly aesthetic base of social harmony in moral philosophy goes *sub rosa* (except in the writings of Bastiat, as I have discussed), theories of consumption and specifically those revolving around the definition of "utility" take up questions like those being addressed in the realm of art, such as the centrality of pleasure in experiencing the object/commodity and the reconciliation of individual subjective tastes with the common good or universal standards of taste. To an extent, Guillory acknowledges these shared concerns when dismissing the importance of the marginalist contribution to the value debate. He quotes Robert Heilbroner (and I quote the part of his long citation dealing with "utility"):

> very few economists actually use utility analysis as a serious means of resolving the value problematic. . . . It is striking in this regard that economists regularly resort to a cost-of-production approach when compiling data for gross national product or when comparing the products of two or more years. From a view that

sees utilities as the fundamental and irreducible building blocks of price, gross
national product is a meaningless concept, the 'summation' of individual
experiences of pleasure and pain. This has no more validity than the summation
of enjoyments of an audience at a concert. (Heilbroner in Guillory 380).

As Heilbroner points out, this way of looking at "utility" may not be
useful to economists, but it is the direction taken later in the
nineteenth century by not only the marginalists, but by forerunners,
like Jules Dupuit whose analyses I discuss later in this chapter.

At the same time, "use" alone, undertheorized, becomes inconse-
quential in the debates surrounding value, almost always assumed, but
never a real variable. Smith, of course, goes on to theorize that labor is
"the real measure of the exchangeable value of all commodities"
(*Wealth of Nations* 33). He recognizes that this measure is hidden
behind another common illusion: that we trade quantities of commodities, not labor: "The one is a plain palpable object; the other an
abstract notion, which, though it can be made sufficiently intelligible,
is not altogether so natural or obvious" (35). The commodity, in his
theory, is dematerialized, or rather its materiality is displaced onto the
human body which creates value through labor. In a way, he valorizes
both abstraction (from the object) and concrete human production;
nature without human industry has no value. But, as Herbert argues,
Smith's attempt to establish value as "an empirical constant" through
measuring quantities of labor, falters on the relativity that enters into a
system of value based in exchange where value is customary and
symbolic (91-94).

Before turning to debates about the meaning of "utility" in French
political economy, we should briefly consider the post-Kantian fate of
utility in aesthetics in France. In Cousin's 1817-1818 lectures on "the
ideas of the true, the beautiful, and the good," he makes explicit
reference to *l'art pour l'art*.[19] But how does he define it, and what
shape does Kant's concept of disinterest take in his aesthetic?

Cousin borrows from Kant (77-79) the notion that ideas of the
beautiful arise from the normal through the rational processes of
abstraction and comparison, but is careful to distinguish an ideal of
beauty that arises only from comparing individual instances, a process

---

[19] Gene H. Bell-Villada notes that Benjamin Constant uses the phrase "l'art pour l'art"
in an 1804 diary in reference to Kant's aesthetics. Bell-Villada conjectures that by the
time of Cousin's lectures, the notion was already circulating in Parisian intellectual
circles (36-7; 39).

based in sensation, from a process whereby reason immediately apprehends the "absolute" in the particular instance, a more neo-Platonic model (131-36). Kant actually argues against any ideal as an aesthetic measure since "the ideal consists in the expression of the *moral*, apart from which the object would not please at once universally and positively" (79) and this precludes any judgment formed according to such an ideal from being purely aesthetic (80). Cousin makes no such distinction, in line with his advocacy of a moral art, as we shall see, and of a firm distinction between the realms of sense and reason. In advocating a neo-Platonic version of the aesthetic, he claims that we measure particular instances of beauty against this ideal, and that the beauty we see is only "l'image, le reflet, le signe de la vraie beauté" (133). He does, however, follow Kant to insist on the disinterested nature of aesthetic judgment, citing as example the Kantian sentiment of the sublime, and specifically excluding need and desire. His aim, in part, is to refute eighteenth-century "sensualist philosophy"; in distinguishing "sensation" from "sentiment" ("feeling"), he asserts that it is the latter that is in play in aesthetic judgment. Arguing against too much "sensation," he claims that the artist who paints "voluptuous forms" troubles, and incites revolt in "l'idée chaste et pure de la beauté" (125). His description of desire is telling: "le désir profane son objet.". He explains:

> Le désir est fils du besoin. Il suppose un manque, un défaut, et jusqu'à un certain point, une souffrance. Le sentiment du beau n'est pas un besoin; il est satisfait par cela seul qu'il existe. Le désir est enflammé, impétueux, douloureux. Le sentiment du beau, libre de tout désir et en même temps de toute crainte, élève et échauffe l'âme, et peut la transporter jusqu'à l'enthousiasme, sans lui faire connaître les troubles de la passion. (139)

While assigning the aesthetic sentiment a near heroic action, free of desire and fear, Cousin's language casts desire as a violation of what is sacred and as sexual appetite: both profanation and lack – "the son of need." By the same token, Cousin casts beauty as a purifying agent: "l'effet certain du vrai beau est d'épurer et d'ennoblir l'âme" (171). His rationale for this assertion relies on an analogy among three types of beauty: physical, intellectual, and moral. One of these types takes precedence over the others: "Le fond de toute beauté, c'est la beauté morale" (170), an ideal that Kant would place beyond pure aesthetic judgment. But for Cousin, since virtue and intellectual rigor are forms of beauty, the true, the good, and the beautiful are one and the same. Effectively, in Cousin's philosophy, Kant's categorical distinctions – for instance between delight and desire, or between the agreeable and the beautiful – take on moral valence. The negations that Kant invokes to clear a space for "pure" aesthetic judgment – lack of personal interest of all sorts – allow Cousin to define aesthetic purity by its difference from the sexual and the sacrilegious. It is a *différance* that will haunt the cult of beauty in the later aestheticism of Gautier and Baudelaire.

For Cousin, the notion of purity thus underlies beauty in three ways: purity and simplicity result from the process of abstraction at the heart of determining the beautiful, as the "absolute" is distinguished from the incidental (136); moral purity represents the foundational type of beauty; and ideal beauty, impossible to embody in a single example, leads to the infinite and hence to God. These three notions are hardly commensurable, as Cousin melds Kantian ratiocination with neo-Platonism and a Christian morality based in self-abnegation and self-discipline.

As *l'art pour l'art* relies necessarily on exclusion for definition, what is excluded and how the exclusion operates is key to understanding the rhetorical trajectory of the phrase in the particular context and generally. Cousin does use *l'art pour l'art* to distinguish the aesthetic function from the ethical, the political, and the religious – but only to a certain extent. He clarifies that art should not be "au service de la religion et de la morale," but should work indirectly to perfect the soul (183). Wanting to retain a moral and spiritual function for art, albeit indirect, he proposes a sort of "separate spheres" scheme for art, ethics, religion, and politics:

> Non, le bien, le saint, le beau, ne servent à rien qu'à eux-mêmes. Il faut comprendre et aimer la morale pour la morale, la religion pour la religion, l'art pour l'art. Mais l'art, la religion, la morale, sont utiles à la société ; je le sais ; mais à quelle condition ? Qu'ils n'y songent même pas. C'est le culte indépendant et désintéressé de la beauté, de la vertu, de la sainteté, qui seul profite à la société, parce que seul il élève les âmes, nourrit et propage ces dispositions généreuses qui font à leur tour la puissance des États. (184)

In a way, to echo Constant's loose articulation of *Zweckmässigkeit ohne Zweck*, "art attains the purpose that it does not have" in itself, but also in the moral and the spiritual. But it is worth noting that Cousin uses the discourse of freedom and servitude to make his argument for such categorical autonomy. (Such master/slave discourse might appear to be utterly figurative and abstract if it weren't for reality of state censorship and direction of the arts by state institutions. In fact, Cousin's own lectures were subsequently suppressed by the government.) "Freedom" while "predicated on negation" like the aesthetic (Harpham 141) was no less powerful a word in Restoration France than it is today. Cousin's emphasis on morality and even patriotism is consistent with the aspirations of his generation, according to Alan B. Spitzer: "Cousin's great appeal to his Restoration audience lay precisely in that assimilation of beauty to truth and goodness, in that cosmic synthesis that was, presumably, to fill the void at the center of the generation's moral universe" (191-92).

Cousin does burden beauty with the task of teaching virtue through form without any intention to do so (agency here is curiously displaced onto an abstraction), and thereby "profite la société"; further, it empowers the State by molding the citizenry. This characterization of the social function of beauty builds on his earlier contention that the judgment of beauty is universal, not individual, since "la beauté, comme la vérité, n'appartient à aucun de nous: c'est le bien commun, c'est le domaine public de l'humanité" (129). So freedom belongs to the realm of the aesthetic as a whole, not to individuals whose judgments, if they differ from the ideal, are matters of personal taste, which is prey to the agreeable, to need and desire.[20] Cousin's stance shares with later configurations of *l'art pour l'art* the sacralization of the aesthetic, but without any consequent demotion or replacement of traditional religion or morality. Here art indirectly promotes the social good, and paradoxically only through such indirection can this happen. Thus disinterestedness in art operates like self-interest in economic behavior: ironically both promote the social good by ignoring it. One might ask, then, if disinterestedness so defined is ultimately illusory, if it proceeds from a blind spot of authorial (un)intentionality, contravened by the social and political resonances of any public discourse. The recourse to "liberty" as part

---

[20] Needless to say, this realm of ideal beauty is represented by the hegemonic European tradition in art, as Cousin's racist example shows: he argues that if a sensationalist basis sufficed for the experience of beauty, then judgment would be relative, and "la Vénus des Hottentots égalera la Vénus de Médicis" which he calls absurd (131).

of this argument proceeds from the assumption of disinterest, yet resembles the discourse of *laissez-faire* predicated on the motivation of self-interest. Tellingly any conflict over the message or intention of a work of art is thereby circumvented, at least theoretically, since art can have no intention other than the aesthetic, except again indirectly. Thus, Cousin, despite his insistence on keeping the moral and aesthetic spheres separate, has clearly introduced a form of instrumentality as a validation of the aesthetic in the cause of patriotism.

Thus even within the mandate of *l'art pour l'art* Cousin allows a sort of indirect utility to art, paradoxically as it is this autonomy that makes art useful. But by the mid-1830's the assault on utilitarianism by artists and critics was much more entrenched, and the rejection of utility in art much more absolute. Théophile Gautier's 1834 preface to his novel, *Mademoiselle de Maupin,* was an influential articulation of this position. Gautier takes aim at Saint-Simonian critics, advocates of engaged art that addresses social malaise and the needs of the poor. But in this broadside against a utilitarian art, he considers the meaning of "utility" itself. First, he notes the relativity and subjectivity of use: that poets have different needs than boot-makers in pursuing their profession. But then he considers what is absolutely necessary to human life, and soon arrives at the position that what is necessary or useful in a conventional sense is ugly, and therefore anathema to the artist: "Il n'y a de vraiment beau que ce qui ne peut servir à rien; tout ce qui est utile est laid, car c'est l'expression de quelque besoin, et ceux de l'homme sont ignobles et dégoutants, comme sa pauvre et infirme nature. – L'endroit le plus utile d'une maison, ce sont les latrines." This position rejects outright the eighteenth-century aesthetic of utility articulated by Hume and Smith among others. In a wry version of Kantian aesthetics, Gautier asserts his own code of utility as paradox : "je suis de ceux pour qui le superflu est le nécessaire" (54). Yet his aesthetic is sensualist in a way that the idealist philosopher, Cousin, would reject ; "car la jouissance me paraît le but de la vie, et la seule chose utile au monde" (55). And a more radical departure from Cousin appears in the decoupling of need from desire, which Cousin explicitly linked in his refutation of the eighteenth-century "utility is beauty" argument. For Cousin, need creates desire which violates beauty. For Gautier, human needs and desires are separate except in his rhetorical paradox of redefining the superfluous as necessary for artists and writers like himself. Indeed, it is the pursuit of desire apart from need, ("de boire sans avoir soif, de batter le briquet, et de faire amour en toutes saisons") that distinguishes humans from beasts (55).

In distinguishing need from desire, Gautier parodies the views of "économistes," but "utility" as a concept in political economy was, in fact, in dispute among political economists, with the relationship between need and desire forming much of the unspoken subtext. Uncertainty about the definition and, ultimately, the usefulness of "utility" to this new "science" stems in large part from Smith's original distinction between "value in use" and "value in exchange", making "value in use" seem somewhat irrelevant to the workings of markets (although he does not say as much), while he shifts the focus of his theory of value to the measurement of labor. David Ricardo, at the beginning of his major work, *On the Principles of Political Economy and Taxation* (1817), cites Smith's distinction between use value and exchange value, and then adds this gloss: "Utility then is not the measure of exchangeable value, although it is absolutely essential to it. If a commodity were in no way useful – in other words, if it could in no way contribute to our gratification –, it would be destitute of exchangeable value, however scarce it might be, or whatever quantity of labour might be necessary to procure it" (11). Ricardo, to be sure, was much more concerned with refining Smith's labor theory of value, as the subheading for this first section implies: "The value of a commodity, or the quantity of any other commodity for which it will exchange, depends on the relative quantity of labour which is necessary for its production, and not on the greater or less compensation which is paid for that labour" (11). But his parenthetical definition of the "useful" as that which "contribute[s] to our gratification" represents a nod towards the judgment of the buyer as definitional within a clearly productionist theory of value. Since Smith had asserted that commodities "which have the greatest value in exchange have frequently little or no value in use," this refinement is more of correction of Smith on this score, a claim that "use" or "utility" is relevant to exchange value and has to do with "gratification."

Ricardo's correspondence with Jean-Baptiste Say, the most prominent French political economist of the first decades of the nineteenth century, helps us see what was at stake in defining utility. Having read Say's *Catéchisme D'Economie Politique*, Ricardo writes to Say in a letter dated 18 August 1815:

You have I perceive a little modified the definition of the word *value* as far as it is dependent on utility, but with great diffidence, I observe, that I do not think you have mastered the difficulties which attach to the explanation of that difficult word. Utility is certainly the foundation of value, but the degree of utility can never be the measure by which to estimate value. A commodity difficult of production will always be more valuable than one which is easily produced although all men should agree that the latter is more useful than the former. A commodity must be useful to have value but the difficulty of its production is the true measure of its value. For this reason Iron though more useful is of less value than gold. (6: 247-48)

Two responses to this letter are extant.[21] In the first, dated September 10, 1815, Say claims that his views and Ricardo's are in perfect accord on the question of the determination of value. Ricardo simply should note the restrictions that Say imposes on this determination later in the volume: "que l'utilité n'est pas l'unique mais la premiere [sic] cause de la valeur" (6: 271). But it is the second response, that perhaps was never sent, that best illustrates the shift to the buyer's judgment implied in Ricardo's own reference to "our gratification": "Il faut que je me sois bien mal expliqué, puisque vous m'accusez d'avoir dit que l'utilité était la mesure de la valeur; tandis que je croyais avoir toujours dit que la valeur que les hommes attachent à une chose est la mesure de l'utilité qu'ils trouvent en elle" (6: 273). Whether or not Ricardo received this response, he clearly saw the difference between the productionist orientation of his economic theory and the implications of Say's definition of "utility". He writes in a letter to Malthus, dated 9 October 1820, in reference to Say's *Lettres à M. Malthus*:

He certainly has not a correct notion of what is meant by value, when he contends that a commodity is valuable in proportion to its utility. This would be true if buyers only regulated the value of commodities; then indeed we might expect that all men would be willing to give a price for things in proportion to the estimation in which they held them, but the fact appears to me to be that the buyers have the least in the world to do in regulating price—it is all done by the competition of the sellers, and however the buyers might be really willing to give more for iron, than for gold, they could not, because the supply would be regulated by the cost of production, and therefore gold would inevitably be in

---

[21] Say's first response, found among Ricardo's papers, was certainly sent; the second may not have been. It was published in Say's *Mélanges* and *Oeuvres diverses*, but no manuscript is extant, according to Piero Sraffa, the editor of Ricardo's correspondence (6: 273n.).

the proportion which it now is to iron, altho' it probably is by all mankind considered the less useful metal. (8: 276-77)

(This is in response to a letter from Malthus in which Malthus refers to Say's "strange and useless application of the term utility" [8: 260].) Ricardo's illustration here relies on a definition of utility as that which is "useful," not that which "contribute[s] to our gratification" for certainly a case could then be made for the greater relative value of gold. In a way, one can accuse him of opening the very door that Say steps through.

In a later letter to Ricardo, dated 19 July 1821, Say insists on the paradoxical nature of Smith's "value in use": "C'est, permettez-moi de vous le dire, ce que ne peut enseigner la considération de la *valeur en utilité* (*value in use*) mots qui me paraissent incompatibles, parce que l'idée de *valeur* ne peut etre [sic] séparé de celle de comparaison et d'échange". He goes on to insist that while "créer de l'utilité c'est créer de la richesse," no other measure of this created utility is possible except the quantity of another good to be had in exchange for it, its current price (Ricardo 9: 32). In other words, for political economy, "use" has no value, yet "created utility" is synonymous with the creation of wealth or value. "Use" diverges from "utility" in these shifts of nomenclature that would preserve Smith's tradition while amending it. Is this analogous to Smith's distinction in *The Theory of Moral Sentiments* between actual use and the beauty of "fitness," for it is this "fitness" which gives the observer pleasure, and inspires the purchase of the flawless timepiece? If so, then like Smith's beauty of fitness, Say's "created utility" also creates pleasure in the observer/consumer and may even have an aesthetic function, distinct from and superfluous to its usefulness.

How is such utility value created? Ricardo's answer is labor, of course. Say's answer, too, emphasizes production, but a further dematerialized production measured not by the physical properties of the product, but instead by the judgment of consumers: "La production n'est point une creation de matière, mais une création d'utilité. Elle ne se mesure point suivant la longueur, le volume ou le poids du produit, mais suivant l'utilité qu'on lui a donnée" (*Traité d'économie politique* 51).[22] In other words, there is nothing godlike about human productiv-

---

[22] Say's point derives from a larger critique of Smith and his distinction between productive and unproductive labor; Say argues that manufacturing and service

ity; people do not *create* anything, but accommodate nature for human use. And, this utility, if we follow Say's reasoning from the earlier excerpt, is measured, albeit imperfectly, by price.

In his essay on "Utility" in *The New Palgrave*, R.D. Collison Black notes that since the British classical economists "were mainly interested in 'natural' rather than 'market' price, that is, in long-run normal values which were mainly determined by supply and cost, the fact that they had no theory to explain fully the relationships between utility, demand and market price was not a matter of concern to most of them." But between 1830 and 1870 these relationships did draw the attention of some, and "not surprisingly some of the best work was done at this time in France, where the tradition of demand analysis was stronger" (296-97).[23] For a contemporary critique of Say which resulted in an understanding of utility much closer to later neoclassical theory, I turn now to a figure who was not a member of the dominant school of political economy at the time, that of Say and his followers, but who was an econo-engineer who took up the question of the definition of "utility" in order to devise a method for measuring public utility. Jules Dupuit's contribution to this debate not only anticipates the direction that neoclassical economics would take much later in the century, but also shares features with the anti-utility rhetoric of writers like Gautier and Baudelaire.

Dupuit was a member of the prestigious and politically independent Corps des Ingénieurs des Ponts et Chaussées, whose duties in-

---

workers both produce utility, "a purely immaterial quality," in the words of Evelyn Forget. See her article analyzing Say's annotations of his copy of *The Wealth of Nations,* "J.-B. Say and Adam Smith : An Essay in the Transmission of Ideas," especially 128-31, and her book, *The Social Economics of Jean-Baptiste Say: Markets and virtue,* 133-37, for an account of Say's utility theory of value and the extent to which he anticipates Walras. Forget defends Say against Schumpeter's charge of "ineptitude" for considering the usefulness of air and water to be so great as to exceed any price; rather, Say saw this as a question of the quantity of the thing exceeding demand. But Forget does finally conclude that "there is no real recognition of the role of scarcity in the determination of natural price in the first edition of the *Traité* nor is there any real recognition of a concept of the margin, despite Say's intriguing use of the phrase the 'degree of utility'" (*Social Economics* 137).

[23] Ekelund and Hébert trace the French emphasis on utility, "not integrity," as the aim of science back to Diderot and Alembert's *Encyclopédie* which inspired the *idéologues* like Say, Pierre Cabanis, and Destutt de Tracy; the latter, "[i]nspired by Étienne Condillac," "broke with British classical economics in connecting (exchange) value to utility" (34-35).

cluded feasibility studies for public projects. His 1844 article, "De la mesure de l'utilité des travaux publics," as well as subsequent follow-up articles, is a critique of an application of Say's specification of public utility by a fellow engineer Navier that vastly overestimated the benefits of constructing a new canal to replace a road (Ekelund and Hébert 82).[24] But it is also a critique of Say's definition of utility, and a review of the concept in Smith, Ricardo, and others.

In his revision of utility, Dupuit begins by citing passages from Say defining utility as "la faculté qu'ont les choses de pouvoir servir à l'homme, de quelque manière que ce soit. La chose la plus inutile, et même la plus incommode, comme un manteau de cour, a ce qu'on appelle ici son utilité, si l'usage dont elle est, quel qu'il soit, suffit pour qu'on y attache un *prix*" (31). Say goes on to stipulate that this price is the measure of utility; thus, utility is fundamental to demand and thereby to value. But this value can rise no higher than the cost of production, for if it did, then the consumer could produce the item himself. Dupuit points out the error in this reasoning: if the public consents to pay a certain amount for transportation, yet the cost of providing transportation actually amounts to half of this sum, due to some improvement in the roads or coaches, is the utility of these roads then only half as much? On the contrary: the original figure marks the minimal utility of these roads, since that is what the public is willing to pay (32-33). Thus Dupuit follows Say in emphasizing the con-sumer's judgment in stipulating utility, and goes further to dispute the limited curtailment of this power that Say would impose by making the cost of production the ceiling of utility value.

In his critique of Say's definition of utility, Dupuit refers to Smith's distinction between use value and exchange value as an au-thority for his own concept of utility, citing J. R. McCulloch's gloss that it would be best to reserve the term "value" for exchange value and "utility" "to express the power or capacity of an article to satisfy our wants or gratify our desires" (37). In a later article, "De l'influ-ence des péages sur l'utilité des voies de communication," Dupuit cites Say's debate with Ricardo to show how Say actually neglects use value by only allowing for that which may be measured by price, hence exchange value. But Smith himself has done as much, as I

---

[24] Ekelund and Hébert's *Secret Origins of Modern Microeconomics: Dupuit and the Engineers* has been extremely helpful to me both for specific information about Dupuit's life and as an introduction and guide to his contributions to economics.

argued earlier. Here Dupuit also cites etymology as an authority for his use of "utility":

> En économie politique, tout ce qui sert, tout ce qui a un usage, est utile (de *uti*, se servir) ; dans le langage ordinaire, on ne dit qu'une chose est utile qu'autant qu'elle a un usage rationnel ; c'est une distinction tellement simple que l'esprit ne peut jamais être embarrassé sur le sens du mot utile; elle existait d'ailleurs déjà dans le langage ordinaire. Que de chose utiles à l'homme du monde qui ne le sont pas pour aux yeux du savant! que de choses utiles au savant qui ne le sont pas pour le philosophe! L'économie politique ne prend pas part à leurs discussions, elle appelle utile ce que chacun d'eux désire. (104-5)

This passage seems almost a direct rebuttal of Gautier's argument against utility; like Gautier, Dupuit recognizes the distinction between need and desire, and the subjectivity and relativity of need (different occupations, different values) in ordinary usage, but insists on the irrelevance of this distinction for political economy which relies simply on the desires of the individual agent. In other words, "utility" for the economic agent may be as irrational and as driven by desire as the delectation desired by the artistic sensibility that Gautier describes. Further, while pointing out that political economy has a special language that must be distinguished from ordinary discourse, Dupuit claims greater authenticity for this discourse which adheres more closely to the word's root, making it a more authentic *poesis*. This claim of the authority of origins is evident in Dupuit's citations of Smith despite the fact that Dupuit's definition of the term is closer to Say's than to Smith's.

Dupuit thus agrees with Say's initial definition of utility as proceeding from desire, not need, despite his use of Smith contra Say in his argument. But Dupuit does critique how Say measures utility, and his confusing introduction of the costs of production into the constraints on this measure. (The idea that use value is intrinsic to the item is by no means dead at this time; in a critical response to Dupuit's 1844 article, another engineer, Bordas, asserts as much in refuting Dupuit's utility measure, concluding that utility is not susceptible to measurement.) It is this critique and the more immediate tasks of estimating the costs and benefits of engineering projects that lead him to new ways of measuring utility that anticipate the direction that economics takes much later in the century with neoclassical economists like William Stanley Jevons, Léon Walras, and Carl Menger.[25]

How, then, does one measure desire, if that is what utility amounts to? Dupuit cites Destutt de Tracy: the measure of utility of an object is the maximum sacrifice that each consumer would be willing to make to acquire it (109). The difference between this amount and the actual price a consumer pays constitutes "relative utility" in Dupuit's terms, or "consumer surplus" in present-day economics, adding to the utility gained by the consumer. By the same token, the difference between the minimum price that the seller could offer and the actual price paid constitutes utility for the seller ("producer surplus" in current parlance).

Dupuit also proposes that an individual consumer's estimation of the utility of a given item may vary according to amount. That is, the price a consumer will pay for water to drink may be well above what he or she will pay for water to bathe or for other uses.[26] And since consumers vary in their desire for commodities or services, that variation can result in different prices for the same product. For instance, the same rail trip would be priced differently depending on whether one chose to ride in first, second, or third class. Dupuit uses the pricing of theater tickets as an example of such catering to variations in the public; he claims, in fact, that an unobstructed view

---

[25] Direct evidence of Dupuit's influence on the neoclassicals, however, is tenuous. According to Ekelund and Hébert, "Walras was alternately antagonistic, flattering, ambiguous, and contradictory in his treatment of Dupuit" (345). Walras wrote to Jevons in 1874 that he was familiar with Dupuit's 1844 article in which, he claims, Dupuit arrives at the mathematical expression of utility without solving it. In 1877, after reading Dupuit's article, Jevons wrote to Walras, "It is impossible not to allow that Dupuit had a very profound comprehension of the subject and anticipated us as regarding the fundamental ideas of utility. But he did not work his subject out and did not reach a theory of exchange. It is extraordinary too what a small effect his publication had upon economists, most of whom were ignorant of its existence" (quoted by Ekelund and Hébert, 346). Thus it seems that Dupuit anticipated the direction that economics would take thirty years hence without directly influencing neoclassical thought in the making. Nonetheless, Mark Blaug credits Dupuit, along with other engineer-economists like Dionysius Lardner in England and Charles Ellett Jr. in the United States, with producing "a concrete institutional base for the rise of marginalism in economics" as they studied the economics of public utilities at the time of the building, financing, and pricing of the railways (306).

[26] A point also made by Say. See Forget, *Social Economics* 136.

of the stage is hardly the sole consideration in ticket price discrimination:

> [L]es entrepreneurs dans leurs tarifs savent mettre à profit tous les caprices des spectateurs, de ceux qui vont pour voir, de ceux qui vont pour être vus, et de ceux qui vont pour tout autre motif. On les fait payer en raison du sacrifice qu'ils sont disposés à faire pour satisfaire leurs caprices, et non en raison du spectacle dont ils jouissent. (142)

The insight is nearly Balzacian, with the entrepreneur, like the novelist, understanding the mixture of "caprices" and willingness to sacrifice at play in the act of exchange. It is an act informed by social and psychological conditions well beyond the category of "need", complexly motivated.[27]

Dupuit refers to the pyramidal structure of wealth in the country (few rich, many poor), and argues that the wise entrepreneur or administrator in the case of public goods takes class structure into account. When devising a toll for a bridge between a working-class district and a factory, workers (who have few funds but for whom the bridge offers great utility) could be identified according to dress, the "livret" they carry, or the tolls could be lower around the time when work starts and finishes. Dupuit recognizes that the greatest number of people would use a bridge or road if there were no toll, but argues that this constitutes an unfair tax on nonusers. This is a recognition that the public affected by such works is not just the consumers, but the greater political entity. But having taken into account such considerations, he fashions a methodology that would devise pricing schedules producing the greatest general utility, maximizing both the users' and producers' utility. According to his tables of gradations of changes in the amount of tolls, the toll that offers the greatest general utility will not be the one that offers the largest revenues to the producers nor the

---

[27] In "The Ongoing 'Soft Revolution'", Žižek compares Angelis Silesius's *rose* with the guard's refusal to allow Primo Levi even a bit of snow to quench his thirst in a Nazi concentration camp as two instances of "no why." "Perhaps the coincidence of these two *whys* is the ultimate infinite judgement of the twentieth century; the groundless fact of a rose enjoying its own existence meets its oppositional determination in the groundless prohibition of the guard done out of pure *jouissance*, just for the sake of it" (318). By the same token, the insight that economic actions may be just as capricious or groundless brings to mind the groundless grounds claimed for the aesthetic. It is an insight both frightening and exhilarating – the freedom to act capriciously and irrationally.

one that encourages the greatest number of users (zero). One conclusion that he draws from such tables is that public works should not be privatized since companies seek to maximize profits, not general utility (131-32; 134-35). Clearly Dupuit's faith in market mechanisms and *laissez-faire* is tempered by concern for general public welfare. It is also worth noting that taking sacrifice into account when measuring utility reintroduces a version of need, inflected by class. Instead of considering value as defined by labor in terms of what workers need to subsist, workers are configured as consumers making choices with limited means.[28]

Despite such an allowance for the limited purchasing power of the poor, Dupuit's "utility" clearly encompasses far more than mere use; it is the satisfaction of desire as he states in the passage above. Whim, caprice, assertion of one's uniqueness and individuality – purchases peculiar to one's occupation or to one's personality and values – the economists' utility encompasses all motivations to buy, including the desires that Gautier would characterize as quite superfluous and beyond utility. This consonance points to an emphasis on consumption over production for both the economists gauging the public's reception of goods and services and the sensualist aesthetes.[29] For both, the object itself no longer has intrinsic value and has virtually disappeared as subjective and variable desire takes front stage as the determinant of value.

There is a danger, of course, in collapsing individual consumer choice, regardless of the buyer's need for the commodity, and access to public works such as bridges and roadways, into a single notion of utility. Rancière, in *The Flesh of Words: the Politics of Writing,* speaks of the engineering projects of the nineteenth century, often

---

[28] Dupuit here follows Say in considering political economy a "science," distinct from political theory. The political economist thereby takes the distribution of wealth as a given rather than a problem of political or social organization that needs to be addressed. Policy recommendations would rely on this positive knowledge. See Philippe Fontaine, "The French Economists and Politics, 1750-1850: The Science and Art of Political Economy" 387. Fontaine notes, too, an interest during this period in designing an art of political economy, defined as application of its principles, and a *theory* of the art of political economy (389).

[29] Gagnier makes this argument for developments in Great Britain later in the century as the British aesthetes (Pater, Wilde) inhabit a consumerist ideology while the Marginalist revolution turns the focus of economics to consumer behavior. See *The Insatiability of Human Wants*, chapter 1.

inspired by Saint-Simonian ideas, as a "writing...inscribed in the very texture of things" (106):

> When the Saint-Simonians go to Egypt, attracted by the dream of the canal connecting the two seas, Michel Chevalier contrasts this actual writing with the mystical and diaphanous ideology of political parties: "We trace our arguments," he said, "on a geographical map." (107)

Dupuit's calculation of fair fares would affect the public's access to new means of travel and communication that are "an actual modification of the perceptible world" in Rancière's words (106) and that have undeniable economic and political consequences. To consider these consumer choices as commensurate with the purchase of a theatre ticket or a new shawl ignores collective need and opportunity by configuring them as aggregated individual choice. Yet Dupuit's acknowledgement of public utility again draws this line, as if to say that there is a difference between general social welfare and individual caprice that his own definition of utility would erase.

Dupuit's interest in general or public utility, of course, echoes the concerns of another major tradition of thought, Benthamite utilitarianism. While, as John Bonner notes, "Bentham himself failed to exploit the potential of a utility theory of value" (30), the Epicurean base of his philosophy and his criterion of "the greatest happiness of the greatest number" in assessing social policy and law are both fundamental to Dupuit's thought. Dupuit follows Bentham in later writings by rejecting natural rights and basing property rights on a utility principle (Ekelund and Hébert 309) and by supporting limits on inheritance rights through consideration of public utility (Ekelund and Hébert 332). Indeed, Dupuit's positivism that would describe the world as he finds it yet advocate for policies to promote public utility betrays not a lack of moral compass, but one which considers preexisting moral codes secondary to considerations of measurable social benefit. Thus Dupuit's concern for public welfare falls into the tradition of philosophical utilitarianism, while his redefinition of "utility" is anything but utilitarian in the ordinary sense.

In *The Body Economic: Life, Death, and Sensation in Political Economy and the Victorian Novel*, Catherine Gallagher coins two terms to discuss the centrality of the body to the thinking of political economists. One of these is "bioeconomics," which concerns population theory and food supply, and the second is "somaeconomics" which refers to economic theory based in emotional and sensual feelings. She notes that this latter tradition derives from British empiricism and that political economy is indebted to Jeremy Bentham for an explicit theory of sensationalism (3-4). This calculus of desire and enjoyment is pronounced in French political economy as well with its embrace of British empiricism through the writings of Smith and Bentham and the growing faith in positivism, supporting the sense that political economy should engage in positive not normative analysis. This calculus holds some paradoxes, however. In British political economy, Gallagher remarks, the production of material objects is seen as healthier for the economy than the production of services or knowledge production. Logically, then, desire dominates over enjoyment in a prosperous economy, or pain over pleasure, a most undesirable result in a Benthamite calculus. But she also notes that Say, in order to bring theories of production and consumption more into alignment, de-emphasizes material wealth in his definition of utility, making the difference between the production of goods and the production of services immaterial to value, as it were (52-53). Dupuit follows Say in this; indeed, as an engineer, he is as interested in the consumption of services (railway journeys, or shortening one's route by using a bridge) as he is in the consumption of goods. Nonetheless, the divide between desire and enjoyment that Gallagher points to is relevant to his hypothetical consumer measuring and balancing anticipated pleasures against the pains of enjoyments postponed or foregone. This focus brings economic theory into line with the preoccupations of poets and aesthetic theorists like Baudelaire and Gautier for whom desire and its dissatisfactions, sensual enjoyment and its ephemerality, are ongoing problematics as they wrestle their sense of the satisfactions of art away from the grip of a more abstract, less sensate neoplatonism.

One aim of this chapter has been to suggest that the relationship between political economy and aesthetics in the first half of the nineteenth century in France is closer and more complicated than the rhetoric of *l'art pour l'art* would imply. But there is also the question of discipline formation: what do these discursive formations (borrowing a Foucauldian term) tell us generally about the construction of knowledge during that era, a construction with resonance still in the discourses of economics and art today? Foucault's classic works on knowledge production, *The Order of Things* and *The Archaeology of Knowledge*, offer frameworks for such an inquiry.

One of the main arguments of *The Order of Things* is that an epistemic shift at the end of the eighteenth century undermined the classical order of knowledge and its metaphysical basis; Foucault characterizes this shift as a "withdrawal of knowledge and thought outside the space of representation," and points to Kant's questioning of the conditions in which representation can take place as evidence of this shift (242). While this chapter focuses on a different course for political economy than what Foucault described – the turn to "labor" as the transcendental that makes possible knowledge of human beings – Foucault's larger point remains relevant to the discursive events that this essay describes. The shift can be discerned within Smith's opus alone: the movement from observable utility in objects of beauty and in the beauty of the economic system to the paradox of water and diamonds where use is divorced from value, and "utility," unhinged from "use," launches on the strange voyage of definition described above. (By the same token, "beauty" in the arts escapes representation, frustrating the poet in Baudelaire's "La Beauté"; it resides in a process of infinite reflection between beauty's eye and the heavens.) Measurement becomes the aim in this new "science" – a form of representation, but one quite distinct from the representation of "non-quantitative identities and differences" (218) of Foucault's Classical Order. Meanwhile, definitions or delimitations of "utility" loosen and include a plethora of relations between subject and object: convenience, need, want, desire, caprice, whim. The inclusion of all these aspects of affective life under the umbrella of a single term suggests the inability or, at least, lack of inclination of this new "positive" science to represent or analyze the human psyche in depth and detail (unlike eighteenth-century moral philosophy's comprehensive examination of motivations and sympathies). A straightforward but probably incomplete explanation of this shift would be the division of labor among the emerging social sciences.[30] Other differences between the age of Hume and Smith and the early nineteenth century may be more germane. "Man" for political economy has changed from the Salon and Club conversationalist to the class-specific user of bridges and

---

[30] Fontaine notes that "scientific progress was indeed associated with the division of knowledge between several branches," hence the imperative to define and respect disciplinary boundaries (389, n 17).

roads, a consumer whose preferences have varied and multiple motivations.[31] In a sense, the human psyche is less knowable when a single familiar type or class no longer represents the universal, and Kant's note that aesthetic judgments must assume universality is a remnant of this eighteenth-century presupposition. Further the logic of unintended consequences, a legacy of the eighteenth century (Mandeville, Smith), suggests that the human subject lives under constant illusions. The mechanism and ideology of the "invisible hand" and economic equilibrium/social harmony relies on this disjunction between intention and effect, the economic subject's lack of knowledge of his function in the broader socio-economic system, which warrants his individual freedom, allowed only if its exercise has determinable effects that preserve, in theory, social harmony. But, in light of the strikes and growing worker discontent during the July Monarchy, the ignorance of the economic subject grew less tenable as an assumption. Foucault describes the larger epistemological question underlying nineteenth-century thought: "How can man think what he does not think, inhabit as though by a mute occupation something that eludes him, animate with a kind of frozen movement that figure of himself that takes the form of a stubborn exteriority?" (323). The new producer of knowledge, the social scientist, would observe and theorize what the human subject cannot; hence, the concern with positive "objective" description, measurability, definition of terms. But this new epistemological condition makes all generators of knowledge suspect, and so derision and satiric caricature of the perpetrators of the "dismal science" flourished.

Aesthetic knowledge, too, evolved, a newly prominent field of philosophy at times out of sync or in conflict with emerging trends in art and literature. In France, this is evident in the broad circulation of Cousin's aesthetic and it rejection by critic-poets like Baudelaire for its ties to a stultifying neoplatonism and to the politics of "juste milieu." But the alternative is not a more rarified *l'art pour l'art* auto-

---

[31] Poovey notes this very admission in J.S. Mill's *Essays on Some Unsettled Question in Political Economy*: "Mill was also acknowledging that the very artifice that political economy needed in order to become a science narrowed the understanding of human nature and, with it, the definition of *value* that the science could acknowledge" (*Genres* 243). While I agree with the first part of this statement, my discussion of "utility" is meant to show the fluidity and breadth that persisted in definitions of economic value within the discipline.

nomy, but articulations of new modes of aesthetic reception for both art and literature as forms of representation changed. Rancière speaks of Flaubert's "petrification of language" as democratic, responding to Sartre's charge that it is ultimately bourgeois: if Flaubert's constitutive indifference produced sentences that are "mute pebbles," then their meaning was not tied to a social and political hierarchy, the product of orators, but instead "the words of literature had to display and decipher the signs and symptoms written in a 'mute writing' on the body of things and in the fabric of language" ("Politics of Literature" 17). This writing is no longer readable within a classical order, but is open to all to decipher, its forms creating new ways not only of reading, but of understanding the extraliterary phenomenal realm.

This brings us to the second phase of Foucault's archaeology: the exposition of his own methodology in *The Archaeology of Knowledge*. What is the "discursive formation" at work here, the "distribution of gaps, voids, absences, limits, divisions," this "space of multiple dissensions" (119; 155)? Foucault is clear that the discursive formation is larger than a single discipline; so, in the case at hand, we are concerned not simply with the formation of political economy as a discipline, or with aesthetics after Kant, but with the discursive formation in which relations between subject and object are articulated, in which relations between the individual and the social body are thought, in which "desire," "need," "utility," "interest" take up stations and sometimes mutually define one another, and sometimes merge, in which "freedom" floats freely, sometimes trumping every other discourse in its nebulous authority, sometimes signifying a threat to order and stability. At this point, we seem to be talking about everything imaginable in nineteenth-century society, and that is a danger and also part of the point: what was imaginable? What was able to be articulated? And how was discourse, chameleon-like, transformed by new contexts of articulation: by political currents, social science, the press, new artistic and literary circles, or even the talk of the man and woman in the street?

From this perspective, the "truth" of market equilibrium is legitimized via a "beauty" that is not directly articulated in political economy, but persists via a legacy of earlier thought and a slew of contemporary isomorphisms: theories of social harmony and aesthetic theories – of a "harmony of contraries" or even of color complementarity (see chapter three). These isomorphisms mutually reinforce one another in a post-Revolutionary world where liberty is requisite while fears of instability and violence linger. Such figures mark both the grounds for broad consensus as well as the potential for contradiction and incomprehension. In a different vein, the fate of "utility" is a divergent, rather than convergent one: its most stable, concrete, and narrow definition remains the commonplace sense, the discourse of noneconomists used to ridicule practitioners of the "dismal science" as unaware of life's pleasures and beauties, while the discipline which theorizes and enshrines "utility" broadens its sense to encompass much of what the rest of society and its poets would call "desire." Meanwhile other fundamental terms like "need" and "use" lose definition within the discipline while an urgency grows in both England and France that something has escaped representation. So others, utopians and advocates for the poor take up this occluded discourse as a counter-discourse to the hegemony of the marketplace, where spectacle has replaced representation and the stable value of things.

II

Spectacles of Consumption:
Art and the Industrial Exhibitions

From this epoch derive the arcades and *intérieurs*, the exhibition halls and panoramas. They are residues of a dream world. The realization of dream elements, in the course of waking up, is the paradigm of dialectical thinking. Thus, dialectical thinking is the organ of historical awakening. . . . With the destabilizing of the market economy, we begin to recognize the monuments of the bourgeoisie as ruins even before they have crumbled.
— Walter Benjamin, *The Arcades Project*

In the interior, [the private individual] brings together remote locales and memories of the past. His living room is a box in the theater of the world.
— Walter Benjamin, "Paris, Capital of the Nineteenth Century" (Exposé of 1939)

It is no longer origin that gives rise to historicity; it is historicity that, in its very fabric, makes possible the necessity of an origin which must be both internal and foreign to it: like the virtual tip of a cone in which all differences, all dispersions, all discontinuities would be knitted together so as to form no more than a single point of identity, the impalpable figure of the Same, yet possessing the power, nevertheless, to burst open upon itself and become Other.
— Michel Foucault, *The Order of Things*

While economists found harmonies in the workings of markets, and theorized subjectivities driven as much by caprice as by cool-headed calculation, in the middlebrow discourses of the press, the values and *value* of industry were also mixed with the aesthetic. Although art and industry were understood as separate categories of human endeavor and productivity – as celebrated by their division into two "palaces" at the Universal Exhibition of 1855, le Palais des Beaux-Arts and le Palais de l'Industrie – their relationship is more complicated and interwoven than this dichotomy would imply. One means of determining the public understanding of this relationship is to examine the coverage of the industrial exhibitions of the July Monarchy (1834, 1839, and 1844) in newspapers and journals of various ideological stamps in light of the well-established practice of reviewing the annual salons, juried exhibitions of contemporary art. Although the industrial exhibitions were forerunners and even models for the Crystal Palace of 1851 and the Universal Exhibitions in Paris beginning in 1855, their exclusive focus on industry – on machines and the products of those machines – without the exhibition of art that occurred in the later international exhibitions, affords comparison of their coverage with the older tradition of salon reviews. Indeed, the salons and industrial exhibitions were parallel events, like public spectacles, each drawing press attention and throngs of visitors in different seasons of the same year. Further, reviewers' evocations of the experience of the industrial exhibitions so resemble as to draw on how the annual salons were reviewed, thus encouraging reactions and ways of navigating the spaces of display that imitate the aesthetic experience of the salons. Contemporary discussion of the relationship between art and industry in both arts-oriented and business-oriented publications also gives a sense of how these spectacles were viewed and evaluated, of their impact on France's national image as guardian of "civilization" adapting to a rapidly industrializing economy. Curiously, as I explore in this chapter, constructions of the past often shape understanding of these new goods, drive design, and work to transform the imagined relationship between viewer and object, between self and commodity.

In a way, these reviews were all about viewing and vision in all senses. While Romantic aesthetics redefined vision and imagination for writers and artists, a redefinition that permeated discourses about the self far beyond specifically creative work, the practical aestheticians – the newspaper critics – tackled the problem of how to observe art at the crowded annual salons and other public exhibitions. Arguably it is this latter group of observers of observation who had the greatest direct influence on ways of seeing and ways of speaking about what one sees. Further, this group includes major writers who themselves defined artistic movements, such as Gautier and Baudelaire. Indeed most writers at the time had to make their way in the newspaper culture as such while frequenting the smaller sphere of artists' and writers' coteries, of salons, cafés, and ateliers. But this influence itself, that is, the assumptions and arguments of newspaper critics, was affected by their awareness of a new public for art and by sensibilities shaped by Romantic aesthetics.

In the newspapers and journals of the July Monarchy, a sense of instability in standards of taste, and thus in class allegiance and formation surfaces, symptomatic of a general unsettling of categories, both social (class) and material (between subject and object). While the bourgeois viewer is frequently caricatured as an object of ridicule, questions about what constitutes this powerful new bourgeoisie were seriously worrying; for instance, an article appears in *Le Corsaire-Satan* in 1844 contrasting the bourgeoisie of the *ancien régime* with this new class which is nothing more than "une chose errante ou l'étiquette d'un objet perdu" ("La Bourgeoisie"). Moreover, according to contemporary accounts, the new audience for art included "le peuple," soldiers, grocers and other shopkeepers – "le petit bourgeois" – and provincial visitors as well as the wealthy bankers, industrialists, and politicians and their wives. In other words, this new public was heterogeneous and included a broad range of types in terms of class, income, and education and yet this new public was often seen as a single force to be reckoned with.

This heterogeneous public that flooded the exhibition spaces of art flocked, too, to these new spectacles, also centered on objects. The industrial exhibitions in the French capital drew large crowds and extensive coverage in the press, often in series of articles similar to the serial reviews of the annual art Salons. Distinctly post-revolutionary spectacles (the first took place in 1798), these exhibitions were showcases for French commodities and industry. At these exhibitions, the public viewed not only the latest in machinery, but strolled through rooms full of luxury goods, such as porcelain, silver items, lamps, furniture, fine fabrics, leatherware, cashmere shawls, clocks, wigs, and even ornate firearms. The exhibitions were sponsored by the government; as publicity for the exhibitions and reviews in the press make evident, they provided narratives of progress for France and French industry. Reviews frequently appeared in the same newspapers that covered the Salons, and even occupied the same *feuilleton* space as the art reviews. It is not altogether surprising, then, to discover an aesthetic of the commodity emerge in these reviews, as readers were taught to view the objects produced by industry with the same eye that assessed the value of new works of art.

In Pierre Bourdieu's work on art as a new field of production in the nineteenth century, he argues that it emerged hand-in-hand, or in a necessary relationship of reflexivity, with the aesthetics of reception of this art, that is, "the pure gaze" ("le regard pur") that perceives the work of art as it is meant to be perceived and appreciated, as autonomous and marked by the personal style of the artist. At the same time, this new aesthetics entailed an education in the consumption of art and produced consumers (*Rules of Art* 299-301). Museums and exhibitions played no small part in this education and production of consumers of art. In this chapter, I extend investigation of the production of consumers beyond the confines of art to the goods on display at the industrial exhibitions, arguing that consumption of goods in the broader sense was formed and motivated by an aesthetics derived from the description and assessment of art, even though this aesthetic gaze, for some, assumed an autonomous object. Indeed, speculation concerning the complex relationship between use and beauty is often a subtext of these reviews. Thus the taste for art that conferred distinction, to borrow Bourdieu's term, also formed and informed the taste for luxury goods quite directly through these reviews of the industrial exhibitions.

Art and Industry on Display: Parallel Spaces

The growth of newspapers in nineteenth-century France has been well documented. Between 1830 and 1845, the circulation of Paris dailies tripled (Terdiman, *Discourse/Counter-Discourse* 118). Newspapers and magazines not only reviewed the annual salons and other exhibitions, but also carried articles analyzing industries, banks, stocks, and retail stores for the middle class. Thus, in many publications, art and commerce appeared side-by-side as like topics of general interest. In comparing reviews of the annual salons and the industrial exhibitions, one is struck by the similarity of the experience for the reviewer in terms of understanding and navigating the space of exhibition itself. It is worth noting, too, that the *feuilleton* space in a daily newspaper, a common location for both kinds of reviews, produces certain reader expectations – the writing is brief, part of a series, and topical. The reviewer of the 1834 Industrial Exhibition in the *Journal du Commerce* is self-conscious about his methodology – what he would like to do and how he is constrained:

Nous aurions désiré, dans le compte que nous nous proposons de rendre de nos fêtes industrielles, suivre un ordre méthodique qui nous permit d'embrasser dans un même système de généralités, tous les objets analogues et, par conséquent, de faire connaître, d'un seul coup-d'oeil, à nos lecteurs, les progrès réels que l'industrie a fait dans telle ou telle partie, depuis la dernière exposition. Mais ce mode de procéder, tout logique qu'il puisse être, présente un grave inconvénient pour un journal quotidien dont les lecteurs veulent être mis jour par jour au courant de tout ce qui se passe, et bon gré malgré il faut bien que le *Journal du Commerce*, dès le troisième jour,[1] entre en matière, et, comme tous ses confrères, entretienne ses lecteurs de l'exposition. ("Feuilleton. Exposition des produits de l'industrie"[1])

Writing for a business-oriented newspaper, this reviewer feels torn between a methodology organized around categories of products, tracing industry-specific progress, and a more entertaining account of the industrial exhibition which gives his readers up-to-date information on what is making news. No doubt this reviewer feels that the more "logical" approach is truer to the aim of measuring industrial progress than the sort of coverage favored by the public. Yet he must interest his readers for he, like the manufacturers, is competing in a marketplace, the same discursive marketplace that shapes Salon reviews. This is an admission that schematic analysis aimed at assessment and measurement will take a back seat to producing a vicarious experience for the reader, the sheer sensation of witnessing the new spectacle. As a result, the reviewer, like so many Salon reviewers, will take his readers through the experience of touring the exhibition, room by room, to produce the illusion of being there.

It is a commonplace of Salon reviews to bemoan the crowds for making viewing difficult, to criticize the organization of the Salon, and to criticize the catalogue for being misleading. The organizers of the industrial exhibitions come in for the same kind of criticism. The reviewer in the *Journal du Commerce* cited above remarks on "ce chaos industriel," and in trying to make sense of it, finds that the catalogue indicates that if a certain item is in room one, the next listed will be in room four, and the following in room two (1). He speculates that the order was set simply by the order of registration by the exhibitors. Other critics comment on the dizzying abundance of items and the difficulty of comprehension for someone outside the industry, particularly when viewing machines. For instance, with a certain measure

---

[1] The exhibition opened three days earlier; this is already the second article covering it in this newspaper.

of class-based condescension, Jules Janin, the reviewer of the 1839 Industrial Exhibition in *L'Artiste*, a major journal advocating for the arts, laments that he is as lost as the crowd is in making sense of the Exhibition: "On a beau n'être qu'un écrivain, on ne veut pas rester perdu, bouche béante, dans cette foule d'idiots qui ont des yeux pour ne pas voir, des oreilles pour ne pas entendre, et qui regardent toutes ces merveilles, récemment créées, avec aussi peu d'attention que d'intelligence" (17). Janin also reviewed the Salon for *L'Artiste* that year and his remark is reminiscent of how the bourgeois crowds are frequently characterized by Salon reviewers. But beyond the poor organization of the exhibition halls and press of the crowds, the sense of chaos and bafflement felt by the reviewers stems also from the sheer novelty of many of the machines and items on display. As Janin puts it, "Je ne crois pas, en effet, qu'il y ait au monde un seul homme capable de deviner toutes ces nouveautés étranges ; je suis même persuadé qu'il y en a bien peu qui soient capables de les comprendre, surtout quand vous arrivez au plus fort de ce silence, quand l'âme, c'est-à-dire la vapeur, manque à toutes ces machines, quand le mouvement et la vie ont quitté ces rouages, quand toutes ces formes fantastiques se présentent à vous, arrêtées dans leur travail de chaque jour" (17). In his eyes, the new machines take on the aspect of silent, inscrutable monsters, creating a nightmarish atmosphere. Note that his bafflement derives from two aspects of the exhibition: the machine's unfamiliarity, its newness, and its decontextualization, removed from worksite and divorced from function, a situation endemic to the exhibition as an institution of selective display. The *frisson* of the novel and the strange undoubtedly adds to the attractions of the exhibition, but also provides a reason and psychological substrate for writing: to counter the new, to make the strange comprehensible and familiar.

For some reviewers, both of the Salon and of the Industrial Exhibition, the sense of chaos takes on a broader meaning, signifying general cultural decline. Arsène Houssaye, editor of *L'Artiste*, begins his series of reviews of the Salon of 1844 on a dour note, berating artists for their penchant for hasty productions—sketches, theater sets—and their love of fame and gain. He bemoans the loss of direction and common purpose in art since the revolution of 1830, and drawing on Romantic themes, he castigates artists for appealing to the eyes, not the soul, that is, for addressing a physical rather than spiritual sense of vision. He proclaims chance—"le hasard"—the only

master heeded today (10 March 1844, 146). And so, in his second
article on the Salon of 1844, he finds that the lack of direction in the
visual arts results in mediocre art and an experience of disorder in the
exhibition space itself:

> J'ai passé vite devant les 2,423 toiles, marbres, plâtres, pastels, dessins et
> gravures qui sont réunis, pour la même fête, dans le palais des chefs-d'œuvre.
> Tout ce que j'ai remarqué vient sans ordre s'agiter sous mes regards. Rien ne se
> fixe encore dans ma mémoire.

And even aided by the catalogue, "je n'y vois pas plus clair" (17
March 1844, 162).

Gabriel Laviron, *L'Artiste*'s reviewer of the 1844 Industrial Exhibition, takes up a similar theme, commenting on the high level of
purposeless frenetic activity in contemporary France, the instability in
laws, institutions, and traditions, and the consequent reliance on
chance, "le hasard," in decision-making. These general comments lead
into his characterization of the architectural spaces of his time as similarly provisional and temporary, including public buildings such as
the Opera, the railroads, and the exhibition space in the Louvre, sup-
plemented for the annual Salon, itself necessitating a temporary displacement of the permanent collection. Then he turns to the subject of
his article: "on construit provisoirement, tous les cinq ans, pour abriter
les chefs-d'œuvre de l'industrie nationale, de méchants hangars déco-
rés avec du papier peint que l'on décore du titre pompeux de Galerie
d'Exposition" (28 April 1844, 266).

Thus, this critic's view of the space for the Industrial Exhibition –
transitory and marked by fakery – is rhetorically linked to his experience of his age, and these features mark the space of the Salon as well.
And, although art and industry tended to be figured as oppositional,
these reviews reveal common cultural and social anxieties triggered
by the exhibitions – suspicion of the spectacle as false and fleeting,
which puts in question the common ideals (nationalist pride and
"Progress") that they represent, as well as common strategies for
comprehending and ordering the experience of these spectacles. After
complaining about the practical difficulties of seeing– the arrangement
of the exhibitions, poor lighting, poor placement of works, misleading
catalogues (guides to direct one's vision) – *L'Artiste*'s reviewers of
both the Salon and of the Industrial Exhibition, as consciously
subjective viewers, alternately give themselves up to the randomness

of the experience of these spectacles, or rely on the catalogue categories to order their experience (genre and authorship for art, or kinds of
goods in the Industrial Exhibition).

Given the growing public for spectacle, Salon reviewers often
assumed an educative role: instructing the public about what constitutes good art, all the while critiquing public taste, evidenced by
which paintings draw crowds. But, in the wake of Romanticism, taste
was subjective, and passion laudatory, and so the aesthetic sensibility
could indulge in and model flights of fancy. A look at the reviews in
the more flamboyant arts-oriented newspaper, *Le Corsaire*, reveals
another strategy for dealing with randomness: to dissolve it into a
dream experience. The critic who covered the Salon of 1844 for *Le
Corsaire* signed himself "F." He makes the usual complaints about the
jury's selection, with charges of partiality and self-interest; he also
criticizes the decision to no longer allow the renting of "livrets" (the
catalogue) and he derides the placement of the paintings as entirely
random – "au hasard". This randomness directs his experience: "moi
aussi je marcherai au hasard." He remarks upon the stupidity of the
crowd, but saves his most vituperative remarks for supercilious connoisseurs: "tout ce qui plait à la foule les jette dans des attaques de
nerfs" (22 March 1844, 1; 2).

F., however, does not rely on randomness to order his review, but
tends to group together the entries of individual artists, although his
last article depicts his descent into the Dantesque underworld of
sculpture. This piecemeal treatment of the salons, again, was typical,
much of the comment on the line of whether an artist's entries were
better or worse than previous years, and why. Indeed, this critic is
aware of how all the reviews of the Salon resemble one another,
blaming this on the word limits imposed on writers and the enormous
number of works exhibited. But to get a sense of his aesthetic values,
it is worthwhile to look at moments when his enthusiasm is greatest.
For instance, he remarks on an immense painting, "which would be
impossible to not notice," for it extends thirty feet in width, twenty in
height, and takes up almost an entire wall of the *Salon-Carré*, one of
the central rooms. It is Auguste Couder's "Fédération des gardes nationales et de l'armée au Champ-de-Mars, à Paris (14 juillet 1790)". F.
notes that the official "exposition" of the subject in the *livret* is nearly
as long as the painting itself! Then he gives his own estimation of the
painting, followed by a telling contrast:

Il y a sans doute dans cet ouvrage un grand mérite d'exécution, une patience infinie, une rare perfection de détails. Choisissez au hasard parmi ces milliers de figurines qui fatiguent l'œil, sans rien dire à l'imagination; vous n'en trouverez pas une qui ne soit, prise à part, un petit chef-d'œuvre de vérité et de finesse. Pour nous, qui connaissons la facilité un peu négligente de M. Auguste Couder, ce soin extrême, ce précieux fini, cette conscience presque scrupuleuse dans les moindres parties d'un si grand tableau, nous a un peu étonnés, et – pourquoi ne pas l'avouer? – nous soupçonnons plus d'un apprenti d'avoir travaillé à cette *Fédération*, sous les ordres et la direction du maître. Où serait le mal? Les grands peintres n'ont jamais dédaigné la collaboration de leurs élèves.— Mais si M. Couder croit avoir fait un tableau, il se trompe; il n'a fait qu'un plan. Cette toile est vide. Il n'y a ni foule, ni bruit, ni mouvement; point d'unité, point d'action, rien de l'enthousiasme qu'a dû éveiller dans le peuple cette imposante céré- monie. Tous ces bons hommes, rangés symétriquement en bataille, nous rappellent les soldats de plomb dont les enfants savent si bien se servir dans les combinaisons profondes de leur invariable stratégie. La place du tableau de M. Couder n'est pas au Louvre, n'est point à Versailles; c'est à la Bibliothèque, section des estampes et des cartes géographiques, ou bien dans les cartons de ministère de la guerre, comme document bon à consulter.

Je donnerais vingt *Fédérations*, dix fois plus grandes que celles de M. Cou- der, pour un tout petit tableau de M. Papéty, qui ne tient qu'un coin modeste au- dessous de cette immense page. Ce n'est qu'un corps de femme, haut de quelques pouces—car le saint n'est mis à côté, apparemment, que pour justifier la *Tentation*. Saint Hilarion ou saint Antoine, qu'importe? le fait est que cet ad- mirable torse, si Dieu ne vient pas en aide à ses élus, suffirait, à lui seul, à dé- peupler le Paradis. Quelle séduction dans le regard, quelle grâce dans la pose, quelle voluptueuse nonchalance dans le mouvement! Comme le plaisir suinte par tous les pores de cette peau d'albâtre! Quels désirs allume cette légère et perfide tunique, semée d'étoiles d'or, et tissue d'air et de rayons! Les détails sont traités avec une science rare, et le festin est digne de la belle tentatrice. (4 April 1844, 2)

One implication of F.'s polemic is worth noting: the division between art and other forms of representation is unstable even though these paintings have won a juried competition in order to be included in the Salon. F. would re-categorize *Fédérations* and banish it from the Lou- vre. How does he judge? Using his own aesthetic eye: *Fédérations* belongs in the department of cartography at the library, or in the min- istry of war by dint of its excessive orderliness, producing an "empty" canvas. F. claims here a category mistake, non-art at the Salon. To clarify his point, F. directs the viewer/reader's attention to another small painting below this "page": the *Tentation*. For F. this painting is the place of desire and ease. Unlike the large tableau that fatigues the critic's eye with its detail, this tiny painting is taken in at a glance, a glance returned by the seductress herself, defining the space of art as a pure screen for erotic projection, the space for the writing of desire. Ironically, while F. berates the first work for not living up to its stirring patriotic subject, he explicitly reads past the genre and intention of this religious painting. His attitude is: who cares about the saint?

What is perhaps most significant in terms of public instruction is F.'s polemic against institutional aesthetics, manifested by the display space itself (huge for *Fédérations*), for which he would substitute his aesthetics of desire and reading against the grain, that is, against the genre and intention of this religious painting. And it is not only the representation of her body, but also of the fabric of her tunic that draws his praise, in tone and attention to detail not so different from description of silks and damasks at the industrial exhibitions. Overall F. leads the reader through the experience of the salon by creating a space of erotic projection at its best moments – or nightmarish space in the worst (the inferno of statues or the chaos of the crowd are examples). He also leads us to imagine that these are the visual delights that draw the populace of Paris – like the populace of Paradise in F.'s quip; the implication of his criticism of Couder's painting is that the work does not sufficiently stimulate the viewer's imagination and desires.

That reviews of the industrial exhibitions would also aim at public instruction is hardly surprising; often, after an initial article describing the exhibition's opening as turbulent and confusing, the writer will do his research and make subsequent columns more edifying. But that many reviewers would be concerned with teaching taste, or would even conjure dream spaces, as we will see, rather than simply providing information about recent innovations in machines or manufacturing processes, is another symptom of the kinship between these kinds of reviewing and, presumably, viewing. This tension between experienced randomness and the ordering structure of the catalogue may help explain the resort to summoning an illusion of a "dream space" for the reviewers and viewers of both the Salon and the Industrial Exhibition. As with F.'s Salon review, considerations of taste can lead to wonderment or to horror.

The influence may go in the opposite direction as well, that is, values associated with the Industrial Exhibitions may appear in Salon reviews. While the focus on measuring progress found in reviews of the industrial exhibitions – and the demonstration of progress in industry is an official aim of these events – may seem anathema to the

aims of Salon reviewers, this is often not so. The reviewer of the
Salon of 1834 in *L'Artiste* evaluates the work of each artist in terms of
his or her "progrès" since the last Salon (only a year earlier). This
critic is on the whole sanguine about the current Salon, but sees this
"progress" as an indication that French painting is beginning to
emerge from the period of decline that followed the "perfection"
reached in the early seventeenth century ("Salon de 1834"162). This
question of whether French art is on the ascendant or in decline is
posed in some form by nearly every Salon reviewer. But the fact that
these public spectacles are competitions that occur at regular intervals
creates an expectation of progress, thereby reinforcing the notion that
"progress" is to be valued. And during the July Monarchy, rewarding
progress was aligned with a political rhetoric of encouraging a merito-
cracy in place of the old aristocratic order. In the words of Louis-Philippe at the awards ceremony for the 1834 Industrial Exhibition,
"Montrons que si nous n'avons pas voulu de l'aristocratie du privilège, nous voulons l'aristocratie de la grandeur d'âme, de l'habileté, du
talent et des services rendus à la patrie" ("Distribution des récompenses accordées à l'industrie" 2). (The account in the *Journal du Commerce*, itself taken from *Le Moniteur*, records the audience's reaction:
"Nouveaux applaudissemens, nouveaux cris de *vive le roi!*") Of
course, defining "progress" is itself a concern of reviewers, for both
art and industry. But the fetishization of novelty, or the view that
novelty in and of itself has value, is clearly one consequence of the
"history as progress" paradigm that such exhibitions encourage, for
industry first and eventually for art.

Thus questions of taste and expectations of progress compose
distinct and often incommensurate threads of analysis in reviews of
both the salons and the industrial shows, incommensurate in that taste
is based in the tradition-bound values of art criticism, while progress
would seem to demand innovation, the disruption of old ways of production, and the appearance of new, strange products. But, even when
covering the industrial exhibitions, with all the talk of French
industrial progress, explicit in the publicity materials and exhibition
catalogues, some reviewers reflected on how elusive the measurement
of progress was and on how the industrial exhibitions failed to represent such progress accurately.[2] Critics saw distortions stemming

---

[2] See, for instance, Fix 4.

from the demand for novelty – that innovation for its own sake would represent progress as opposed to a real increase in the product's utility, and from the incentive to create spectacle – to exhibit rather than simply represent an industry. Some reviewers opined that progress should be defined in terms of lower costs of production, resulting in lower prices for consumers rather than the "tours de force" that, as display and sensation, make the greatest impact.[3] Clearly critics at that time were ready to dispute the official rhetoric that such exhibitions were meant to measure and represent progress in French industry by noting the invidious effects of the drive to innovate and the lure of display, exhibitors' interests in enticing consumers and building reputation through the pleasure of spectacle.[4]

Given that reviews of the industrial exhibitions and salon reviews often appeared in the same places in newspapers and evoked parallel experiences, and that sometimes the same writer would review both events, it was perhaps inevitable that the question of the relationship between art and industry arose. The most obvious answer would seem to be "no relationship" at a time when the ideology of *l'art pour l'art* was on the ascendant, yet instead one finds characterizations of an intimate relationship, even among advocates for the arts. In 1834, the reviewer of the Industrial Exhibition for *L'Artiste* begins his series of articles with the assertion that in no other country do the arts exert more of an influence over industry than in France. This reviewer, like many others, notes the superiority of French luxury goods, although even greater perfection would be achievable were artists to have a direct role designing for industry. In a later article, as this reviewer re-marks on items in bad taste, this suggestion recurs and the question of taste itself is addressed within the framework of French achievement in art:

> Le sentiment du beau dans les arts, que les progrès de notre siècle tendent chaque jour à inspirer avantage au public, doit amener, dans les ameublemens, dans tous les produits, le goût du bon, autrement dit du beau; les fabricans seront bien alors forcés de se convertir et de venir demander aux artistes le pardon et le

---

[3] See, for instance, J.B., "Feuilleton. Exposition des produits de l'industrie. (1er article.)" 1.

[4] Philippe Hamon sees this tension between representation and display as an ambiguity inherent in "exposition" both architectural and textual: "The exposition is simultaneously utilitarian and picturesque – a place both for entertainment and for the exhibition of knowledge" (10).

remède de leurs erreurs. . . . Nous croyons généralement, et bien à tort, que les
arts sont un vain exercice de la pensée humaine, sans influence immédiate sur
notre bien-être et nos plaisirs. Les artistes auraient intérêt à prouver le contraire,
en mettant au besoin leurs facultés au service de l'industrie ; refuseraient-ils
d'ailleurs de faire aujourd'hui ce que les artistes et des artistes éminens comme
Cellini et tant d'autres ont fait à des époques célèbres. (251)

In other words, French taste is a consequence of public exposure to
French art, and French industry would do well to draw on the talents
of artists, giving art a clear utility. The French then would emulate
other societies notable for their artistic achievement, such as the city-
states of Renaissance Italy. But this reviewer also sees resistance to
such an accommodation between art and industry in the consumers of
luxury goods: no longer royalty and aristocracy, they are the newly
rich who value money above all and would have ostentation, the sign
of wealth, dominate over taste in the goods they prefer. But the ideal
traced by this reviewer is revealing of the dynamic between art and
industry: just as the aesthetic gaze assesses the goods on display, so
ideally production itself would aim at satisfaction of this sense. In
other words, the aesthetic puts a value on goods that conform to its
values, and so gives industry an incentive to create aesthetically-
pleasing goods, as opposed to the cheap, useful, or efficiently produced. In 1844, this ideal continues to be invoked. In the very same
opening piece in which he decries his own "provisional" era, Laviron
explains why *L'Artiste* would review the Industrial Exhibition by
summoning a vision of a future *belle époque* of the arts supported by
industry, similar to past golden ages in Venice, Florence, and Pisa. He
looks forward to a time when industry will require "strange palaces"
and create work for architects, painters, and sculptors, a solution to the
problem of the provisional itself (28 April 1844, 266-67).

Although business-oriented newspapers, like *Le Commerce*, tend
to argue for utility and affordability as value in the goods displayed at
the industrial exhibitions, we find arguments for aesthetic value in
such publications as well. In the feuilleton of *Le Commerce*, of 10
February 1839, an article, "Du goût dans les arts industriels," takes
just such a position in publicizing the appearance of a new journal,
Exposition. The author argues that the "je ne sais quoi" that produces
the sense of beauty is not only possible in the "arts industriels," but
gives French goods their competitive edge. Thanks to the taste of
French artists and manufacturers, French exports excel "par l'élégance

de ses dessins, par l'harmonie de ses formes, par la riche variété de ses conceptions" (1). It is this "je ne sais quoi" – by definition undefinable yet productive of pleasure – that bridges the divide between work of art and product of industry:

> Qu'est-ce qui fait d'une maison un morceau d'architecture? Qu'est-ce qui donne aux produits des fondeurs et des ciseleurs ce charme qui leur fait accorder le nom de production de l'art? C'est précisément cette entente de la forme, qu'on peut puiser dans une étude attentive du dessin, mais qu'on ne peut assujétir à des règles certaines, parce qu'elle participe de l'imagination.

The Romantic invocation of the imagination is hardly new in 1839, but that it characterizes the potential of commodities to aspire to the status of art is worth noting. According to this view, art has had its impact on industry, and the consumer's eye has been trained in aesthetics. In the *Journal des Économistes*, Théodore Fix goes so far as to assert a moral function for taste in industry. If "du bon marché, de la qualité et du goût" are the three factors that matter in judging the achievements of industry, "le goût, qui est . . . la condition morale du l'industrie, l'épuration de ce que les instincts, les besoins et les jouissances peuvent avoir de grossier, le goût est à lui seul le véritable sceau de la perfection, et peut devenir, dans le luxe et dans l'abondance, un moyen de purification et la source de certaines perfections morales (3).

This equation of the good and the beautiful is no doubt itself a product of the aesthetic philosophy of Victor Cousin and adds the argument of moral edification to the benefits of visiting the industrial shows and buying items like those on display.

Art is also blamed for the aesthetic failures of industry. In 1844, Laviron, the critic reviewing the Industrial Exhibition for *L'Artiste*, complains of the "culte du laid" learned from the dominant trend in art and literature of the last twenty years:

> Le culte du laid, que l'on essaye depuis tantôt vingt ans d'ériger en théorie dans les hautes régions de l'art et de la littérature, a fini par s'étendre jusqu'aux plus intimes; et là, dépouillé du prestige de grandeur qui protège les compositions importantes, il s'étale dans toute sa honteuse nudité. (3 May 1844, 12)

In this negative vein, the dividing line between art and industry seems especially nebulous; it is a "prestige of greatness" that keeps art from disgusting us when this same aesthetic applied to everyday objects does provoke such disgust.

Art's Gift to Industry, or the Nostalgia Fashion

Laviron's diagnosis of what is wrong with the art-influenced products of French industry (he likes the machines on display) points to another trend that complicates the narrative of progress: the nostalgia fashion, including the desire for reproductions of the work of earlier eras. He complains: "Tous les styles sont mélangés, toutes les époques sont confondues; on fait du neuf à l'imitation des plus hideuses vieilleries; le culte du laid, porté jusqu'au fanatisme, ne connait plus de mesure, et pour peu que cela continue, nous ne désespérons pas de voir les dames à la mode porter, en guise de collier, un chapelet de vertèbres humaines, et déposer le soir ces étranges bijoux dans un crâne monté en baguier" (12). The aesthetic of the grotesque to which he alludes emerged, of course, out of the Romantic romance with the medieval which has spilled over into the world of everyday objects, a complaint made by other critics as well. And it is notable that Laviron is as critical of the confusion of styles as he is of the ugliness imitated. But he doesn't complain of historical reproduction itself as a trend. And this is typical of the reviews of the industrial exhibitions as a whole. Indeed, new processes that make possible the mechanical reproduction of artifacts from the past are typically praised both for the ingenuity of the technology and for the consequent reduction in price, making such objects affordable. Thus the irony that technological progress was lauded for making possible the illusion of living in the past.

While Laviron complains of the ugliness of many items meant to evoke past eras, many reviewers found much to admire aesthetically and technologically in these historical reproductions. Typical is a remark that praises the cabinet-makers of the faubourg St.-Antoine in Paris for their broad range of furniture styles, including ornate pieces in medieval, Renaissance and Empire styles as well as more simple ones –"selon le goût du jour." This year, 1844, the dominant style is Louis XV: "et l'on se croirait parfois transporté dans les boudoirs musqués de Mme de Pompadour, en voyant ces guéridons en bois de rose, ornés de petits amours peints sur porcelaine, et de figures à la manière de Boucher" (Z. 2) After praising the evocative power of this furniture, this reviewer, like so many others, sounds the note of

progress in the furniture's "execution." W. Dickson, in *Le Commerce,*
June 26, 1844, admires a "petit service de thé, dit *vis-à-vis*, dont on ne
peut considérer les détails sans un sourire ou un souvenir, un espoir ou
un regret, est dans le goût caractéristique du XVe siècle; c'est de la
Renaissance pure" (3). He credits the literature of the time with
forming public taste, and consequently industry's success in evoking
memories through such pleasing detail is evidence of industry's
liaison with the reigning aesthetic. In the feuilleton of *La Presse* of
May 5, 1844, the reviewer praises stained-glass imitations of the rose
windows of the cathedrals of Chartres, Paris, and Reims: "Ce qui était
un embellissement royal est devenu désormais un objet d'ameuble-
ment bourgeois, et il n'est pas un seul cabinet d'étude, pas un boudoir
où, pour quelques centaines de francs, on ne puisse se procurer ces
demi-jours mystérieux si propices à l'étude et à la reverie" (1). The
stained glass not only inserts a medieval note in interior décor, but
also creates an atmosphere conducive to the pleasures of study and
daydreaming for the bourgeois consumer. One critic in 1834 even
suggests the possibility of a house full of rooms reminiscent of
different past eras. Praising the achievements of one manufacturer, he
enthuses:

> Grace à M. Chenavard, quel plaisir peut se donner un homme riche et
> d'imagination? qu'il meuble tous les appartemens de sa maison, chacun dans un
> style différent et qui rappelle un siècle célèbre ; le voilà successivement et au gré
> de son caprice, transporté au milieu de siècle qu'il veut apercevoir. Qui
> n'éprouverait un charme infini à étudier l'histoire du seizième siècle ? qui n'en
> comprendrait mieux le sens, assis dans une chambre dont tous les meubles ainsi
> que ce lit retraceraient à ses yeux la physionomie matérielle de l'époque?
> ("Exposition de l'industrie française" 194)

In other words, the wealthy can use interior décor to turn their
domiciles into escapes back in time; they can enjoy the sensation of
being transported into other eras to study history first hand, as it were,
elevating the role of consumer to that of scholar. Thus, at this time of
rapid industrialization, national pride in innovation is mingled with a
strong desire for the past. One is tempted to speak of a forerunner of
postmodernism here – nostalgia reacting to and afforded by rapid
technological change, the melding of the two in virtual realities, a
phantasmagoria of past in present. And a feature of the reviews of the
industrial exhibitions reinforces this impression: the writing of little
histories to ground the objects on display.

Typically reviews of the industrial exhibitions begin with accounts of the history of the industrial exhibitions themselves. Sometimes the writer has a particular argument to make; for instance, an anonymous writer in *L'Artiste* in 1839 contends that the spacing of the exhibitions (every five years) and the lack of a permanent structure to house them allows the large manufacturers to avoid the competition that more frequent exhibitions and a better space for exhibiting would make possible ("De l'exposition des produits de l'industrie" 2). But most reviewers seem to emphasize through these histories the extent to which the industrial exhibitions are a product of postrevolutionary France, often with mention of the work liberalization law of 1791. These accounts often do point to the purpose that the exhibitions served for different governments – for the Directorate, for Napoleon, for the Restoration, and now for the July Monarchy – with an emphasis on how peace encourages industrial progress. The long period of the Napoleonic Wars during which there were no exhibitions is frequently cited as evidence of this. That industrial successes serve as substitutes for or supplements to military ones was implied from the start with the use of the Champs de Mars as the site of the first industrial exhibition in 1798. During the July Monarchy, Louis Philippe explicitly argues that economic competition is a better form of warfare than military campaigns in his speeches at the closing of the exhibitions. Such boosterism is evident in these brief histories, too, as the growth in size and duration of the industrial exhibitions is seen as a sign of the growth and health of French industry.[5]

Many reviewers also provide narratives of the history of particular industries. Obviously, industries that are quite new – the making of steam engines, for instance – lack such introductions. But for some industries – wool, cotton, cashmere, certain kinds of decorative metalwork (niello) – such histories almost inevitably appear. On one level, like the exhibition histories, they are narratives of progress: for instance, the story of the introduction of merino sheep in France, a gift from Spanish king in 1780, and the improvement of the French stock

---

[5] See, for instance, J.B., "Exposition des produits de l'industrie (1er article.) Des expositions des produits de l'industrie en général." The author cites the growth in public interest, evidenced in the lengthening of the time of exhibition, as a sign of progress among others (1).

over time, appears in more than one review.[6] But such stories also
serve as a reminder that these new commodities are rooted in an older
France, that the high-quality, soft woolen fabrics on display have their
own ancestors in fabrics available only to the royalty and nobility of
the Ancien Régime. Shawls tend to carry an especially heavy
symbolic load. Memories of shawls brought back from Napoleon's
campaigns in Egypt signify both Oriental luxury and military victory.
Laviron, for instance, noting that cashmeres "arrivèrent chez nous
comme une part du butin, tachés de sang et percés de coups de sabre,"
tells of "une vieille dame qui montre encore avec orgueil un châle
magnifique, un des plus beaux ouvrages des ouvriers de l'Inde, qui lui
fut offert par le défunt général, son mari, alors capitaine de cavalerie.
On y a laissé, très apparente, la trace du terrible coup de sabre qui le
fit passer, de la tête d'un aga des Mamelucks, aux mains de l'officier
français" ("Exposition des produits de l'industrie. Tissus – meubles –
machines" 217). The new shawls on display, manufactured in France
in imitation of high-quality, highly-prized handwoven shawls from
India, afford middle-class women a share of such nationalistic triumph
over foes both through the evocation of Napoleonic victories and
endorsement of French industry that, in replicating exotic goods, will
triumph on the battleground designated by the July Monarchy, that of
the international marketplace.[7]

   More than one reviewer in 1834 told the story of niello,
decorative metalwork, from Renaissance Florence to the "Orient" to
the courts of the Russian czars to finally nineteenth-century France,
through a bit of serendipity:

> Transporté d'abord de l'Orient en Europe, il est au bout de quelques siècles
> forcé de rentrer dans sa patrie; il y sommeille long-temps, ne s'occupant que
> d'embellir les sabres, les poignards et les chibouques des Asiatiques; puis, après
> un long et obscur repos, il s'échappe par les déserts, et gagne le nord de
> l'Europe, demandant quelques encouragemens à l'aristocratie tartare de la cour
> du czar. Là, un voyageur prend par hasard une tabatière niellée dans sa poche,
> puis le voilà à Paris, et grâce à lui cet art, depuis trois siècles chassé de notre
> Occident industrieux, y est rétabli avec gloire. ("Exposition de l'industrie
> française. Les nielles françaises. – La lithographie. Les bronzes" 249)

---

[6] For one example, see J.B., "Exposition des produits de l'industrie. Salle des tissus. –
(1er article.) – Des laines" 1.
[7] For an analysis of the semiotics of the shawl in nineteenth-century France as an
indicator of feminine identities and consequent anxieties regarding class mobility and
authenticity, see Hiner.

So told, the present-day object encapsulates the history, the product's voyage over time and space, evoking a fantasy of other times and places, a frequent trope of Romanticism. The notion that the object serves as an embodiment of history or the starting point for the imagination of dramatic histories becomes a commonplace, as in this *feuilleton* on the "Exposition des manufactures royales de Sèvres, des Gobelins et de Beauvais" by Théophile Gautier: "Les vases mexicains, par exemple, avec leur attitude épatéc, leurs mascarons hideux, leurs anses tordues, n'ont ils pas quelques chose de sauvage, de féroce, qui rappelle les monstrueuses idoles de Vitzliputzli que M. de Humboldt désigne sous le nom de Huitzilopochtli. Ces vases-là ne sont-ils pas faits pour être remplis de sang ?" (2). Gautier implies that the object asks to be read into the viewer's own fantasies of the primitive and exotic, in the guise of history.[8]

Thus the allure of these products of industry was constituted through reconstructions of the past, whether a history of the product – a story of progress and improvement, but also a reminder of a pre-revolutionary France – or an evocation of an imagined exotic history. In effect these reviewers evoked for their readers the comforting or thrilling thought of a past present in the contemporary commodity. Product-viewing was inflected with the pleasures of manufactured memory which gave a context for the new and thus diminished the shock of the unfamiliar. Further, the new styles, especially in household furnishings, were often copies of grandiose decor from past eras. Consequently while the industrial exhibitions encouraged and provided a showcase for the cult of the new, this was a showcase imbued with a pleasurable sense of the past.

The power of the experience and discourse of the industrial exhibitions, a discourse with aesthetic, literary, and historical overtones, to motivate consumption activities is clear. At times, it is explicit as in a *feuilleton* from *Le Corsaire* covering the 1844 Exhibition of the Products of Industry (May 6, 1844) which makes the passage from exhibition space to the space of consumption a theme. It appears in an ongoing series of *feuilletons* entitled "Paris Industriel"

---

[8] See Natalia Majluf on the misreadings of art by Peruvian and Mexican artists, especially Francisco Laso's "The Inhabitant of the Cordillera of Peru," at the Paris Universal Exhibition of 1855 as French critics represented national difference in the mold of travelers' picturesque.

which covers everything from new factories to new stores for "des dames" to life insurance. (Indeed, the latter topic appears often enough to suggest an avid interest among the readership or a particularly strong marketing campaign among insurers.) There is undoubtedly a subtext of progress in this coverage – for instance, the writer, Charles Desolme, praises one manufacturer for refining the process of making porcelain like "tendre vieux Sèvres" at much less cost. A certain nationalistic pride appears here, too, as Desolme notes that, with these advances, nothing now could keep the French from building a monument comparable to the tower of Nanking.

After discussing the porcelain, in this first piece on the Exhibition, (in later articles he covers other luxury goods, like other critics devoting much attention to shawls in particular), M. Desolme is restless; he must move on: "[d]es salles de l'Exposition aux galeries de la maison Chambellan la transition est toute naturelle." That is, the transition from a spectacle of production – the exhibition of the products of industry – to the place of consumption, the new stores, *is* natural. Caught up in the circulation of publicity, Desolmes presents himself as a reader, infected by desire wrought of discourse, specifically what he has read in the newspapers: "nous sommes entrés chez MM. Bossuat et Tuquet pour voir, de nos propres yeux, toutes les merveilles que nous annoncent les journaux depuis quelque temps, et que nous avaient racontées sincèrement plusieurs personnes de notre connaissance, qui déjà étaient allées rendre visite à ces magasins remarquables" (2). As writer, he proceeds to give his readers a vicarious tour, praising the light made possible by glass roofing, the displays, and the arrangement of the store such that the buyer may circulate freely in pursuit of needs and fantasies. The organization of the store is full of significations: statues of the inventors of production methods stand to indicate the goods which their inventiveness have made possible, an instantiation of industrial inventor as great man (the cult of genius) and work of art (the commodity as human labor transformed into commodity as human thought). Finally, Desolme notes that the owners have plans to add further embellishments to this "immense exposition permanente": if these projects materialize, "MM. Bossuat et Tuquet auront véritablement arraché une page des Mille et une Nuits pour la livrer toute resplendissante aux regards étonnés de la population parisienne" (3). To quote Colin Campbell on the hedonist imagination that drives modern consumerism: "Whatever one experiences in reality it is possible to 'adjust' in imagination so as to make appear more pleasurable; thus the illusion is always better than the reality: the promise more interesting than actuality" (90).

Thus even in publications with an arts-oriented bias, it is difficult to sort the aesthetic from the commercial gaze as goods and *magasins de nouveautés* promise literary fantasies, and exhibits at the Industrial Exhibition serve as vehicles for Romantic dreaming and vicarious pleasures. Such dreaming serves an obvious practical end for the exhibitors: creating desire for goods. Richard Terdiman in his chapter on "Newspaper Culture" in *Discourse/Counter-Discourse* describes the commercialization of the newspapers through surreptitious advertising in "bought" articles, especially after the launch of Emile de Girardin's *La Presse* in 1836 with its lower subscription rates and greater reliance on advertising revenue (123-25). Whether or not this was the case with "Paris Industriel," the commercial incentive is undeniable.

In sum, reviews of the industrial exhibitions show the influence of Salon reviews in their themes (the crowds; taste), conventions (room-by-room organization; appraisal of individual manufacturers as artists), and Romantic overtones (dreaming, transport) and they give us a window into the aesthetic education of the consumer through the construction and representation of interest in the objects on display. They also offer insights into the psychology of an age. Despite the sense that crowds flocked to the exhibitions to witness "Progress" first hand, these reviews show how complicated that experience was. Svetlana Boym, in *The Future of Nostalgia*, observes that nostalgia "inevitably reappears as a defense mechanism in a time of accelerated rhythms of life and historical upheavals" and is "coeval with modernity." Susan Stewart's comment on the gap that attaches nostalgia to the souvenir seems to apply to these manufactured "souvenirs" as well:

> As in an album of photographs or a collection of antiquarian relics, the past is constructed from a set of presently existing pieces. There is no continuous identity between these objects and their referents. Only the act of memory constitutes their resemblance. And it is in this gap between resemblance and identity that nostalgic desire arises. The nostalgic is enamored of distance, not of the referent itself. Nostalgia cannot be sustained without loss. (145)

These reviews reveal how nostalgia mingled with the emerging historical consciousness, both wrought of the repeated and cataclysmic political upheavals in France since the 1789 Revolution and of the changes in everyday life broadly associated with modernization. So the little histories and recreations of the past are symptoms and responses to an epistemic rupture; they feed off the new historical consciousness and feed into it; memory becomes a collective event, informed by a visual display; its artifice is known – it is manufactured, and yet suppressed through the objects as metonyms for a past that is willed.

Terdiman, in his article, "Deconstructing Memory: On Representing the Past and Theorizing Culture in France since the Revolution," lists three determinants "in the realm of production of the social" of the nineteenth century's creation of memory in its modern form:

1. "a quantum leap in the productive power of human labor: the coming of the machine, the rapid, virtually endless replication and dissemination of objects which the machine makes possible" resulting in an altered perception of time itself;

2. the discipline which feeding on the "increasingly powerful analytical inclination in middle-class thought" took the production process as its object with "*time* as its problem" (here I assume Terdiman is referring to political economy and other theories of the social);

3. "the early development of the 'culture' or 'consciousness' industry," as it was called by the Frankfurt School: "rise of the media, embracing an educational system, an increasingly massified press, increasingly programmed collective experiences in shopping, in entertainment, in sport and in national-political collective celebration." This new industry "institutionalized an innovative – and frequently a bewildering – cultural memory," in Terdiman's words (19).

Of course, one finds powerful cross-fertilization among these determinants: machines on display as national and cultural indices; reviews of such displays inflected with the theories and values of political economy; and interplay among aspects of the "culture" industry in that the exhibitions as institutions decontextualize, recategorize, and evaluate the things on display while the press works to acknowledge and overcome bewilderment by writing about change and its concrete manifestations, those machines and their products, and in so doing manufacture and circulate collective memory as history.

Thus in the industrial exhibitions, all three determinants are in play and are interconnected. The nostalgia fashion offset the sense of bafflement and disorientation that many visitors to the exhibitions felt and, no doubt, in a broader context, soothed the sense of historical dislocation of the time. For the impact of political and social upheaval, of a recent history of revolutions, wars, and irreversible social transformation, also haunts these reviews. A latent symptom of this turmoil is the national pride evident in the emphasis on aesthetics itself, on French preeminence in the arts; the reviewers, even in business-oriented publications, provide a vivid sense of how aesthetic attitudes fashioned the reception of commodities and even the comprehension of machines. So, while these exhibitions were evidence of the dominance of progress as an organizing paradigm for the historical consciousness in the early nineteenth century, accounts by contemporary observers belie a countervailing desire to imagine and posit an origin that predates industrial modernity as it is being experienced, an origin, to repeat Foucault's articulation, "in which all differences, all dispersions, all discontinuities would be knitted together so as to form no more than a single point of identity, the impalpable figure of the Same, yet possessing the power, nevertheless, to burst open upon itself and become Other." It is this dream of the Same, of the spectator and potential consumer transporting him or herself back to the origin via the object which inevitably ends in a disjuncture of object and origin, and of self and imagined other, which may be a mechanism in the insatiability of desire produced in consumerism.

But these objects were not simply commodities in the sense of placeholders for exchange value. As Bill Brown reminds us, "even when the commodity form saturates society, . . . culture works to singularize objects"("Reification" 177). Romantic literature and art furnished a framework of meaning, a way of comprehending the attraction of things for the viewers; in other words, literature invented the plot for reading the social text, as Rancière argues. He points to the curiosity shop in Balzac's *The Wild Ass's Skin* as an instance of literature making each object into a "poetic element, a sensitive form that is a fabric of signs as well" ("Politics of Literature" 19). Here was the enabling condition, as it were, for Marx's understanding of the commodity as phantasmagoria (21).[9] Coverage of the industrial

---

[9] Rancière here is also giving his explanation of how Benjamin could read Baudelaire's imagery through the lens of Marx's commodity fetish which also informs the

exhibitions gives strong evidence of the decipherment and animation of objects through literary fashions and story-telling.

The work of illusion itself is powerful as an antidote to bewilderment. The reviews of the industrial exhibitions make us aware of the pleasures of viewing these displays for the public of the July Monarchy, of their desires for transport to other places and times and for the certitude of origins. In the frenzied pursuit of innovation and novelty, hyper-signified by the awards structures of both the Salons and industrial exhibitions, the tempering of novelty with intimations of the past endowed these objects with a double-coded aura: the latest thing, plus a whiff of past grandeur.

---

dreamscape of the arcades. That is, nineteenth-century literature provided the "model of intelligibility – the model of deciphering the unconscious hieroglyph" that made Marx's analysis possible and that Benjamin seized upon to "read" Baudelaire symptomatically ("Politics of Literature" 20-21).

III

Baudelaire's *Salon de 1846*
and the Education of the Bourgeois Viewer

> L'art est un bien infiniment précieux, un breuvage rafraichissant
> et réchauffant, qui rétablit l'estomac et l'esprit dans l'équilibre
> naturel de l'idéal.
> – Baudelaire, *Salon de 1846*

In 1846, a young poet and critic, little known outside a circle of
writers and artists in Paris and the staffs of the newspapers that he
wrote for, published a slim volume on the Salon of 1846 which eventually came to be seen as the augur of modernity in art. One way to
understand the role of this early work in theorizing art's modernity is
to deem it, in the words of Pierre Bourdieu, among "the first systematic formulations of the theory of art for art's sake." Bourdieu characterizes this theory as "this singular way of living through art, whose
roots lie in an art of living that rejects the bourgeois lifestyle, notably
because it is founded upon the act of refusing any social justification
for art or the artist himself," and notes that "no one contributed more
than Baudelaire" towards creating the image of the artist as a disinterested loner, a "dandy," and "an aristocrat indifferent to society's
honours and who looks only to posterity ("Link" 32). Yet, Baudelaire's presentation of the situation of art vis-à-vis the bourgeoisie and
their lifestyle in the *Salon de 1846* may be read quite differently – as
both a strategic play for their support for the arts and an undermining
of the already banal artist/bourgeois antithesis. He opens with an
address and a dedication "Aux Bourgeois," and attempts to negotiate a
position for the contemporary critic that takes bourgeois interests into
account and views the bourgeois public as an audience worthy of address, denigrating instead other more "elite" audiences like the denizens of the ateliers, and other critics. As Eliane Jasenas argues, Bau-

delaire is interested in defining his role as a critic: one who would help shape the critical abilities of this powerful audience.[1] It is a role that requires not simply evaluation of the works of individual artists appearing in the *Salon*, but more importantly the argument for a whole new vision of art that literally entails learning to view in new ways. Indeed, for the Salon as a whole, his aim may be understood as public instruction, an effort to influence the aesthetic sensibilities of this new audience for art drawn from diverse social classes.

Yet the stakes in how we read the *Salon de 1846* are greater than simply registering the rhetorical stance taken by a young poet in defending (some) contemporary art in an era of bourgeois ascendancy. As Baudelaire is often seen as the originator of modern poetry in France, and, in general, of the idea of modernity, so "art for art's sake" or aestheticism is often seen as setting the trend for the separation of art and literature from engagement with the political, social, and, above all, economic in the industrial and post-industrial age. Aestheticism may be defined as a doctrine whereby art purifies itself of content other than itself, and the audience for such art and poetry is largely other like-minded artists, poets, and critics.[2] A corollary to the trend towards self-reference is the move towards abstraction in visual art and poetry. Art thereby buys its autonomy from the values and system of assigning value of the marketplace at the price of a broad audience, forfeiting the opportunity to affect the political or social conscience, or ideology, of that audience.

In light of this version of the progress of art in modern culture, Baudelaire's *Salon de 1846* merits our attention both for what it tells us about the cultural climate in 1846 and for its impact on the future of art and literature. But to cast Baudelaire's thought as the theoretical groundwork for *l'art pour l'art* is to miss his representation and indeed advocacy of art's and artists' interests in the *Salon* that are many-layered and more complicated than any outright refusal of a social role and meaning for art, a refusal, for that matter, absent from

---

[1] Jasenas sees in this dedication Baudelaire's recognition of the need to educate the powerful bourgeoisie in contrast with the highly critical stance towards the problem of their power taken by Stendhal in *D'un nouveau complot contre les industriels* (1825).

[2] In "The Market of Symbolic Goods," Bourdieu describes the production of high art since the 1830's in France as a "field of restricted production" regulated by writers, artists, and critics who basically form "mutual admiration societies" that assume the function of "cultural consecration," buying the autonomy of the field of high art at the price of divorcing themselves from the broader public (115-16).

the *Salon*. Instead if we use Bourdieu's own framework for understanding the sociology of art, we may read the *Salon de 1846* as a document whose aims include the positioning of the artist and writer within the larger spectrum of social meaning and discourse and as a map of that attempt.[3]

Bourdieu, in *The Rules of Art*, outlines a sociological approach to this history that discerns an interplay of homologies among the different arts as fields of production and distribution, and between those fields and the field of power:

> Because they are all organized around the same fundamental opposition as regards the relation to demand (that of the "commercial" and the "non-commercial"), the fields of production and distribution of different species of cultural goods – painting, theatre, literature, music – are structurally and functionally homologous among themselves, and maintain, moreover, a relation of structural homology within the field of power, where the essential part of their clientele is recruited. (161)

He finds a double valence, composed of two economic logics, that becomes automatic or self-propagating around 1880, but has its sources in the early decades of the century in the growth of markets for literature and art, and in documents like Gautier's preface to *Mademoiselle de Maupin* that could be interpreted as reactions to these markets (203). The antinomy between commercial art and literature, pitched to a growing audience, hence market, and "pure" art and literature whose audience is confined to peers, that is, other like-minded writers and artists, creates a curious inversion of commercial versus symbolic capital, according to Bourdieu. Those works with the smallest audience, the audience of other producers of art, accrue the most prestige, or symbolic capital, while current fame, popularity, and commercial success become indicators of works aimed at a large, presumably undiscerning audience and thus lacking in prestige in the long run, while profitable in the short run. In this way, both "economies" take on their own dynamics and, at the same time, rely on interplay between them for these dynamics. Bourdieu is careful,

---

[3] See Robb on how, as a young critic, Baudelaire distinguished himself from other reviewers of the Salon by publishing *Le Salon de 1846* as a separate volume rather than as a series of feuilletons, and on his relationship with the older critic at the *Corsaire-Satan*, Courtois. Wettlaufer cites Robb's research as evidence of Baudelaire's interest in securing an audience for his criticism and thus reason to take "Au Bourgeois" at face value (141).

however, to represent the indirect nature of individual producers' involvement in these dynamics overall. He uses his notion of "habitus" to ground these economies historically vis-à-vis the individual artists and writers. Works emerge from "a space of possibles" that "impresses itself on all those who have interiorized the logic and necessity of the field as a sort of *historical transcendental* [Bourdieu's emphasis], a system of (social) categories of perception and appreciation, of social conditions of possibility and legitimacy which like the concepts of genres, schools, manners and forms, define and delimit the universe of the thinkable and the unthinkable, that is to say, both the finite universe of potentialities capable of being thought and realized at a given moment – freedom – and the system of constraints inside which is determined what is to be done and to be thought – necessity" (236). In other words, a critic and poet like Baudelaire, a player in the field, intuits the strength and legitimizing structure of the critical status quo, the dominance of particular ways of seeing and judging, but also senses how those modes might be transformed. This sense grows from not only a comprehension of the current lay of the land in art, but also from an awareness of the position of the arts within the larger field of the social.

Hence Baudelaire's awareness and use of legitimizing discourses and his assertion of his difference and freedom from some of these, strategically, give us a window into his sense of the cultural field – how he might position himself within it and how he might transform it. Looked at in the context of existing aesthetic discourses, we get a sense of the possibilities for contention – how Baudelaire draws on key terms in aesthetic schools he would undermine and replace. Bourdieu deems Baudelaire a "nomothète" ("founder" or "founding hero") of the trend towards autonomy in art. Indeed, Bourdieu's point is to explain how art as an autonomous field is able to provide the rewards to rebellious or disaffected artists – with Baudelaire as a case in point – that contemporaneous bourgeois society and/or state institutions would deny them, a function of the double economy. Hence Bourdieu's emphasis on the meaning of Baudelaire's failed bid for a seat in the Académie Française in 1862 for the ideology of Aestheticism. The danger in assigning the role of "founding hero" to the quixotic poet is an implication of uniformity in Baudelaire's thought, an assumption of consistency in his self-positioning in the literary field and the field of power which an application of Bourdieu's own methodology to the *Salon de 1846* would belie. (Bourdieu does acknowledge the impact of the events of 1848 and the defeat of the Second Republic as turning points for Baudelaire and his generation [58-60].) Further, the fundamental opposition between "commercial" and "noncommercial" as regards demand on which Bourdieu bases his homologous economies is unstable, both through the cross-fertilization between the fields of art and industry, or transferable aesthetics, and the very notion of the popular, which may be identified through the simple marker of commercial success or more indirectly as that which many people, especially *le peuple,* value. This latter meaning of "popular" is necessarily an aim for a critic and poet who would educate the public, while crude commercial success may well be disdained.

If we following the logic of Bourdieu's system for Baudelaire's own critical position, we may well discern allegiances, strategies, and signs of positioning within the contemporaneous cultural field. We can, of course, reading backward, find aspects of the theory of *l'art pour l'art* – as it later emerged to define modern art in Clement Greenberg's terms – in the *Salon de 1846.* Certain elements are articulated in a way that makes Baudelaire's critical eye seem prescient of the innovations, indeed revolutions that would transform the art world in the next one hundred years. For instance, the move towards abstraction may be presaged in the consideration of color for color's sake in the lyrical "De la couleur." Baudelaire is also keenly aware of differences in taste, or level of connoisseurship between different segments of the audience for art, indicating, for instance, that Delacroix, his exemplar of Romantic – i.e. modern – art, had poets and artists as his audience (2: 474). But *l'art pour l'art* had already gone through a series of instantiations to produce competing schools, divided along generational lines, and differing as well in terms of what *l'art pour l'art* was defined *against.*[4] This ambiguity of oppositional object, masked by the simplicity of the slogan, may well shed light on Baudelaire's own inconsistencies in his articulated positions about *l'art pour l'art.* Indeed, not only does Baudelaire neglect to embrace any one school of *l'art pour l'art* in the *Salon de 1846*, but he carries on a polemic with Cousin's philosophy in his heavy criticism of

---

[4] Further, as I discuss in chapter four, Baudelaire's own quest for a fully sensate aesthetic entailed a questioning of the preciousness and superficiality of the *l'art pour l'art* poetics of his day, associated mainly with the Parnassians.

eclecticism and his own redefinition of morality in art which appropriates the key term – *la morale* – of Cousin's neoplatonism. Baudelaire's positioning vis-à-vis Gautier is more complicated – an embrace of the sensual and the outré in art, most pointedly in referencing cross-dressing at one point in the *Salon* (2: 444), but avoiding the full-blown anti-utilitarian strain of Gautier's famous preface.

If we look at the *Salon de 1846* as motivated by a desire to transform the perception and appreciation of art, to educate the public about art, and, following the thrust of the dedication, to win the allegiance of the powerful interests, those of the *haute bourgeoisie*, to the kind of art that Baudelaire prizes, we might say that Baudelaire embraces a program of art for the body's sake rather than art for art's sake, that is, the promise in art of a fully sensual experience – the exercise of all five senses, as he puts it, derived from the viewing process (2: 415). Baudelaire makes the case that the experience of art is not only sensual, but synaesthetic, which makes possible and imaginable an expanded sensual terrain for the experience of both visual art and literature, and adds a transcendent dimension in the symbolic frameworks implied by such reciprocity.

Moreover, the *Salon of 1846* is informed by discourses that are hardly purely aesthetic in the Kantian sense, but which derive from the emerging fields of human science and political economy. Such discourses not only support Baudelaire's argument for the integral role of art in modern society, but are evidence of extra-literary authorities that he calls on to ground and assess the experience of pleasure proffered by art and poetry.

Pitching the Pleasures of Art: the Promise of Equilibrium

Baudelaire voices a desire to reach out to the bourgeoisie as a potential audience for art at least twice before the *Salon de 1846*: in the *Salon de 1845* and in a piece appearing early in 1846, "Le Musée classique du Bazar Bonne-Nouvelle." Already, in 1845 Baudelaire was very aware of the price (literally) the world of art would pay for turning their collective backs on the group he would define as "la majorité, – nombre et intelligence; – donc . . . la force" (2: 415) in the opening of the *Salon de 1846*. In these earlier texts, Baudelaire makes clear the responsibility of the critics and artists to educate the bourgeois eye. In "Le Musée Classique de Bazar Bonne-Nouvelle," he designates the villain as "l'artiste-bourgeois"

> qui a été créé pour s'interposer entre le public et le génie; il les cache l'un à l'autre. Le bourgeois qui a peu de notions scientifiques va où le pousse la grande voix de l'artiste-bourgeois (2: 414).

Thus "l'artiste-bourgeois" has a twofold effect on the public: he not only misleads the unknowing and unlearned "bourgeois" but also blocks his view, as it were, of the works of genius that otherwise could teach him. Here Baudelaire makes clear the malleability of the observer of art: the bad taste of the bourgeois is due to exposure to solely mediocre art, which instills a poor sense of what is valuable in art. By the same token, exposure to great art can, of itself, train the bourgeois eye. Baudelaire seizes upon the stereotypical "petit-bourgeois" – the grocer – to make his point:

> Si on supprimait celui-ci [l'artiste-bourgeois], l'épicier porterait E. Delacroix en triomphe. . . . Ne le raillez point de vouloir sortir de sa sphère, et aspirer, l'excellente créature, aux régions hautes. Il veut être ému, il veut sentir, connaître, rêver comme il aime; il veut être complet; il vous demande tous les jours son morceau d'art de poésie, et vous le volez. Il mange du Cogniet, et cela prouve que sa bonne volonté est grande comme l'infini. Servez-lui un chef-d'œuvre, il le digérera et ne s'en portera que mieux! (2: 414)

While Baudelaire's language of degustation in speaking of the tastes of the grocer is no doubt a form of mild mockery, this language of appetites and tastes, the rhetoric of sensual desire and satiation, is one that he will use to woo the bourgeois viewer in the aesthetic system of the *Salon de 1846* and is symptomatic of his own experience of art as *jouissance*. And his playful sympathy with the petit-bourgeois also implies a strategic stance against particular schools of art and the self-promotion of some painters in the broader discursive field of criticism. Cogniet, Baudelaire points out, was one of the organizers of the exhibition (2: 411) who had been a disciple of Guérin (Pichois, n. 1, 2: 1292). Baudelaire takes him to task for not only "hiding" two drawings by his teacher, but for the prominent placement of his own mediocre work and the absence of works by Delacroix who also studied with Guérin: "M. Cogniet, qui a si bien dissimulé son illustre maitre, a-t-il donc craint de soutenir son illustre condisciple?" (2: 414). Further, we sense his own fatigue with anti-bourgeois discourse as unfortunately clichéd, the rant of mediocre artists (*rapins*) attempting to distinguish themselves from the tasteless crowd.

There seems to be some consensus now that Baudelaire's embrace of the bourgeoisie in the opening section or dedication of the *Salon de 1846*, "Aux Bourgeois," is honest, not a colossal piece of irony, even in light of Baudelaire's later anti-bourgeois statements or his contributions to the construction of the image of the artist as anti-bourgeois, as a cultural aristocrat, and so on.[5] Much of the dedication is, indeed, unabashed praise, or more precisely, recognition of the importance and the accomplishments of this social class. Baudelaire has here gone beyond the "épiciers" to the bourgeois in power – the landowners, legislators, merchants, even the king (this is still the July Monarchy of Louis-Philippe), and he lauds this powerful group for founding collections, museums, and galleries (2: 416).[6] Clearly, this group is assuming the role of patrons of the arts through such funding activities that, moreover, make art accessible to a broader audience – the grocers and their ilk. I would like to note two aspects of this appeal in particular: one, that Baudelaire uses language that he feels evidently will appeal to the bourgeois mind: that of rights (reminiscent of the discourse of the Revolution) and of investment and return. He declares that the bourgeoisie have the right "de sentir et de jouir" (2: 415), a right the "monopolists" ("accapareurs") of spiritual things would deny them, and here he alludes to those who distribute praise and blame, the critics.[7] The enjoyment of art, however, is also a need:

---

[5] For a brief overview of this debate, see Jasenas 192-93. For an astute close reading of the arguments of "Au Bourgeois" as a recognition of the part of the bourgeoisie in the consumption and production of art, see Van Slyke. Burton sees a bogus embrace of the bourgeoisie insofar as it is born of necessity (37). Be that as it may, Baudelaire does reject repeatedly the stereotypical anti-bourgeois position of the artistic "rapins" that he so clearly disdains and his desire to educate this new public for art seems entirely genuine.

[6] Chambers points to the neoclassical tradition of dedicating works to powerful members of the nobility as a model for "Au Bourgeois" which "imposes a heritage of inflated stylistic and rhetorical conventions that inevitably suggest flattery or – even worse ironic overstatement" (9). Since Baudelaire is so clearly seeking patronage for art, the comparison is especially apt. Baudelaire's choice of the bourgeoisie as opposed to an aristocratic patron, of course, is part of the message of the dedication – that support for the arts has shifted, or should shift, to the newly powerful bourgeoisie.

[7] See Jasenas on how Baudelaire borrowed this term from Stendhal, *D'un nouveau complot contre les industriels* (1825) and redefined it: instead of social "monopolists" of power (Stendhal's sense), Baudelaire attacks the "monopolists" of art (199-200).

Or, vous avez besoin d'art.
L'art est un bien infiniment précieux, un breuvage rafraichissant et réchauffant, qui rétablit l'estomac et l'esprit dans l'équilibre naturel de l'idéal. (2: 415-
16)

Thus the "utility" of art that Baudelaire invokes in the next paragraph.
But it is a utility defined in terms of pleasure – not utilitarianism in the
commonplace sense of only fulfilling basic needs, but rather in the
sense of subjective pleasure, of "jouissance" and "volupté" (2: 416).
In describing the fulfillment of this need as something earned, Baudelaire invokes the language of investment and return:

Quand vous avez donné à la société votre science, votre industrie, votre travail,
votre argent, vous réclamez votre payement en jouissances du corps, de la
raison et de l'imagination. Si vous récupérez la quantité de jouissances nécessaire pour rétablir l'équilibre de toutes les parties de votre être, vous êtes heureux, repus et bienveillants, comme la société sera repue, heureuse et bien-
veillante, quand elle aura trouve son équilibre général et absolu. (2: 417)

Baudelaire here links the personal health of the bourgeois patron,
nourished by the art he or she has funded, to the general health of the
social body.
    What sort of discourse is this? What kind of picture of an ideally
functioning society? In *La Mystique de Baudelaire* (first published in
1932), Jean Pommier located evidence of Fourierist discourse (56),
but more recent scholarship has made clear the limited nature of this
influence.[8] The parallels between Baudelaire's formulations, and those
of a nascent political economy, however, extend well beyond the use
of the term "equilibrium"; Baudelaire mimics this discourse, which
represents a pervasive mode of thought and a means of framing social
issues. David Kelley has argued that Baudelaire's notion of a natural

---

[8] Burton points out that Baudelaire probably knew Fourier's thought second-hand
from reading *La Démocratie pacifique* and *La Phalange*. Burton goes on to argue that
despite using "Fourierist categories of thought" Baudelaire, in his most Fourierist section of Le Salon de 1846, "Des écoles et des ouvriers," produces "a thoroughly anti-
Fourierist conclusion" (17). See Burton 14-23 for evidence of Baudelaire's lack of
allegiance to Fourierist or Republican politics at this time. Van Slyke also discounts
Fourierist readings, noting that this equilibrium "est présenté comme une possibilité
réelle dans la 'civilisation' qui, pour Fourier, constituait l'étape ultime de la barbarie"
(59). These views are congruent with my argument that Baudelaire is drawing on
larger notions of social harmony, homologous with his emerging aesthetics, not the
doctrine or politics of any given school of thought.

equilibrium between the individual and the social body is part and parcel of his Romantic view of a universe governed by the law of complementary contrasts, or contraries. Thus the synthesis of individual and collectivity, artist and bourgeois in the social realm is consonant with the synthesis of line and color, unity and variety, in the aesthetic realm. This parallel, then, offers a means of reconciling the socio-political with the aesthetic for Baudelaire, a parallel which virtually endows the realm of the socio-political with the qualities of the aesthetic: harmony and the complementarity of contrasts are homologous with the doctrine of equilibrium in political economy, the reconciliation of price competition. Baudelaire is hardly alone in spinning theories of socio-economic and aesthetic harmony side-by-side during the 1840s; Jennifer Phillips notes that both socialist art critic Théophile Thoré and Fourierist Désiré Laverdant invoke formal aspects of color harmony that may generate a harmonious sense of the world (352-53). But, in his invocation of the potential for social harmony, Baudelaire explicitly employs a vocabulary of practical and personal economics, outlining a form of exchange: social harmony depends on the bodily equilibrium wrought by the enjoyment of art's harmonies by the bourgeoisie; art needs the practical support of bourgeois purses. It is clear that he recognized the entanglement of the aesthetic with the economic in concrete and symbolic terms and here is constructing a theoretical base for the reconciliation of such diverse interests as he confronted the problem of the value of art in the society in which he lived.

His use of this discourse shows how far he is from the tenets of *l'art pour l'art*. His description of art as "un bien infiniment précieux, un breuvage rafraichissant et réchauffant, qui rétablit l'estomac et l'esprit dans l'équilibre naturel de l'idéal" relies on a notion of use value, but this use is defined as not only bodily and spiritual but a bringing together of body and spirit in an equilibration. Art creates harmony in the state of being of the individual. Earlier in "Aux Bourgeois," Baudelaire remarks: "Vous pouvez vivre trois jours sans pain; – sans poésie, jamais" (2: 413). Obviously both these assertions rhetorically present art as a need, not a superfluity or luxury. Its preciousness is like that of water, which as Adam Smith showed in comparing water with diamonds, has little to do with its exchange value or market value; as "infinitely precious" it is beyond measurement. But while Baudelaire makes the argument that art's utility is a basis for its value, that utility consists solely in subjective enjoyment, not religious, moral, or political edification. Baudelaire also invokes another aspect of economic theories of value: labor. Here art accrues exchange value for it is the nonaesthetic labor of the bourgeois that buys his right to enjoy art, the product of the artist's labor.[9] Note that the value of art is not a measure of the artist's labor, but of the "labor" of those paying for it as well as their other monetary contributions to society, i. e. capital. So, despite invoking labor to establish the bourgeois right to art, Baudelaire places the emphasis on consumption, not production, although consumption does *produce* a transformed consumer (art is a good and a service). Baudelaire ignores any conflict of interests to assert the ideal: that this exchange of art for society-building labor (and capital) establishes a social equilibrium: "équilibre general et absolu." This social equilibrium relies, we presume, on its bodily counterpart, the "l'équilibre naturel de l'idéal" of the individual body refreshed by art.

As discussed in chapter one, by the 1840s, the concept of economic equilibrium was accepted by most political economists, but the definition of "utility" was less settled. The economist in France whose model comes closest to Baudelaire's own ideal "economy" is Dupuit. To recall Dupuit's characterization of utility: In 1849 (three years after Baudelaire's *Salon*) he wrote that "the term utility can be applied to everything that satisfies a desire, whether it be in conformity with reason or not" (75), making "utility" a subjective measure and recognizing the difficulty of distinguishing the needs of the economic agent from his desires. Such desires would then be accounted for within his economic model:

> Man's desires, the energy of which directed toward one object or another varies in intensity according to the circumstance, play the same role in society as attraction in the material world. . . . This science [political economy] must embrace not only material objects susceptible to being exchanged but the satisfactions of the spirit and of the heart, all that satisfies our desires, whatever they may be, everything that men endeavor to acquire or to retain by means of sacrifice. (*my translation*) (77)

---

[9] As Sewell has shown, "labor" was a focus of intense scrutiny in the 1840s, praised by some worker-poets like Charles Poncy as a fount of social order and spirituality while other social observers like Louis Villermé bemoaned its degrading, even brutalizing capabilities. See Sewell, ch. 10, "The paradoxes of labor," 219-42.

Thus value should be calculated from the point of view of the consumer and his desires, or, in Baudelaire's terms, according to "la quantité de jouissances nécessaire pour rétablir l'équilibre de toutes les parties de votre être." It is calculation, but one that aims at an ideal amount of pleasure, measured subjectively.

It is striking that Baudelaire weaves this subjective calculation, this impulse behind exchange, into his argument for investment in art. While Baudelaire shows how complicit the art world is with the world of commerce and industry, he limns an aesthetic return based in satisfactions of body and spirit. Baudelaire, too, defines a "utility":

> Vous en concevez l'utilité, ô bourgeois, – législateurs, ou commerçants, – quand la septième ou la huitième heure sonnée incline votre tête fatiguée vers les braises du foyer et les oreillards du fauteuil.
> Un désir plus brulant, une rêverie plus active, vous délasseraient alors de l'action quotidienne. (2: 416)

If we hold Baudelaire to the terms of his argument, this "utility," this experience of pleasure, is theoretically quantifiable, based on his social equilibrium model: the bourgeois has paid for his pleasures with his labor. (Of course, Baudelaire makes no attempt to propose any formulas to take such a measurement.) While his invocation of "utility" may be tongue-in-cheek, Baudelaire is all too aware of the quantification of art's value: he acknowledges that artists and critics owe the bourgeoisie a debt for erecting the museums and galleries, and building the collections; they now gain their livelihood, directly or indirectly, from this newly powerful class. If these bourgeois patrons don't gain the pleasure promised them, the return on their investment, then they may well withdraw their patronage and the general good will be harmed. (Of course, in light of Baudelaire's earlier remarks about the grocer, and remarks made elsewhere, we see behind this "threat" his fear that they will fund art, but of the wrong sort.)

In other words, this equilibrium model does more than simply suggest a means of measuring pleasure: it represents a social body, too, an ideally functioning society where "les savants seront propriétaires, et les propriétaires savants" (2: 415). It is isomorphic with other models drawn from political economy which seek to define the means by which value is established within a society of conflicting interests.[10] This isomorphism brings to the fore two issues: the legitimacy of social theory framed in aesthetic terms (equilibrium as harmony) which after all implies that the system functions fairly and adequately. Of course, Baudelaire refers only to the possibility of a future equilibrium when the bourgeoisie have learned how to nourish themselves with art, and thus feel the return on their investment. Secondly, how does Baudelaire's "equilibrium" function? In other words, how would such a utopian system be achieved? According to the system articulated in *Le Salon de 1846*, the just and healthy social body depends on the satisfactions of the individual bourgeois body. But, as opposed to Adam Smith's "invisible hand" which turns the greed of the rich into opportunity for the rest, Baudelaire's system, in order to make this exchange of labor and capital for physical, intellectual, and spiritual enjoyments work, requires a rather visible hand: the hand of the critic.[11] (Recall the fate of the *épicier*: poor art does not nourish.)

Educating the Bourgeois Eye

In the first essay of the *Salon de 1846*, "A quoi bon la critique?" which immediately follows the dedication to the bourgeoisie, Baudelaire takes up directly this topic of what the critic should be teaching the bourgeois public. Here he famously states: "pour être juste, c'est-à-dire pour avoir sa raison d'être, la critique doit être partiale, passionnée, politique, c'est-à-dire faite à un point de vue exclusif, mais au point de vue qui ouvre le plus d'horizons" (2: 418). The explanation that follows makes it clear that Baudelaire feels that art criticism must go beyond staking out positions on the line versus color controversy (or Ingres versus Delacroix); and that both art and criticism should bear the mark of the temperament of the producer –

---

[10] See Van Slyke for instances of the contradictions hidden in this utopian equilibrium, for instance, the acknowledgement that the wealthy bourgeoisie have all the power, and that their interests oppose those of even the petit-bourgeoisie, "les épiciers" (59; 64).

[11] British advocacy for political economy also involved educating members of all classes to become more like the ideal subjects of the political economists' system. This education included an emphasis for the working class reader on developing a taste for more and better goods which would in turn create a population of prudent consumers consistent with the principles of Malthus's moral restraint. I thank Brian Cooper for this insight.

hence the passion and partiality. Later in the *Salon*, Baudelaire will fashion the obverse of this argument, his case against eclecticism. Baudelaire's heroic image of the artist and critic owes a great deal to Romantic theories of the imagination, borrowed from Germany and England, as many have noted, but as we look at his specific instructions on how to observe art, we find him indebted at some level to new ideas about physical sight and the composition of light that emerged in the first decades of the nineteenth century.

Anyone who reads "De la couleur," the third chapter of the *Salon de 1846*, from the point of view of the early twenty-first century would be struck by the degree to which Baudelaire anticipates the "discoveries" of Impressionism. One is struck, too, by the scientific vocabulary: references to molecular constitution, to the work of the caloric, to chemical affinities. This conjunction is not coincidental. Jonathan Crary, in *Techniques of the Observer: On Vision and Modernity in the Nineteenth Century*, details how the positivism of scientific and popular culture reorganized the way vision and perception were themselves perceived in the first few decades of the nineteenth century, long before such notions were "represented" on the canvases of the Impressionists. Crary argues that research on the physiology of the eye and on the nature of light participated in a paradigm shift from eighteenth-century views of a stable relationship between perception and the world viewed, in which the eye worked as a sort of camera obscura, to views that emphasized the extent to which vision is produced by the eye, such that "external procedures of manipulation and stimulation . . . have the essential capacity *to produce experience for the subject*" (92). Notions of the illusory or deceptive nature of vision were disseminated to the broader public through the invention of devices originally intended for scientific research but soon adapted and marketed for popular entertainment, such as the thaumatrope, phenakistiscope, stereoscope, and kaleidoscope. (Baudelaire mentions the kaleidoscope in this *Salon* [2: 453] and other devices such as the stereoscope elsewhere.) So, within this broad awareness of the illusory aspects of vision, Baudelaire certainly may have been encouraged that perception, and thereby taste, were indeed malleable. Furthermore, as Bernard Howells and Jennifer Phillips both argue, it is likely that Baudelaire was familiar with the color theory of chemist Michel-Eugène Chevreul who published *De la loi du contraste simultané des couleurs* in 1839 and who gave lectures regularly at the Gobelins between 1824 and 1852.[12] Chevreul's experiments demonstrated the subjectivity of the color perception, most notably the heightened effect of complementary colors when juxtaposed.[13]

Baudelaire begins his chapter on color by exhorting his readers to notice the dynamic character of color, its vibration and movement:

> Supposons un bel espace de nature où tout verdoie, rougeoie, poudroie et chatoie en pleine liberté, où toutes choses, diversement colorées suivant leur constitution moléculaire, changées de seconde en seconde par le déplacement de l'ombre et de la lumière, et agitées par le travail intérieur de calorique, se trouvent en perpé-tuelle vibration, laquelle fait trembler les lignes et complète la loi du mouvement eternel et universel. (2: 422)

And he later, in the same paragraph, compares the effect of the seasonal mist on the appearance of this natural scene to that of a top "qui, mu par une vitesse accélérée, nous apparait gris, bien qu'il résume en lui toutes les couleurs" (2: 423), thus using an optical illusion to illustrate how the perception of light works in natural circumstances. This focus on the dynamic, ever-changing character of color and light leads him to this synaesthetic analogy: "Cette grande symphonie du jour, qui est l'éternelle variation de la symphonie d'hier, cette succession de mélodies, où la variété sort toujours de l'infini, cet hymne compliqué s'appelle la couleur" (2: 423).

Yet the artist will not paint well if he or she simply follows the dictates of the eye for "[l]'air joue un si grand rôle dans la théorie de la couleur, que, si un paysagiste peignait les feuilles des arbres telles qu'il les voit, il obtiendrait un ton faux; attendu qu'il y a un espace d'air bien moindre entre le spectateur et le tableau qu'entre le spectateur et la nature" (2: 425). So the artist makes use of "lies"

---

[12] Howells 176. Both Howells and Phillips demonstrate strong affinities between Chevreul's color theory and Baudelaire's treatment of color in "De la couleur." Reviews of Chevreul's book appeared in *L'Artiste* in 1842 and in the *Bulletin de l'ami des arts* in 1844; as Howells notes, Baudelaire was actively seeking a place on the editorial staffs of both of these journals at the time and so it is very likely that he would have read the reviews and have had at least second hand knowledge of these theories.

[13] Phillips especially emphasizes how Chevreul and Baudelaire share a sense that color perception exceeds the distinction between subjective and objective in that both understand a physical basis for color even while it is constituted through a perceiving subject. She notes this approach is consistent with Baudelaire's challenge to the dualism of the line/color debate elsewhere in *Le Salon de 1846*.

("mensonges") like nature itself. (This point goes along with Baudelaire's insistence elsewhere that the artist interpret, not copy nature.) The spectator, then, must train his or her eye to appreciate art which avails itself of the dynamic character of color while obeying the aesthetic principles of harmony, melody, and counterpoint that Baudelaire propounds: "La bonne manière de savoir si un tableau est mélodieux est de le regarder d'assez loin pour n'en comprendre ni le sujet ni les lignes. S'il est mélodieux, il a déjà un sens, et il a déjà pris sa place dans le répertoire des souvenirs" (2: 425). Baudelaire is literally recommending means to manipulate visual perception so that certain qualities in painting become evident. The resulting perceptions would not be unlike the raw material of vision as described by the researcher, Hermann von Helmholtz: "Everything our eye sees it sees as an aggregate of coloured surfaces in the visual field – that is its form of visual intuition" (Crary 95). Baudelaire then asserts the emotional tenor of color, which brings him to the notion of synaesthesia and a passage by E.T.A. Hoffmann on "une réunion intime entre les couleurs, les sons et les parfums" (2: 425), thereby wedding assumptions about visual perception based in positivist science to German Romantic theory.

Baudelaire would advise this "long view" or focus on color as an abstract interrelational system to the point of ignoring other minor defects in the painting. In viewing a work by Delacroix, he remarks:

> Dans un article qui a plutôt l'air d'une prophétie que d'une critique, à quoi bon relever des fautes de détail et des taches microscopiques? L'ensemble est si beau, que je n'en ai pas le courage. . . . Les défauts de M. Delacroix sont parfois si visibles qu'ils sautent à l'œil le moins exercé. On peut ouvrir au hasard la première feuille venue, où pendant longtemps l'on s'est obstiné, à l'inverse de mon système, à ne pas voir les qualités radieuses qui constituent son originalité. (2: 441)

Again, Baudelaire emphasizes the importance of learning to observe in a particular way – according to his system to which he has attached the authority of science – to comprehend what is not evident to the less trained eye. Note that here Baudelaire is assuming the universal subject of science rather than the class-constructed subject of the dedication in order to establish a common ground between himself as a right-minded critic and the bourgeois public.

Insisting that colors "n'existent que relativement" (2: 424), as Chevreul demonstrated empirically, Baudelaire refers to one set of complementary colors, red and green, in several places in a way that show how he understands this scientifically verified experience to have emotional and nearly metaphysical effects. In the opening paragraph of "De la couleur," after evoking a natural scene dominated by the play of red and green, "où tout verdoie, rougeoie," he emphasizes green as a bass note in nature: "Les arbres sont verts, les gazons verts, les mousses vertes; le vert serpente dans les troncs, les tiges non mures sont vertes; le vert est le fond de la nature, parce que le vert se marie facilement à tous les autres tons. Ce qui me frappe d'abord, c'est que partout – coquelicots dans les gazons, pavots, perroquets, etc. – le rouge chante la gloire du vert" (2: 422). Thus the red by contrasting green brings out its glory, part of the harmony of nature's color scheme. Elsewhere he notices a paler version of this contrast: "Une lumière rose ou couleur de pêche et une ombre verte, c'est la que gît toute la difficulté" (2: 454). But the experience of color contrasts is not one of unmixed pleasure : "J'ai eu longtemps devant ma fenêtre un cabaret mi-parti de vert et de rouge cru, qui étaient pour mes yeux une douleur délicieuse" (2: 425). Lest we dismiss this reflection as incidental or symptomatic of urban decadence in this broader evocation of the harmony of color, we should note that Baudelaire finds a like experience of painful pleasure in Delacroix's use of red and green. In the section of *Le Salon de 1846* on Delacroix, Baudelaire repeats the remark of a friend and painter about Delacroix's painting, "peinture de cannibale," and responds:

> À coup sûr, ce n'est point dans les curiosités d'une palette encombrée, ni dans le dictionnaire des règles, que notre jeune ami saura trouver cette sanglante et farouche désolation, à peine compensée par le vert sombre de l'espérance !
> Cet hymne terrible à la douleur faisait sur sa classique imagination l'effet des vins redoutables de l'Anjou, de l'Auvergne ou du Rhin, sur un estomac accoutumé aux pâles violettes du Médoc.
> Ainsi, universalité de sentiment, – et maintenant universalité de science ! (2: 436)

Blood red, evoking bodily pain, and green, symbolizing hope: these colors signify individually, but together construct the tension between suffering and hope, intoxicate the viewer, and thus the science of color supports what is already known through feeling. Color contrasts, in heightening tonality, amplify the psychological agon. Praising paintings of Native Americans by Catlin, he notices the same harmonious and meaningful contrast:

> Quant à la couleur, elle a quelque chose de mystérieux qui me plait plus que je ne saurais dire. Le rouge, la couleur du sang, la couleur de la vie, abondait tellement dans ce sombre musée, que c'était une ivresse; quant aux paysages, – montagnes boisées, savanes immenses, rivières désertes, – ils étaient monotonement, éternellement verts; le rouge, cette couleur si obscure, si épaisse, plus difficile à pénétrer que les yeux d'un serpent, – le vert, cette couleur calme et gaie et souriante de la nature, je les retrouve chantant leur antithèse mélodique jusque sur le visage de ces deux héros. – Ce qu'il y a de certain, c'est que tous leurs tatouages et coloriages étaient faits selon les gammes naturelles et harmoniques. (2: 446)

Color, even in its harmonies, is sublime in that it is "difficult," hard to know, but more pointedly in that it induces negative pleasures, delicious pains. This heightened aesthetic sensation of intense saturated harmonies is ultimately disharmonic, and it is this sensation that Baudelaire most highly prizes. The effect of color contrast leads to a new understanding of harmony as potentially its opposite: disturbing, arresting, sharp, discordant. (Baudelaire's delectation of this experience poses a contrast with Benthamite theories of pleasure and pain in political economy in which the subject desires pleasure alone.)[14]

Let's step back now, as Baudelaire suggests, from the details of the *Salon de 1846* to its place within the broader context of changes in artistic institutions and as a consequence means of evaluating art in the nineteenth century. Michael Moriarty in his essay, "Structures of cultural production in nineteenth-century France," very usefully summarizes the sea-change that profoundly affected the art world in postrevolutionary France. In the ancien régime the authority of the Académie Royale de Peinture et de Sculpture dominated the production of art; only Academicians could exhibit at the biennial Salons (15-16). Art thus served the interests of a single elite public. Yet, already in the eighteenth century, the public for art began to broaden as unofficial Salon reports "tinged art criticism with coded political implications, impugning the social order through its products; and artists like David reacted to these responses" (16). As William Ray, drawing on Habermas, points out, in the eighteenth century, display creates a discursive forum that undermines the hierarchies of the

---

[14] I thank Brian Cooper for this point of contrast.

institution supporting the display (the Académie, for instance), and yet discursive practices themselves create conventions and grounds for consensus:

> [F]rom a practical point of view the effect of the salon and of the theories of autonomous response it occasioned was to encourage people to express themselves in public who otherwise might not have. The physical conditions of the exhibit itself encouraged this by their 'spectacular' structure. By providing a large, anonymous arena where the exchange of personal assessments and the formation of consensus could be observed firsthand, the salon made visible for the people the mechanisms of opinion formation and discursive authority. It made a spectacle out of the play between individual expression and collective voice and fostered in the public an awareness of the mechanisms, risks, and benefits of discursive economies. (537)

The critic emerged as the "amateur" (in both senses of the word) authority, promoting particular kinds of appreciation and reading under the banner of critical individualism and freedom.[15]

The nineteenth century saw the decline of the Académie-Salon system, and with it, profound changes in the system of patronage and the audience for art. Moriarty details the growth in importance of the dealers in the new market system on whom the artists were dependent and the newly important function of the critic of which Baudelaire himself was so cognizant. And the newspapers made this art criticism available to a growing literate audience. So, broadly speaking, we see in the *ancien régime* an art world overshadowed by the prestige of the Academy and its neoclassical values whose elite audience was educated in these tastes. By the mid-nineteenth century, not only had the painters and poets of Romanticism revolted against the dictates of Neoclassicism, but the institutions that had enforced these values were beginning to lose sway. With the advent of a broader, more diverse, more segmented public came a loss of consensus over what aesthetic qualities were valuable in art. A critic like Baudelaire, then, is in the exhilarating position of articulating new aesthetic norms, yet has to sell these ideas to a public that is no longer unified or "educated" in aesthetic judgement or "taste". Hence Baudelaire's explicit awareness of the issue of popularity, and of the fickleness of public taste: "À mesure que le public voit de la bonne peinture, il se détache des artistes les plus populaires, s'ils ne peuvent plus lui donner la même

---

[15] Brian Cooper and I make this point in "Object Lessons" 4-5.

quantité de plaisir" (2: 485).[16] As Baudelaire promised in his dedication, "Aux Bourgeois," art correctly appreciated will afford pleasure. But will this happen without his mediation as a critic, as this comment seems to imply? Baudelaire's explicit directions on how to view make clear that such pleasure comes only after the eye has been initiated into the art of viewing. Another paradox haunts this passage: that of the public becoming disaffected with the popular, the product, as it were, of their own choice. But, as I note earlier, Baudelaire blames misleading "bourgeois artists" for the public's want of taste, not their natural inclinations, in that he values "naïveté."

But Baudelaire understands another force behind the public's embrace of bad art: ideology. That Baudelaire perceives the influence of the political on the aesthetic is already clear in his call for a criticism that is "partial, impassioned, political." In the section of the *Salon de 1846* on Horace Vernet, Baudelaire assails his work on aesthetic grounds – "ses tableaux ne sont point de la peinture, mais une masturbation agile et fréquente, une irritation de l'épiderme français" (2: 470) – but accounts for its popularity in its nationalism and militarism, a popularity "qui ne durera d'ailleurs pas plus longtemps que la guerre" (2: 469). He champions instead a cosmopolitanism that prefers beauty to glory (2: 470) and sees himself as a representative of a new generation that abhors war and "des sottises nationales" (2: 471) – an acknowledgement of the power of the public to draw attention to certain artists and make their reputations. "Popularity" has entered the critic's vocabulary, something to wrestle with, appeal to, or reject as a criterion for value, just as the critic must wrestle with, appeal to, or reject the bourgeois public as audience.

Tawdry Seductions, Dissonant Pleasures

There is another sort of popularity that Baudelaire treats in *Le Salon de 1846*, but these works lure him despite his critical eye which recognizes their aesthetic failings. In the section entitled "Des sujets amoureux et de M. Tassaert," Baudelaire describes his own pleasures in viewing erotic images as an experience of expanding time in public and private spaces (although spaces of leisure), and of equivocal desire whose addictive quality transforms it into need. Here the

---

[16] See, too, his comments about the waning popularity of Ary Scheffer once the public was exposed to some "real" painting (2: 475).

rhetoric of utility receives a new inflection as Baudelaire reveals the pleasures of the consumption of images. So, while he would argue that, for the bourgeois, pleasure proceeds from meeting an unrecognized need, in his account of his personal experience, need arises from the experience of pleasure. Furthermore, in these two versions of enjoyment derived from viewing, there are two versions of temporal consciousness: the time-bound consciousness of the well-regulated day as opposed to a state of consciousness in which time inflates and is "lost." In "Au Bourgeois," these versions are compatible if one restricts the latter to a firmly defined leisure time. Yet, as described by Baudelaire in "Des sujets amoureux et de M. Tassaert," scheduled time is threatened by the sense of losing oneself and time when in the state of *jouissance*.

Although much of *Le Salon de 1846* theorizes about the experience of viewing art, and breaks new ground in that respect, this section is unique in giving us Baudelaire's view of himself viewing and enjoying images. Baudelaire begins by addressing his reader as a possible fellow connoisseur of such images: "Vous est-il arrivé, comme à moi, de tomber dans de grandes mélancolies, après avoir passé de longues heures à feuilleter des estampes libertines?" (2: 443) For Baudelaire, this is, of course, a characteristic gesture towards the reader, a request – acknowledge your complicity, your resemblance to me – that also recognizes the suffering that results from such viewing. While the kind of images that the bourgeois, in his armchair, would view is left undefined in "Au Bourgeois," Baudelaire does promise that "[u]n désir plus brûlant, une rêverie plus active, vous délasseraient alors de l'action quotidienne" (2: 416). But here where we get a glimpse of Baudelaire's own experience viewing images that inspire desire and reverie, we hear that the hours passed were long: "Soit dans les interminables soirées d'hiver au coin du feu, soit dans les lourds loisirs de la canicule, au coin des boutiques de vitrier, la vue de ces dessins m'a mis sur des pentes de rêverie immenses, à peu près comme un livre obscène nous précipite vers les océans mystiques du bleu" (2: 443). Although the hours were long, the experience of time changes as the viewer enters the state of erotic reverie, a state troped as a return to nature, to a landscape or seascape, with its immense slopes and mystical blue oceans, a sly insinuation of it naturalness. The place of viewing has changed as well, a consequence of the difference in social station between the house-proud bourgeois and the bohemian who enjoys art free in the libraries or in the corners of bookstores as well as by the home hearth. In a spirit of mock boosterism, Baudelaire suggests an ideal and imaginary site: a museum of love that "le poète, le curieux, le philosophe" could enjoy. (The bourgeois, too, just needs funding!) While in the dedication, "Au Bourgeois," Baudelaire speaks of viewing art in the private domestic space and lauds the bourgeoisie for supporting the funding of museums, hence public art, it is worth noting that in discussing his own experience a third space for viewing is mentioned – in the "boutique," that is, the marketplace, although he's not buying.

Later in this section, Baudelaire mentions a different marketplace, one represented in the paintings of M. Tassaert displayed at the Salon. He comments at length on a painting of the sale of women – hence desire: "Le Marchand d'esclaves." Not only is the focus of the painting women for sale, but they appear to be "femmes civilisées" as signified by the commodities they wear while in the state of undress: "Celle qui est vue de dos, et dont les fesses sont enveloppés dans une gaze transparente, a encore sur la tête un bonnet acheté rue Vivienne ou au Temple. La pauvre fille a sans doute été enlevée par les pirates" (2: 445). Baudelaire's comments on the painting make it clear that he is critical less of its subject matter — easily dismissed as Oriental barbarism (the buyer is "un Turc bête et sensuel") than of the Westernization of the women, or the all too clear reliance of the painter on Parisian models. Baudelaire, in representing his own viewing of this painting, perhaps unwittingly occupies the place of the "Turc bête et sensuel," while as a Westerner, he recognizes the signs of commodities. Baudelaire's tacit, equivocal identification with the "Turk" brings to the fore a comparison of acts: Is the consumption of erotic images, whether viewing or buying, an ethically superior act to the purchase of the woman herself? What separates him – in control of such consumption – from the Turk, who controls the woman? Is the bonnet bought on the rue Vivenne or Temple ironically what separates the civilized woman, the faux slave, from the authentic item? Yet he seems to prefer his women without bonnets, and so this veil of distinction – the illusion of civilization – drops.

I mentioned earlier that Baudelaire sees suffering as well as pleasure in this viewing: "Plaisir et douleur mêlés, amertume dont la lèvre a toujours soif! – Le plaisir est de voir représenté sous toutes ses formes le sentiment le plus important de la nature, – et la colère, de trouver souvent si mal imité ou si sottement calomnié" (2: 443). So the pain is the result of aesthetic failings, but it is this mixture that he desires, like red and green in painting. Would a museum of love, full of works by Ingres, Watteau, Rubens, and Delacroix (all mentioned as creators of an immense poem of love whose hands are the purest) solve this problem? Why not simply take his pleasures from great works of art? What seduces Baudelaire here? The desire that is never satiated is again the mixture of pleasure and pain, this potent blend of bad art and vital subject matter. It is a degradation of the aesthetic, an incommensurability of pleasures, a gap between the judgment of the aesthetic eye and a bodily response, that reproduces the gap between self and desire that even the greatest Romantic art produces in the experience of reverie before immensity. Here pleasures are dissonant, and the clash heightens the effect, like red next to green. Here we have a glimpse of the future of the Baudelairean aesthetic, the failure of harmony in modernity and the collapse of the aesthetic as distinction between fine art and the patently commercial image (parallel to the collapse of the guise of civilization).

Possibly for Baudelaire it is the simultaneous consciousness of illusion and self-deception that is most desired. Jean Baudrillard explains why seduction, which aptly characterizes this experience of viewing, is so powerful:

> The strategy of seduction is one of deception. It lies in wait for all that tends to confuse itself with its reality. And it is potentially a source of fabulous strength. For if production can only produce objects or real signs, and thereby obtain some power; seduction, by producing only illusions, obtains all powers, including the power to return production and reality to their fundamental illusion. (69-70)

One could read the entire *Salon de 1846* as one grand seduction, proceeding from the initial dedication to the bourgeois, where Baudelaire flatters the powerful bourgeois and promises pleasure if the challenge is met. (For Baudrillard, all discourse, through its appearance, its surface, its nuances and inflections, is seductive and resists interpretation through this seduction.) In *Seduction*, Baudrillard opposes seduction to production; his description of this *agon* fits Baudelaire's discursive strategy in *Au Bourgeois* beautifully:

> Seduction is stronger than power because it is reversible and mortal, while power, like value, seeks to be irreversible, cumulative and immortal. Power par-

takes of all the illusions of production, and of the real; it wants to be real, and so tends to become its own imaginary, its own superstition (with the help of theories that analyze it, be they to contest it). Seduction, on the other hand, is not of the order of the real – and is never of the order of force, nor relations of force. But precisely for this reason, it enmeshes all power's *real* actions, as well as the entire reality of production, in this unremitting reversibility and disaccumulation – *without which there would be neither power nor accumulation.* . . . Do you think that power, sex, economics – all these real, really big things – would have held up for a single moment unless sustained by fascination, a fascination that comes precisely from the mirror image in which they are reflected, from their continuous reversion, the palpable pleasure borne of their imminent catastrophe? (46)

Elsewhere, in a section entitled "I'll be your mirror," Baudrillard expands on the necessary mirroring in the seduction process. He quotes Vincent Descombes from *L'Inconscient malgré lui*:

What seduces is not some feminine wile, but the fact that it is directed at you. It is seductive to be seduced, and consequently, it is being seduced that is seductive. In other words, the being seduced finds himself in the person seducing. What the person seduced sees in the one who seduces him, the unique object of his fascination, is his own seductive, charming self, his lovable self-image... (68)

And, so Baudelaire would seduce the bourgeoisie with the image of their power and the image of their discourse. He directly acknowledges their power and its legitimacy: "Vous êtes la majorité, – nombre et intelligence; – donc vous êtes la force, – qui est justice." As I discussed earlier, he uses the language of social order and rights, of bourgeois class consciousness, and of business and political economy. Finally, the promised society, one of perfect equilibrium, would culminate in a state of utter reversibility, a state of mutual and ongoing seduction: "un jour radieux viendra où les savants seront propriétaires, et les propriétaires savants. Alors votre puissance sera complète, et nul ne protestera contre elle" (2: 415). In other words, you bourgeois will be all powerful, but we will be each other. In "Des sujets amoureux et de M. Tassaert" we come to understand more about this "other": a complex viewer, self-aware of his own self-deception, pained by his own tawdry desires – not because they are immoral, but because they lack taste. And yet this pain only adds to his equivocal pleasure. His anatomy of seduction is a search for the truth of pleasure's source and reason.

There is a moral here, too, for political economists. Despite the seductiveness of this utopian vision, the consumption of images that Baudelaire has recommended for the mental and physical health of the hearty bourgeois and the consumption of erotic images that he confesses to as an addiction give us a sense of what consumption promises in general, at least, in Baudelaire's time. It is the seduction that is perhaps most addictive, not the acquisition. Baudelaire notes that M. Tassaert as an artist is appreciated only by "flâneurs" and that the public doesn't know him well enough. Somehow it is appropriate that the denizen of the boulevards, the embodiment of the urban glance, should know these pleasures that Baudelaire would democratically reveal to the broader public. And, for all that Baudelaire senses that bourgeois support for the arts is necessary for their survival, it is clear that the seductions of art run counter to the order of the bourgeois world, its sense of time, the function of its spaces, and its moral pretensions. Perhaps it is Baudrillard's illusion that the order of seduction can trump that of production, just as for Baudelaire the seductions of art trump class division and class-specific temporal and spatial regimens that arise from the demands of production.[17] But ultimately it is the illusions of consumption, the illusions of a life of free choice among pleasures, pleasures that may even disrupt the regimens of production, that make production profitable, that tempt the viewer to buy.

In conclusion, at the same time that Baudelaire was formulating and articulating the theory that would define aesthetic value as residing not in content, but in more abstract, formal qualities, thus undermining any vestigial notions of art's sacral or didactic purpose, he framed an appeal for art's utilitarian function within bourgeois society: one of sensual satisfaction and specifically of the fullest, or most efficient use of leisure time. As abstraction for Baudelaire is a realization of the materiality and emotional tenor of the components of art, like color, art as abstraction offers the viewer a sensual and emotional experience. As a critic, Baudelaire defines his own role as

---

[17] Rancière argues this point using an example, described in a workers' newspaper during the Revolution of 1848, *Le Tocsin des travailleurs*, of a joiner who stops working to take in the arrangement of the room or the view of a garden; this constitutes a "disconnection between the activity of the hands and that of the gaze," "the means of disrupting the adequation of a body and an ethos." This aesthetic "dissensus" opens up a politics for the worker ("Aesthetic Dimension" 7-8).

more than just an arbiter of art, or even aesthetic theorist: he will also educate his readers about how to view, recognizing the plasticity of vision, the functioning of illusion in even ordinary seeing. Through such lessons, Baudelaire hopes to make the bourgeoisie into connoisseurs of aesthetic experience, or as he puts it: "un jour viendra où les savants seront propriétaires, et les propriétaires savants." This consciousness on Baudelaire's part, his willingness to mold his aesthetic theory into an appeal to the bourgeois spectator, reveals an important aspect of aestheticism that the slogan of art-for-art's-sake belies: efforts on the part of those affiliated with the art world to negotiate a position for themselves and a function for art within the everyday praxis of bourgeois society, a function, that is, beyond the simple commodity status of the individual work. Further, to suggest his position as critic is unprejudiced against the bourgeoisie, he directs his invective against so-called bourgeois artists, a demonstration of his ability to rise above the clichés of the artist-versus-bourgeois opposition. In other words, as artist and critic, he does not *need* to define his own taste *against* the bourgeois, but chooses as foil the pretensions of the bourgeois artist instead, a complication of distinctions and a strategic distinction for his own position as artist and critic. It is, however, an argument that presents the work of art as an item for consumption – for degustation, if not simply possession. Baudelaire brackets issues of production in this focus on the experience of enjoying or consuming art.

In employing a rhetoric of investment and return in this appeal, Baudelaire implies that the experience of art itself is quantifiable, that it enters a relationship of equivalence. This notion is incommensurable with Baudelaire's definition of the Romantic aesthetic that he would teach to the bourgeois public. He repeatedly defines the Romantic as "intimité, spiritualité, couleur, aspiration vers l'infini" (2: 421), thus experience of such art only piques desires that cannot by definition be fully or at least temporarily satisfied, as the appetite for a good *pot-de-feu* or a decent wine can. The synesthetic process itself is epitomized by a train of desires: as soon as the senses apprehend the aesthetic in one form, such as color, its fuller appreciation or pleasure necessitates the apprehension in another form, such as sound. As aesthetic pleasure, then, entails an unending movement, the dissolution of one form of apprehension into another, this process, the essential or deepest aesthetic experience for Baudelaire, in and of itself ceaselessly postpones satisfaction, or satiation. Thus even if the bourgeois spectator were to transform his or her habits of perception and attain the aesthetic experience Baudelaire proffers, satisfaction cannot be guaranteed. It is instead a "douleur morale," the stridency of red against green, that for Baudelaire hits the most authentic aesthetic note. There is also a desire for the tawdry within the ideal to which Baudelaire confesses, and which he admits into his aesthetic experience.

In the final and perhaps best-known section of *Le Salon de 1846*, "De l'héroïsme de la vie moderne," Baudelaire famously describes what his contemporaries miss by looking for beauty in ancient subjects and classical forms: "La vie parisienne est féconde en sujets poétiques et merveilleux. Le merveilleux nous enveloppe et nous abreuve comme l'atmosphère; mais nous ne le voyons pas" (2: 496). It is a call for art that opens the public's eyes to their own new world, to a vision both tawdry and pleasurable, of dissonant harmonies.

IV

Baudelaire after 1848:
Towards a Cosmopolitan Aesthetic

Le beau est toujours bizarre.
– Baudelaire, "Exposition universelle – 1855 – Beaux-arts"

In *Le Salon de 1846*, the announcement and articulation of a new aesthetic in visual art inspired by Delacroix's painting, of new optical and color theories, and of the import of a growing heterogeneous public for art, Baudelaire argues for an expansive sense of place and meaning of art in the lives of everyday French people that would lend itself to a harmonious social structure. Any quarrel about taste is aimed at the pretentious "artistes-bourgeois" rather than the actual or authentic bourgeois themselves. Certainly, as his career progressed, Baudelaire did not always maintain his enthusiasm for instructing the uninstructed. Yet the recognition of problems of taste that underscored his desire to reform taste did continue to be a concern for him. Perhaps of greater concern was the further articulation of a visually-informed aesthetic, a liberation from the hegemony of a lingering neoclassicism, represented by an entrenched academic art, but also a departure from *l'art pour l'art* aestheticism and its limitations. The writings discussed in this chapter span the period from 1851 to 1863 and represent a series of moments in his interrogation of accepted norms and his desire to broaden and redirect the aesthetic, or what is recognized as aesthetically valuable. From a post-1848 appreciation of poetry from *"le peuple"* and analysis of the sources of its popularity to the reinvention of the universal as a culturally relative sensibility, not a single norm of beauty, to, finally, the idea of an exotic domestic, a cosmopolitan lens focused on the details of everyday life, these texts reveal a Baudelaire attentive to art's contexts, theorizing the relationships between art and its environment, and eventually theorizing an aesthetic of the bizarre whose objects are no longer confined to art itself. Looking at both his positive program for a universal or cosmopolitan sensibility and at his disparagement of certain *idées fixes* of his day, we find a trajectory towards an ever more heterogeneous aesthetic, a broader compass for the aesthetic view, and a radically new definition of beauty by that attempts to account for the impact of beauty on the viewer once European norms and traditions are cast off.

***

> Pascal dit que les toges, la pourpre et les panaches ont été très heureusement inventés pour imposer au vulgaire, pour marquer d'une étiquette ce qui est vraiment respectable; et cependant les distinctions officielles dont Delacroix a été l'objet n'ont pas fait taire l'ignorance. Mais à bien regarder la chose, pour les gens qui, comme moi, veulent que les affaires d'art ne se traitent qu'entre aristocrates et qui croient que c'est la rareté des élus qui fait le paradis, tout est ainsi pour le mieux. –Baudelaire, *Salon de 1859*

This passage from *Le Salon de 1859* seems to represent a dramatic shift in attitude from the earlier Baudelaire who would educate the *épicier*. Many critics have characterized the post 1848 Baudelaire as disillusioned, depoliticized, conservative, and even reactionary in his politics.[1] And yet even this aristocratic posing and longing for a bygone era of clear social hierarchies needs to be considered within its context: a defense of Delacroix against any and all critics and a Salon, written, like those by Diderot, as letters to a friend, hence addressing the "elect" – although, since his friend is M. le directeur de la "Revue Française," they are letters intended for publication. Baudelaire's tone

---

[1] This position was widespread until the early 1970's, according to Richard D. E. Burton, who identifies the influential scholar of Baudelaire, Claude Pichois, as an important proponent of this view that depicts Baudelaire's revolutionary tendencies as short-lived, peripheral to his thought and career as a poet, and essentially expressions of an instinct for revolt without a true politics. From this perspective, his statement of 1852, "LE 2 DÉCEMBRE m'a *physiquement dépolitiqué,*" represents the completion of his disgust with politics through the events of the Bonapartist coup rather than its cause (Burton v-vi). Burton cites a group of German scholars beginning in the 1970s, influenced by the work of Benjamin, who radically question this consensus, producing a group of studies that, in Burton's view, read "Baudelaire's experience of *quarante-huit* and its aftermath through their authors' own recent experience of *soixante-huit* and its aftermath" (vii). While less focused on Baudelaire's politics per se, my study is concerned with how his aesthetic is enmeshed in the social and economic, and is shaped by an acute awareness of the contextual.

of intimacy is also one of complaint, including many complaints against his time. Yet if this aristocratic past were still present, if marks of status were fixed and universally recognized within French society, then his role of cultural analyst, deciphering fashion and ornament (*Le Salon de 1846*; *Le Peintre de la vie moderne*), and the possibility of self-invention through fashion that he celebrates in his depiction of the dandy and women dressing in "Éloge du Maquillage" would be impossible.

Putting aside inconsistencies of position, for consistency itself is a dangerous assumption for a writer who elsewhere promotes artifice and self-invention, we might consider for a moment what has changed since 1846. Perhaps most obvious are the tumultuous changes of political regime between 1848 and 1851 which culminated in the establishment of the Second Empire. As for art, in 1859 Baudelaire begins his essay complaining of the banality of the work in the current Salon, evincing a general disaffection with contemporary French painting. In a sense, his disaffection betrays a disappointment that French painting has not changed enough from the time when he disparaged the Vernets and Scheffers, hence that the public's taste is still in need of education. But if Patricia Mainardi is correct in understanding support for Ingres' "timeless and eternal" art as code for political monarchism (76), then Baudelaire's very support of Delacroix signals a different political allegiance. Thus before we conclude that Baudelaire has entirely given up on the broader public and longs for an aristocratic past, it is worthwhile to look carefully at his remarks about public taste in the 1850s. His stated political affiliations may swing from socialist to conservative, but his concern to define and refine a new aesthetic in defiance of the dominant schools of his time is ongoing. This concern is affected by his consciousness of the various publics of his time, is molded by the modern experience of the spectacle, and finally embraces its opposite in the everyday, that is, the extension of aesthetic understanding beyond art to the flagrantly anti-aesthetic. In this chapter, I consider three moments in this undertaking that help us chart the progression of his thought: his essay on Pierre Dupont's collection of workers' songs (1851), his review of the Beaux-Arts exhibit in the Universal Exhibition of 1855, and finally his most far-reaching analysis of modernity, *Le Peintre de la vie moderne* (1863). In each, in contest with other schools of thought about art of the time, we see a striving to define an art that is sensate, but not superficially so, an art of engaging objects and new contexts for those objects that change the meaning of what can be art. We hear less about the potential for social harmony found in *The Salon of 1846*, but more that throws light on the subject's relationship to the (art) object in an era of proliferating things – ready matter for cultural interpretation, an activity that itself recreates the subject as the chameleon observer/critic/lover. In contradistinction to both conventional bourgeois and academic tastes, Baudelaire's new aesthetic develops from a complicated subject/object dialectic, fed by immersion in new forms of spectacle.

The Poet-Worker: Songs of the Laboring Body

In an essay that appeared as the preface of the first volume of Pierre Dupont's *Chants et Chansons* (1851), often seen as atypical because of his embrace of a politically conscious art, Baudelaire takes swipes at bourgeois taste, but, similar to his earlier criticism of bourgeois artists, his most searing attacks are aimed at certain producers of art, in this case, wrong-minded poets, not the audience. Hence his famous invective against *l'art pour l'art*, often taken as anomalous for the poet who would serve as avatar of that movement for future generations of poets and critics: "La puérile utopie de l'école de *l'art pour l'art*, en excluant la morale, et souvent même la passion, était nécessairement stérile."[2] He pairs this attack with sharp criticism of the reign of Louis-Philippe, particularly of the youth in the final years of the July Monarchy, for its focus on gaining wealth in a "système éclectique et propriétariste" (2: 28) associating the economic system with the leading philosophical school headed by Victor Cousin. Like the July Monarchy in which it gained prominence, *l'art pour l'art* is derided for its materialism. In other words, the aural richness of such poetry, its showiness, "ces accents purement matériels, faits pour éblouir la vue tremblante des enfants ou pour caresser leur oreille paresseuse" (2: 27), masks an emptiness of signification equivalent to

---

[2] Benjamin sees this rejection of *l'art pour l'art* as only an "attitude": "It permitted him to announce the latitude which was at his disposal as a man of letters" (*Charles Baudelaire* 27). Certainly Baudelaire was always eager to take up the position of the contrarian. But, in context, this rejection has important ramifications for his aesthetic: the refusal of an empty gorgeousness as he sought a more authentically modern, yet sensate art.

the striving for riches for their own sake that smothers "l'enthousias-me, la charité, la philosophie, et tout ce qui fait le patrimoine com-mun" (2: 28). In contrast, he lauds this poetry of the working class "non pas tant à cause de sa valeur propre, qui cependant est très grande, qu'à cause des sentiments publics dont cette poésie est le symptôme, et dont Pierre Dupont s'est fait l'écho" (2: 26). These songs signify beyond the literal sense of their lyrics: they are symp-toms of the body politic, a means of diagnosing social ills. They do not lack aesthetic value, but ground that value in a close semiotic rela-tionship, a signification of what he implies is quite legitimate public sentiment. In other words, Baudelaire not only recognizes the legitI-macy of public feeling to be voiced through poetry, but lauds such voicing, a quite different semiology from the "étiquette" that would point to what deserves recognition in pre-revolutionary times, the signs of status that Baudelaire in 1859 assumes were means of silenc-ing dissent concerning eminence, "pour imposer au vulgaire."

Baudelaire is clearly thinking about value in art, and here it is both intrinsic and lodged in the works' symptomaticity, in this con-text, reflective of popular feeling. Indeed, public feeling is deemed the source of poetry here. There is also the clear implication that these songs have a substance that showy *l'art pour l'art* verse lacks. Moreover, Dupont's songs from *Les Paysans* serve as a breath of fresh air in bourgeois salons – "déjà les pianos bourgeois les répétaient avec une joie étourdie" (2: 28) – a healthful substitute for "cette nourriture indigeste de crèmes et de sucreries dont les familles illettrées bourrent imprudemment la mémoire de leurs demoiselles" (2: 30). In other words, they are capable of affecting bourgeois taste, even if their messages may be contrary to bourgeois interests.

Baudelaire speculates about what makes a particular writer attractive to the public when, prefacing his own account of Dupont's story, he analyzes the appeal of biography:

> Le public aime à se rendre compte de l'éducation des esprits auxquels il accorde sa confiance; on dirait qu'il est poussé en ceci par un sentiment indomptable d'égalité. "Tu as touché notre Cœur! Il faut nous démontrer que tu n'es qu'un homme, et que les mêmes éléments de perfectionnement existent pour nous tous." Au philosophe, au savant, au poète, à l'artiste, à tout ce qui est grand, à quiconque le remue et le transforme, le public fait la même requête. L'immense appétit que nous avons pour les biographies naît d'un sentiment profond de l'égalité. (2: 28)

Is Baudelaire mocking the public here? Yes, gently, but his observation of what moves the heart appears in an essay in which he uncynically praises a poet for his appeal to feeling. Furthermore Baudelaire understands that biography is popular because the reader identifies with the subject of the writing, and his depiction of Dupont strives to shape that sympathy. The case in point does have an egalitarian edge: Dupont's biography illustrates how an industrial city gave birth to and bred an artist with a social conscience. But Baudelaire also explicitly sketches Dupont's life and formation as typical of that of an artist, characterized by both work and revolt. He recounts Dupont's liberation from stultifying employment in a bank through the notice gained by a first book of poetry using the trope of freedom from slavery bought by poetry (2: 29). In other words, Dupont went through an experience of personal revolt while becoming the poet of revolution, whose songs were immensely popular in 1848. Baudelaire represents him in typical boho guise, while lauding his moving depictions of workers and their suffering. Rancière, referring to his research on the self-image of worker-poets, writes that "The first worker-militants began by taking themselves for poets or knights, priests or dandies. An allodoxia that is the only way to heterodoxia" (*Philosopher* 200). Baudelaire, forging his version of the artist-hero, gives us the other side of the coin: the poet as worker and militant, and not just in the fields of art. He also saw how the public yearning to identify with their heroes was an instantiation of their desire for equality, and he would establish the aesthetic worth of that poetry of equality. Indeed, he goes so far as to suggest that Dupont's poetry is powerful because it awakens another taste: "dans ce je ne sais quoi qui s'exhale incessamment de sa poésie, que j'appellerais volontiers le gout infini de la République" (2: 33).

   Thus Baudelaire's analysis of public taste here, post-1848, is twofold and relies on class distinctions while suggesting how such distinctions may be elided or overcome. First, his attitude towards the wealthy bourgeois has changed from the direct appeal for support of the dedication of *Le Salon de 1846* to a polemic against materialism and greed on moral and aesthetic grounds. On the other hand, he finds a positive force for reforming taste and political views in Dupont's songs through their intrinsic beauty and representation of the feelings of another, poorer class; their popularity with segments of the bourgeois public is testament to their effectiveness at some level. He himself self-consciously fuels this popularity by incorporating Dupont's biography into his essay, yet also, as cultural analyst, reveals its paradoxical mechanism: the heroic poet up from the working class, yet down from his pedestal for such stardom works through sentimental identification and the ethos of equality.

Critic as Cosmopolite

Whether or not Baudelaire's socialist enthusiasm was short-lived, his concern with understanding the power of art and literature, its signification vis-à-vis its social context, and its potential effect on the public, is ongoing and central to his essay on the 1855 Universal Exhibition. The Exhibition inspires a new aesthetic theory for Baudelaire, a crystallization of his interest in the cosmopolitan that dates back, at least, to *Le Salon de 1846*. In 1846, as a young critic (age 25), he would rally French youth against the militarist nationalism of the work of Horace Vernet which he deemed eminently French, as discussed in the preceding chapter. He explains Vernet's popularity in that "il vous raconte votre gloire, et c'est la grande affaire. – Eh! qu'importe au voyageur enthousiaste, à l'esprit cosmopolite qui préfère le beau à la gloire?" (2: 470). Here his invocation of the cosmopolitan is tied to his abhorrence of unthinking nationalism.

At the Exhibition, Baudelaire finds a fresh version of the "universal," a new ideal potentially free of the tradition of Western classicism and a rebuff to French cultural hegemony. In a note to the Garnier edition of *Curiosités esthétiques L'Art romantique*, the editor, Henri Lemaitre describes the page of Baudelaire's *Exposition universelle – 1855 – Beaux-arts* in which he outlines his new aesthetic of *l'insolite* as "une des plus importantes de toute la littérature esthétique moderne, car elle annonce cette grande révolution que sera le remplacement, par une esthétique de *l'insolite*, de l'esthétique néo-classique de *beau idéal* (et tout aussi bien d'ailleurs de l'esthétique romantique superficielle du *pittoresque*)" (212). Certainly the occasion for the articulation of this new aesthetic is crucial. While Great Britain hosted the first international exhibition in the Crystal Palace of 1851, France by including the fine arts would mount the first "Universal" exhibition, intended to stimulate "progress" and "emulation" in art and industry (Mainardi 42). Works from twenty-eight countries were exhibited, and so the challenge to the many critics who covered the exhibition was to find a critical framework that would offer a single vantage point. The officially sanctioned approach was the Eclecticism of Victor Cousin, both as an overarching approach to art generally and the distinctive feature of French art. Hence, as Gautier argued, French art as "eclectic" is "universal" and thus superior to the art of other nations (Mainardi 69-70). So when Baudelaire speaks of "beauté universelle" it is worth remembering the context: of the first "Exposition universelle des Beaux-arts" covered by critics for whom "universelle" is a byword for "eclectic," hence judged according to the official French aesthetic philosophy.

Baudelaire would define the "universal" differently. In 1846, he vehemently denounced both the eclectic and the national in art. And so his review of the Universal Exhibition, not surprisingly, takes a different course from that of mainstream criticism. Indeed, stimulated by art and artifacts from around the world, Baudelaire interprets the "universal" as the "cosmopolitan"[3] and thereby expands and develops his notion of relative beauty. In a way, he is able to counter the presumption of universality in a Platonist aesthetic with a redefinition of the universal as cosmopolitan. How he articulates this new aesthetic is important, setting his coverage apart from the run-of-the-mill nationalism and ethnic stereotyping of other critics, but more important looking forward to the reconfiguration of the notion of beauty that

---

[3] "Cosmopolitan" can have different meanings. For instance, Natalia Majluf, in discussing Latin American artists residing in and/or trained in Paris or other Western art centers, calls them "marginal cosmopolitans," as "participants in a world culture"who have been marginalized by a "discourse of authenticity" imposed on what were deemed "exotic" cultures (869-70). She also discusses the anxiety of French critics covering the Exposition Universelle over the homogeneity bred of technological "progress" and "universalism." This resulted in an understanding of "cosmopolitan" as sameness or lack of national difference, of which they were critical (873-75). Her essay is wonderfully illustrative of the misreadings of art by Peruvian and Mexican artists, especially Francisco Laso's "The Inhabitant of the Cordillera of Peru," given the penchant of critics to look for a national difference in the mold of travelers's picturesque. But her brief mention of Baudelaire's criticism does not take into account his sense of the cosmopolitan as one who values difference in art to the point of transformation of viewer subjectivity and aesthetic understanding. Her analysis of a "double standard of value" is astute: that Latin American painters would be judged according to their "authenticity,"an emphasis on the collectivity, content over form, and the expression of an unchanging national "core," while the emerging Modernism valued individual expression, form over content, and newness. But she ignores Baudelaire's more radical delineation of the "cosmopolitan," which will open the door to the eventual embrace of nonEuropean aesthetic norms by Modernism.

would undergird the aesthetic of modernity that he articulates in *Le peintre de la vie moderne.*

He begins his review by acknowledging that what is essentially the program of the Universal Exhibition – the comparison of nations and their products – generates "surprise" and "revelations" for the critic:

> Il est peu d'occupations aussi intéressantes, aussi attachantes, aussi pleines de surprises et de révélations pour un critique, pour un rêveur dont l'esprit est tourné à la généralisation aussi bien qu'à l'étude des détails, et, pour mieux dire encore, à l'idée d'ordre et de hiérarchie universelle, que la comparaison des nations et de leurs produits respectifs. Quand je dis hiérarchie, je ne veux pas affirmer la suprématie de telle nation sur telle autre. Quoiqu'il y ait dans la nature des plantes plus ou moins saintes, des formes plus ou moins spirituelles, des animaux plus ou moins sacrés, et qu'il soit légitime de conclure, d'après les instigations de l'immense analogie universelle, que certaines nations – vastes animaux dont l'organisme est adéquat à leur milieu, — aient été préparées et éduquées par la Providence pour un but déterminé, but plus ou moins élevé, plus ou moins rapproché du ciel, — je ne veux pas faire ici autre chose qu'affirmer leur *égale* utilité aux yeux de CELUI qui est indéfinissable, et le miraculeux secours qu'elles se prêtent dans l'harmonie de l'univers. (2: 575)

Although Baudelaire's subject is the fine arts, he uses "produits" which has a particular resonance in an essay on the Universal Exhibition: they could be works of art or the products of industry or both. Indeed, his repeated use of the word "produits" in this essay signifies the degree to which he is reacting to the entire exhibition of art and industry. Later he refers to "les different ateliers de notre fabrique artistique" (2: 578), suggesting an equivalence between the studio and the factory. The poet who praised Dupont's workers' songs maintains an identification with labor. But "produits" also suggests fruits of the earth, the results of natural processes (a meaning already overdetermined in the discourse of political economy in modeling industrial production on the historically more prestigious agricultural production). Official decrees regarding the ordering of the Universal Exhibition, while at times referring to "les œuvres d'art," also include this tripartite classification, "les produits de l'agriculture, de l'in-dustrie et de l'art" (*Rapports* xi). Thus the idiom of the entire exhibition, of art and industry, inflects this art criticism with an emphasis on the similarities between art and industry rather than the distinctions, which contrasts what a strong advocate of *l'art pour l'art* would insist upon.[7] Since the products of industry on display included objects representing the applied arts—metalwork, porcelain, furniture, and other luxury goods—Baudelaire's use of this broader category may well indicate his interest in objects that did not fit in the category of "fine arts."

The stimulation that he has felt as a spectator is implied by words like "surprises" and "révélations." That he characterizes himself as a critic who is a "rêveur," one prone to dream of a universal order and harmony, would seem to prepare the way for a grand utopian scheme, but later in the essay, he utterly disavows any such aim, citing his own failures at creating enduring systems in the past and the inevitability of some surprise or unexpected disruption to the system: "Et toujours un produit spontané, inattendu, de la vitalité universelle venait donner un démenti à ma science enfantine et vieillotte, fille déplorable de l'utopie. J'avais beau déplacer ou étendre le critérium, il était toujours en retard sur l'homme universel, et courait sans cesse après le beau multiforme et versicolore, qui se meut dans les spirales infinies de la vie" (2: 577-78). Thus he will not stipulate the hierarchy of this universal order, deferring before the all-seeing eye who judges all equally useful, no matter what their place in the order;[4] two pages later it is a "vitalité" that is universal, and "l'homme universel" is part of an everchanging beauty of many forms and colors, linked to the "infinite spirals of life."

He takes direct aim at contemporary neoclassicists and the inadequacy of the aesthetic of absolute beauty to account for the beauties on display:

> que ferait, que dirait un Winckelmann moderne (nous en sommes pleins, la nation en regorge, les paresseux en raffolent), que dirait-il en face d'un produit chinois, produit étrange, bizarre, contourné dans sa forme, intense par sa couleur, et quelquefois délicat jusqu'à l'évanouissement ? Cependant c'est un échantillon de la beauté universelle ; mais il faut, pour qu'il soit compris, que le critique, le spectateur opère en lui-même une transformation qui tient du mystère, et que, par un phénomène de la volonté agissant sur l'imagination, il apprenne de lui-même à participer au milieu qui a donné naissance à cette floraison insolite. Peu d'hommes ont, — au complet, — cette grâce divine du

---

[4] As Claude Pichois notes, "analogie universelle" is a Fourierist term, but in 1855, Baudelaire adheres to no utopian or mystical system (2: 1386, n 3). In the context of the opening paragraph of his essay on the occasion of the Exposition universelle, he clearly is employing this language to dislodge "universal" from the more obvious, state-sanctioned meaning of the world-wide reach of an exhibition that shows off the ability of the French to dominate in art and goods on a world stage.

cosmopolitisme ; mais tous peuvent l'acquérir à des degrés divers. Les mieux doués à cet égard sont ces voyageurs solitaires qui ont vécu pendant des années au fond des bois, au milieu des vertigineuses prairies, sans autre compagnon que leur fusil, contemplant, disséquant, écrivant. Aucun voile scolaire, aucun paradoxe universitaire, aucune utopie pédagogique, ne se sont interposés entre eux et la complexe vérité. Ils savent l'admirable, l'immortel, l'inévitable rapport entre la forme et la fonction. Ils ne critiquent pas, ceux-là : ils contemplent, ils étudient. (2: 576)

Of the thirty art critics who covered the Universal Exhibition, only Baudelaire and Gautier mentioned the Chinese art, and Gautier distinguished between the Greek "beau idéal" and Chinese "laid idéal," making Baudelaire the only critic to discern beauty in the Chinese works.[5] The Chinese object is, moreover, a "specimen of universal beauty" in Baudelaire's eyes, and as he emphasizes elsewhere in the essay, such beauty is not uniform, but "multiforme et versicolore" (2: 578). For Baudelaire the truly cosmopolitan critic would see freshly – "contemplate," "study" – and avoid judging works according to preexisting academic systems that blind the critic to their "complex truth," including the functionality of the object's form. In other words, in a move away from a doctrine of formal autonomy, Baudelaire represents the relationship between form and function as part of the object's aesthetic impact, a perception of the embeddedness of the object within its original cultural context and the contribution of that embedding to the object's beauty.

Before discussing in detail the transformative critical process that Baudelaire here theorizes, I will turn briefly to Gautier's longer article on Chinese art, for the difference between Gautier's appraisal of this collection and Baudelaire's emerging cosmopolitan aesthetic is instructive. Although Baudelaire in a later essay will praise his wit as "cosmopolitan,"[6] Gautier's approach to the Chinese collection falls short of what Baudelaire calls for here in a "cosmopolitan" critic. The difference between their approaches to the Chinese collection helps us see what is novel about Baudelaire's "bizarre" or "insolite" – how these terms anchor a cosmopolitan criticism that diverges even in its basic assumptions about the nature of the aesthetic experience from

---

[5] Pichois, note 2, 2: 1368, citing an article by Yoshio Abé (*Le Monde*, 28 November 1968) and Gautier, *Les Beaux-Arts en Europe*, Michel Lévy frères, chap. 12.

[6] "[S]on esprit est un miroir cosmopolite de beauté" ("Théophile Gautier [I]," 2: 108). The context is important: Baudelaire wants to stress romantic aspects of Gautier's sensibility for all that he defends classical beauty.

that practiced by the older poet and critic whom Baudelaire publicly admired.

Gautier's article first appeared in *L'Artiste* entitled "L'Art chinois" in the October 7, 1855, issue, and was reprinted in Gautier's 1857 collection of his reviews of the Universal Exhibition of 1855, *Les Beaux-Arts en Europe*, published by Michel Lévy frères, as "Collection chinoise". This minor change of title may well be significant, for Gautier's tone is derisive when he speaks of Chinese art while he greatly admires Chinese objects – the porcelain, furniture, and other luxury goods that are ordinarily found on the "industrial" side of the Exhibition. He begins his article with the usual tired stereotypes of the Chinese as an ancient but "immobile" people who "ont tout inventé et n'ont rien perfectionné; ils connaissaient la boussole, la poudre, l'imprimerie, le gaz, bien avant que le reste du monde se doutât de ces précieuses découvertes" (130). Such a remark owes something to the general temper of exhibition coverage, since the exhibition is meant to measure and compare "progress," and so the relevance of technology and inventions that were not exploited, symptoms, perhaps, of the immobility that he deems a national trait. In describing the Chinese "genius," Gautier employs some of the same vocabulary as Baudelaire, but the inflection is entirely different:

> Ils ont un génie bizarre, maniaque et patient, qui ne ressemble au génie d'aucun peuple, et qui, au lieu de s'épanouir comme une fleur, se tortille comme une racine de mandragore. Nuls pour la beauté sérieuse, ils excellent dans la curiosité ; s'ils n'ont rien à envoyer aux musées, en revanche ils peuvent remplir toutes les boutiques de bric-à-brac de créations baroques et difformes, du caprice le plus rare. Vous avez sans doute vu ce nain de la rivière des Perles qu'on avait enfermé dans une potiche pour qu'il s'y rabougrit d'une façon curieuse ; c'est l'image la plus juste du génie chinois. (131)

Thus, for Gautier, the "bizarre" implies deformity, stunted growth, and the production of shop goods, not art.[7] He contrasts their aesthetic vision directly with that of classical Greece: "Les autres nations, à commencer par les Grecs, qui l'ont atteint, cherchent le beau idéal; les Chinois cherchent le laid idéal; ils pensent que l'art doit s'éloigner autant que possible de la nature, inutile selon eux à représenter,

---

[7] Quoting Balzac from *Cousin Pons*, Susan Stewart notes the association of "bric-a-brac" with barter, that the term itself "implies the process of acquisition and exchange" (159). Hence the commercial overtones of Gautier's descriptor.

puisque l'original et la copie feraient double emploi" (131-32). Gautier's move here is revealing: ideal beauty is ultimately representational, legitimized by the doctrine of mimesis, and thus a more "natural" flowering, while the Chinese pursue an antimimetic aesthetic, symptomatic of a "deformed" genius that produces "curiosities." This aspect of Gautier's aesthetic philosophy seems more classical than romantic, but more important to our investigation of the "bizarre" are his underlying assumptions. He assumes here a close relationship between nature and beauty and the universal recognition of this relationship. For him Chinese art and artifacts reflect a particular "genius" but not a different way of viewing nature. Rather, it is a "genius" that subverts or distorts the relationship between art and nature and thus produces deformed and stunted products. He mocks Chinese painting in terms of both composition – "faire tenir dans le même cadre des objets que la perspective sépare" – and use of color – "Une tigre bleu-de-ciel, un lion vert-pomme, sont bien plus curieux que s'ils étaient tout bêtement colories de leurs nuances naturelles" (132). He concludes that " le laid est infini et ses combinaisons monstrueuses offrent à la fantaisie des champs illimités" (132). Of course, in retrospect, we discern here the features of modernist painting that emerged later in the century, influenced by the art of Japan and other "exotic" cultures: the nonnaturalistic, arbitrary use of color, the telescoping of objects within the picture plane, and the crucial antirepresentational turn.

Gautier's tone changes when he describes Chinese luxury goods, "la partie vraiment sérieuse de la collection composée des objets les plus rares et les plus précieux en émaux, bronzes, porcelaines, laques, cabinets et meubles de toutes sortes" (136). The materials, the work, and the provenance – imperial palaces – all add value to these objects. He explicitly contrasts Chinese antimimetic painting with the art of ornament, where whimsy is to be applauded: "dans l'arabesque pure, dans l'ornement capricieuse du bronze, de la porcelaine, du bois, de la laque et des pierres dures, les Chinois sont des maitres inimitables, et l'on ne peut qu'admirer les mille produits de leur imagination inépuisablement fertile" (137). His use even of the word "arabesque" is telling, for he adopts Orientalist lenses fashioned by Western perspectives on the Islamic world to stimulate interest in these objects and the world he suggests they intimate. For example, the beauty of Chinese characters and their use in ornamentation remind him of the

Alhambra (133), and he imagines apartments for Chinese women "aussi fermés aux Européens que les harems des pachas d'Asie" (134). Indeed, the general idea of mystery, of a hidden world, and of this exhibition as the exposure of what is normally veiled or forbidden to Western eyes is a leitmotif throughout the review, which begins with the visitor passing by what Gautier characterizes as a guard, the faux-Chinese figures, "deux bronzes de Jules Cordier, un mandarin et son épouse, purs types de l'empire du Milieu qui grimacent avec un sérieux jovial sur leurs piédouches" (130), and ends, not surprisingly, with the assertion that this "merveilleuse collection ... vous fait franchir pour quelques instants la muraille de la Chine" (142).

In contrast with Gautier's presentation of this exhibit as a sneak peek into the world of imperial China, Baudelaire theorizes that for any understanding of the object, itself a specimen of "universal beauty," a more profound change in the spectator is required: a "trans-formation" dependent on the imagination – that is, a full imagining of the locale that produced this art or artifact. Thus Baudelaire invokes a cosmopolitanism rooted in a local (foreign) imaginary. Further, the Chinese object is a "produit" of a "floraison insolite," tropes which suggest a natural process. But, in contrast with Gautier's mimetic ideal, Baudelaire's view of the relationship between art and nature emphasizes analogous harmonic systems rather than representation, and thus redefines the aesthetic worth of these productions within a different ontology, a different sense of the interconnection between art and nature and of natural processes *tout court*. Understanding Chinese art is just one window to understanding "la beauté universelle" which, he implies, is not fully knowable because of its infinite potential configurations or "correspondances" among sensorial instantiations.

Since the *Salon of 1846*, Baudelaire has intimated that the viewing of art may change the alert and receptive spectator. In this 1855 essay, the transformation is so radical that he sketches a solitary traveler in nature, rather than the typical cosmopolite, as the subject best suited for such a transformation, in line with his valuing naiveté and freshness.[8] But he goes on to imagine a voyage to a foreign country by "un homme du monde, un intelligent" with the capacity to feel a sympathy that will "créera en lui un monde nouveau d'idées, monde qui fera partie intégrante de lui-même, et qui l'accompagnera,

---

[8] Jenine Abboushi Dallal helpfully points out the influence of Emerson and Thoreau in this "New World pioneer analogy" (263, n. 53).

sous la forme de souvenirs, jusqu'à la mort" (2: 576). Baudelaire emphasizes a process of surprise, of a subject disconcerted by difference, who gradually is penetrated by "quelques milliers d'idées et de sensations" that "enrichiront son dictionnaire de mortel" and so change his aesthetic allegiances as to cause him to do "comme le Sicambre converti, qu'il brûle ce qu'il avait adoré, et qu'il adore ce qu'il avait brûlé" (2: 577). In contrast, "l'insensé doctrinaire de Beau" will not only be blind to these beauties and the cultures they evoke, but is blind to nature and finally blocked from all sensual experience:

> enfermé dans l'aveuglante forteresse de son système, il blasphémerait la vie et la nature, et son fanatisme grec, italien ou parisien, lui persuaderait de défendre à ce people insolent de jouir, de rêver ou de penser par d'autres procédés que les siens propres; — science barbouille d'encre, goût bâtard, plus barbares que les barbares, qui a oublié la couleur du ciel, la forme du végétal, le mouvement et l'odeur de l'animalité, et dont les doigts crispés, paralysés par la plume, ne peuvent plus courir avec agilité sur l'immense clavier des *correspondances* ! (2: 577)

Thus Baudelaire posits in the object the capacity to elicit its own original environment under the gaze of the receptive and imaginative spectator. If we take the hypothetical Chinese "produit" as an example, he notes its tortuous form, the intensity of its color, and its almost ethereal delicacy, evidence for the cosmopolitan critic of "l'admirable, l'immortel, l'inévitable rapport entre la forme et la function," without, of course, saying what that function might be. Thus a formal appreciation of the object is insufficient; the apprehension of function is needed in order to imagine the culture that produced it. In other words, this visionary eye sees form, color, and near inutility, and imagines the object's making and use. The aesthetic experience of the object – appreciation of its formal qualities – has the power to evoke not only a foreign world but also functionality within that world, the object's use value, as it were, a different register of value from that of exchange, relevant to Gautier's references to the shop-worthiness of the Chinese collection and to the commercial subtext of the Universal Exhibition as a whole.[9] Like Dupont's workers' songs, the object on display is

---

[9] Here I disagree with Dallal who notes that the evanescence of the object "facilitates the detachment of Chinese art from its cultural context and specificity" (244), when the thrust of Baudelaire's description of that encounter is to use it to imagine the object's context. Nonetheless she sees this discussion of the object and its apprehension as evidence that Baudelaire "defines the aesthetic in terms of cultural

symptomatic, but its foreignness requires imagination of that which it signifies.[10] He also imagines the object as a specimen of universal beauty, but not as a model or ideal type; rather, it is an instantiation of harmonies, analogous with those in the natural world, something quite different from Gautier's ideal beauty.

But, to belabor his metaphor, these are harmonies in a new key. In this brief essay, Baudelaire, as Lemaitre remarks, develops his new aesthetic that will eventually replace the dominant aesthetic of the time: *"Le beau est toujours bizarre"* (2: 578).[11] This "bizarrerie" itself "dépendante des milieux, des climats, des mœurs, de la race, de la religion et du tempérament de l'artiste" (2: 578-79); thus the bizarre is not simply the exotic, in other words, the effect of foreignness, but depends on its own cultural context for its effect. That is, as there are many diverse beauties, so there are many "bizarreries," and they are bizarre through their relationship with their own context. The aesthetic critic/theorist requires an anthropological understanding. This is a cosmopolitanism that would be firmly non-Eurocentric by recognizing

---

renunciation," like Gautier in the preface of *Mademoiselle de Maupin*, which may indeed be an important aspect of Baudelaire's cosmopolitanism. See Dallal 244-45.

[10] Debarati Sanyal emphasizes the colonialist agenda of the Universal Exhibition, and thereby reads this transformation of the viewer as "a profound physiological and spiritual penetration that resists the assumed conversion and convertibility of a conquered nation 'penetrated' by the colonial presence" (123). While agreeing with her general sense of Baudelaire as a critic of Western cultural hegemony, her focus on the colonial seems misplaced when the hypothetical object is Chinese, the product of another empire. I also situate this transformation within the larger trajectory of Baudelaire's inquiry into the aesthetic, and, in this context, the "reversal of visual power in the exhibition of foreign merchandise" (123) represents a new stage in Baudelaire's theorization of the ideal of imaginative receptivity for the cosmopolitan critic rather than the experience of the common viewer (see Sanyal 120-3).

[11] It is ironic that the "bizarre" in later decades would become associated with decadence since Baudelaire attempts to forestall such an association by making a case for the real decadence of its opposite: the decadence of the commonplace, of Everyman of the Second Empire, the complacent reader of newspapers who has forfeited his free will in the very expectation of inexorable technological progress, the complacent viewer of art whose judgment relies on moribund models of beauty. There is, however, some etymological support for Baudelaire's aesthetic of the bizarre in Emile Littré's *Dictionnaire de la langue française* of 1863. Littré proposes two possible origins for the word: from the Basque for "beard," since "bizarre" seems to have come to French from Spanish and first meant "valiant, brave," and from the Arabic "bāshāret"—"beauty, elegance, whence valiant, chivalrous, then the sense of anger, fiery, extravagant" (352)—a reminder from one of Baudelaire's contemporaries of the cosmopolitan roots of the French language and nation.

that the bizarre itself is locally meaningful, and not simply the effect of distance from the familiar. Further, the bizarre brings to the foreground the ideational or cognitive in the aesthetic by playing the same role as taste or seasoning in food, which reveals an "idea" to the tongue and the "individuality" of the object:

> Cette dose de bizarrerie qui constitue et définit l'individualité, sans laquelle il n'y a pas de beau, joue dans l'art (que l'exactitude de cette comparaison en fasse pardonner la trivialité) le rôle du goût ou de l'assaisonnement dans les mets, le mets ne différant les uns des autres, abstraction faite de leur utilité ou de la quantité de substance nutritive qu'ils contiennent, que par l'*idée* qu'ils révèlent à la langue. (579)

Thus the aesthetic is reliant on individualism in the object which is also an ethos for the "idea" of the bizarre, the individual, the different, which sets off the transformative process. Here he implies that the rest of the aesthetic effect, that which does not partake of the bizarre, is blandly utilitarian, the nutrition found in the dish, to use his analogy, so ordinary as to have lost its capacity to please or to mean.

This is in part a defense of his methodology – or argument for lack thereof—for throwing over the tired language of salon reviews and approaches to beauty which stifle the imagination. His authority is Balzac, who responded to a painting of a winter scene by wondering about the lives of those depicted: "Que c'est beau! Mais que font-ils dans cette cabane? à quoi pensent-ils, quels sont leurs chagrins? Les récoltes ont-elles été bonnes? *ils ont sans doute des échéances à payer?*" (2: 579). Again, the aesthetic response leads to consideration of content, or context, here even the economic conditions of the painting's subjects. Baudelaire concludes: "Il m'arrivera souvent d'apprécier un tableau uniquement par la somme d'idées ou de rêveries qu'il apportera dans mon esprit" (2: 579), and generalizes that "La peinture est une évocation, une opération magique" (2: 580). Thus the sine qua non of his alternative aesthetic lies in the object's capacity to conjure ideas, provoke daydreaming, in an utterly subjective process, and yet this process is the means to a more profound understanding of the work's context, whether foreign or domestic. His argument is that only through such transformation of the subject can an authentic cosmopolitanism emerge.

It is striking how enthusiastic he is about "cette belle Exposition, si variée dans ses éléments, si inquiétante par sa variété, si déroutante pour la pédagogie " (2: 579), and how it has worked as the impetus for his aesthetic of the bizarre. The contrast between this enthusiasm and his dismay before the banality of the Salon of 1859 is equally striking. Is Baudelaire so seduced by the beauty of the objects on display at the Universal Exhibition that he is drawn into its official rhetoric? Rather he plays off this rhetoric in his repeated use of "products" for the art objects on display, undercutting the official divide between the fine arts and products of industry. This vocabulary suggests, too, the alliance of artists and workers as producers. His critical awareness, however, of the rhetoric surrounding the Exhibition becomes obvious when he turns to the notion of "progress." Since the first industrial exhibition in 1798, the display and measurement of "progress" has been a central aim of the government in launching these shows and has been part of the official rhetoric in both documents of authorization and publicity. (See chapter two.) We find such a rationale in the official documents associated with the Universal Exhibition, for instance, in the decree from Napoleon the Third that calls for the fine arts portion of the Exhibition, "considérant qu'un des moyens les plus efficaces de contribuer au progrès des arts est une Exposition universelle, qui, en ouvrant un concours entre tous les artistes du monde et en mettant en regard tant d'œuvres diverses, doit être un puissant motif d'émulation et offrir une source de comparaisons fécondes" (*Rapports* i). The institutional apparatus also encourages the measurement of progress explicitly in the awarding of prizes.

But Baudelaire's argument is not so much with any implied equivalence between industry and art. Rather he takes issue with the broader conception of history behind the contemporary notion of progress, for which technological innovation and industrial production serve as bellwethers. Baudelaire admits that progress can occur – specifically, in questions of morality, in the careers of individual artists from year to year, in the price and quality of goods. But he objects to the belief in the inevitability of progress, seeing this as both a constraint on liberty and a delusion. He critiques the idea of progress in the arts among individuals, arguing that the greatest artists rarely had important predecessors: "Toute floraison est spontanée, individuelle" (2: 581). Further, in the individual careers of the greatest living French painters Ingres and Delacroix, Baudelaire discerns no "progress" as such.[12]

The same holds for nations: contemporary excellence does not guarantee future greatness. As evidence, he cites the discrepancy between contemporary Italian, German, and Spanish art and that of Leonardo, Raphael, Michelangelo; Dürer; and Zurbaran and Velasquez, respectively. This remark about the mistaken expectations of the public, viewing contemporary art from these countries for the first time, was made frequently by critics covering the fine arts at the Universal Exhibition. More startling is Baudelaire's contention that the expectation that progress is inevitable is itself a sign of decadence: those "races" who persist in this delusion "s'endormiront sur l'oreiller de la fatalité dans le sommeil radoteur de la décrépitude. Cette infatuation est le diagnostic d'une décadence déjà top visible" (2: 580). In other words, this assumption induces inertia, indolence, stagnation, and ultimately decay, and thus serves as, and produces, a sign of decadence. This charge echoes his derision of those who idolize the modern Winckelmanns as "paresseux," another instance of the acceptance of the commonplace and of intellectual complacency. Physical or material progress as signified by new technologies should not be confused with "l'ordre spirituel," and so Baudelaire decries the loss of responsibility, or moral duty, and concomitant loss of freedom and free will that the assumption of the inevitability of progress entails, and the misguided thinking of the average man "tellement américanisé par ses philosophes zoocrates et industriels" who would confuse the physical and moral, the natural and supernatural (2: 580).[13]

---

[12] Compagnon observes that despite Baudelaire's attack on the notion of progress, the modern tradition in art "has redeemed itself" through "the ideas of progress and dialectics," thus the concept of modernity that laid claim to Baudelaire as a founder ignores Baudelaire's critique of one of its crucial premises and harbors a fundamental contradiction between the drive to innovate and its special status as an enduring cultural object (xvi).

[13] Sanyal points out that such "vitriolic denunciations of progress are usually read within a Catholic or de Maistrean framework of original sin and providentialism," yet "Baudelaire's anti-progressivist stance consistently dislocates the Western civilizing mission to assert the value, dignity, and energy of preindustrial peoples and nations against the apparent supremacy of Western nations and their modes of production" (121). Her point underscores the consistency between Baudelaire's description of the ideal cosmopolite critic as a wanderer in the wilderness and this denunciation of the ideology of Progress, all part of his critique of Franco-centricity at the Universal Exhibition.

In effect, Baudelaire's critique of progress is a critique of the epistemological basis of such belief, which he characterizes as information gleaned from the daily newspaper: "Demandez à tout bon Français qui lit tous les jours *son* journal dans son estaminet, ce qu'il entend par progrès, il répondra que c'est la vapeur, l'électricité et l'éclairage au gaz, miracles inconnues aux Romains, et que ces découvertes témoignent pleinement de notre supériorité sur les anciens" (2: 580). The exhibition itself, offering exposure to diverse cultures, serves as an antidote by discrediting the idea of inevitable progress, taking, for instance, "decline" in Italian and Spanish art as cases in point. In other words, the Romans' lack of technological sophistication from the vantage point of the nineteenth century, from the point of view of the reader of daily news, is countered by the inferior state of Italian art in comparison with their Renaissance forerunners. Further, in Baudelaire's view, the Exhibition offers the spectacle of diverse beauties, no matter what the level of "civilization" of the country of their origin; thus art represents knowledge of a different order from that of technology that leads to different conclusions about cultural superiority among nations.

Indeed Baudelaire's aesthetic of the bizarre is a challenge to the idea of levels of civilization, to the ideology of civilization as a marker of progress.[14] Ironically, in his view, the exhibition as a cultural cosmopolis undercuts the rhetoric of progress that the display of technological innovation would support. Here the knowledge of art – visual and remembered – trumps journalistic commonplaces about "progress," and so Baudelaire promotes an aestheticism in that art reveals the fuller truth about the state of current culture and the ontology of history itself, an aesthetic approach to social and cultural critique. But clearly it is not the aestheticism that considers art as ultimately self-referential, existing in a sphere apart from politics, history, and "life," but one that gives art epistemological priority over everyday discourse and that sees in art critical categories for understanding social and historical trends. Of course, for Baudelaire, art is a complex vehicle of social truth, for, at its most bizarre, art has "ideas"

---

[14] Compagnon notes that later assumptions that the cult of the bizarre is part of the aesthetic of the new, requiring novelty in order to elicit surprise, is a misinterpretation of Baudelaire (10), as is clear here where this "bizarre" beauty is realized in the foreign object and in paintings by the "geniuses" of Western art, no matter what their era.

that are best apprehended imaginatively rather than delivered didactically. Patricia Mainardi argues convincingly that the official policy of eclecticism and the use of the retrospective in the 1855 Beaux-arts exhibition took politics out of art by reducing differences among schools to differences of style, not politics, and by shifting emphasis onto individual careers rather than schools and traditions with their political affiliations. Baudelaire, however, would retain for art a role in assessing the state of current society by dint of art's own level of aesthetic accomplishment. Furthermore, art, specifically its "bizarre" beauty, serves as an entrée into understanding its social and cultural context, as in the case of the Chinese objects.

Cosmopolitanism has recently come under attack as the cultural adjunct to and discursive cover for globalization that well-meaning leftist academics have not sufficiently interrogated. Timothy Brennan, for instance, asserts that "an attempt to imagine the relations between emergent financial interests and scholarly models is widely lacking in scholarship itself," while research "finesses" its embeddedness in a social system beholden to corporate interests (661). For Brennan, the cosmopolitan is *"local* while denying its local character" (660), by which he means American: based on an American model of pluralism with American aspirations of global management. He also accuses academia of forgetting and thus unconsciously abetting the repeating of the history of cosmopolitanism.

We might look at the Universal Exhibition and its coverage as a nineteenth-century case in point. The aim of engendering interest in the cosmopolitan was openly commercial: not only was the Universal Exhibition meant to promote industrial competition and desire for the commodities on display, but, in a departure from protocol in earlier industrial exhibitions, prices were attached and some objects were literally for sale. Further, the relationship between the financial interests that would promote French goods and the official school of aesthetics, eclecticism, that helped define French superiority in art as universal was strong in the sense that both were aspects of a single governmental campaign. How might we judge Baudelaire's concept in this light? Should we then be suspicious of Baudelaire's promotion of the "bizarre" as aesthetic value? Undoubtedly his admiration, indeed, desire, for such objects was whetted by the Exhibition, but the image of the cosmopolite that he sketches is radically different from the more conventional type of the, frankly, touristic shopper. He limns a transformation of subjectivity, as I described above, that would come to understand the "bizarre" or "strange" (*insolite*) as an idea within its own context. Granted, this desire to universalize an aesthetic that for him serves as an escape from the burden of neoclassicism is unwittingly local for a Parisian in the capital of the nineteenth century, and his imagining the effect of this aesthetic as a transformation of subjectivity belies a reliance on and obsession with a form of subjectivity, an individualism particular to the West. But, in the context of contemporary discourse, when measured against the notion of the bizarre as deformed, ugly, and alien, his aesthetic implies an ethos of cosmopolitanism that seeks to understand foreign cultures through self-transformation that other inflections of the word at the time lacked. For instance, in the *Rapport sur l'exposition universelle de 1855*, a more familiar sense appears:

> Ajoutons que Paris est le séjour d'une colonie nombreuse d'étrangers qu'y appellent les affaires, le plaisir, l'étude, etc. que par ses collections, ses musées, ses bibliothèques, il se prête plus qu'aucune autre capitale aux travaux d'ensemble sur l'industrie, les sciences et les arts ; que par l'urbanité de ses mœurs, par son hospitalité envers les étrangers, notre capitale a véritablement un caractère cosmopolite. (139)

The report points to the cosmopolitan character of Paris as a reason for its suitability for future grandiose international exhibitions; it is urbane and hospitable, quite unlike the wanderer enamored of the "primitive" who serves as model for Baudelaire. Moreover, for all that Baudelaire, by valuing foreign goods, was complicit with the capitalist system – which is basically what Brennan charges intellectuals today with – he also critiqued the major ideology of that system: the assumption and value of progress, with technology and increased productivity as its indicators. Further, he questioned the meaning of the apparent superiority of French art over that of other nations, seeing no sign there of a greater degree of "civilization," but simply a phase in the life of a nation.

   In sum, a transformative cosmopolitanism, such as Baudelaire envisions, should be distinguished from a cosmopolitanism that is a guise for an assumption of French or European superiority in art and industry by way of contrast with the products of other cultures and the imposition of Western aesthetic norms. (Indeed, the arrangement of the Beaux-arts exhibition, with the central placement and preponderance of French art, is enough to undercut any fair notions of the Exhibition as a truly cosmopolitan event.)[15] We might go further: Baudelaire's cosmopolitanism escapes the rationale for the official cosmopolitanism – a contest among nations that is nonmilitary, which nonetheless reinforces the ideology of the national. Sheldon Pollock has described the "coercive cosmopolitanism" of the Roman Republic and Empire and its Latin language and literature where participation in the cosmopolis is militarily "compelled by the state" (596) in contra-distinction to the "voluntaristic cosmopolitanism" of the spread of Sanskrit as a literary culture through "the circulation of traders, literati, religious professionals, and freelance adventurers" (603). In nineteenth-century France, we see a sort of replay and ultimate failure of the first kind in Napoleon's military conquests and imposition of the Napoleonic code, replaced by the "peaceful" competition of trade. While Baudelaire's solitary traveler conjures the romance of earlier traders and adventurers, the "voluntaristic cosmopolitanism" of Pollock's Sanskrit culture, Baudelaire emphasizes the influence of the foreign on the French, not the hegemony of any single culture, language, or literature. This difference from the official "cosmopol-itan" aim of promoting French superiority in a commercial and cultural arena in the shadow of military defeat forty years earlier, through an exhibition overseen by Prince Napoleon Bonaparte, or-dered by another Emperor Napoleon, is important.[16] For Baudelaire, the cosmopolitan offered a solution to the debate over ideal beauty at the heart of aestheticism: here was evidence that beauty is relative, not absolute, a visual refutation of the academic or neoclassical ideal. The aesthetic ideal is neither singular nor definable through abstract traits; rather relative beauty, known through its embodiments, signifies in multiple realms. Rancière's contention that in "the aesthetic regime" language is not autotelic, but participates in the "distribution of the sensible" is relevant to the practice of the cosmopolitan critic. Objects evoke historical and social worlds, and so enter into the construction of history. Rancière, too, uses Balzac as a reference point in describ-

---

[15] As Raser notes, "[t]he official catalogue lists 10,691 exhibits from France, Algeria, and French colonies; the rest of the world contributed 10,148" ("Politics" 344, n. 5).

[16] Despite the official rationale that the Universal Exhibition would replace war with peaceful competition, France and England were at war with Russia (the Crimean War of 1853-56). This paradox is explicitly acknowledged in government documents, for instance, in the editor's introduction to *Le Travail universel*.

ing how constructions of fiction give shape and meaning to fact-based history, creating "a regime of equivalence between the signs of the new novel and those of the description or interpretation of the phenomena of a civilization" (*Politics of Aesthetics* 37). For Baudelaire, imagination, modeled on Balzac's fiction-making, makes possible of a kind of anthropological investigation. His reference to "correspondances" in this essay is evidence that this revision of the "universal" is an expansion of his idea of harmonies among sound, color, taste, and scent that unlock meaning. Thus, his ongoing interrogation of existing aesthetic systems and his own aesthetic theories are instances of such a striving after materiality through language, with the experience of the visual arts and art objects as model, and a resistance against an aesthetic that moves beauty away from the human sensorium. In "Exposition universelle – 1855 – Beaux-arts," Baudelaire is especially interested in how, in Rancière's words, the "silent language of things or the coded language of images" makes imaginable the traits of other, non-European historical and social worlds, and the transformation of the subject-spectator that accompanies this imagining.

Culture Clash and the Hermeneutics of Modernity

The "coded language of images" and the idea of relative beauty are topics that Baudelaire takes up again in *The Painter of Modern Life*, his fullest articulation of the aesthetic of modernity. In it he famously writes:

> Le beau est fait d'un élément eternel, invariable, dont la quantité est excessivement difficile à déterminer, et d'un élément relatif, circonstanciel, qui sera, si l'on veut, tour à tour ou tout ensemble, l'époque, la mode, la morale, la passion. Sans ce second élément, qui est comme l'enveloppe amusante, titillante, apéritive, du divin gâteau, le premier élément serait indigestible, inappréciable, non adapté et non approprié à la nature humaine. (2: 685)

Thus the "relative, circumstantial element" in this model of beauty plays a similar role to the "bizarre" in the previous one: it is the "aperitif" that makes the unchanging, eternal, and frankly nonhuman in beauty digestible, like the "seasoning" offered by the bizarre. But in *The Painter of Modern Life*, Baudelaire famously chooses fashion as his central example of this relative and circumstantial aspect of beauty. In the passage quoted above, fashion is on a par with the era, its morals and passions; again, analogous to the "bizarre," this aspect of beauty reveals the culture to itself. But this is not just Baudelaire the cynic, the contrarian who would insist that the conventionally unbeautiful is beautiful for the sake of paradox, or that fashion is art simply to gall the academic critics. If we take seriously his idea of the "bizarre" as essential to beauty, then we should expect to find a similar notion in his analysis of the beauty of modern life in Paris. The "bizarre" is the element within a culture that is arresting to that culture as well as to others, and here fashion fits the bill. In other words, the couturier's dream is finally not so different from the "surprise" and "revelation" of cosmopolitan discovery, and similarly functions as a distillation of cultural meaning. And, just as art bears the imprint of the artist's personality for Baudelaire, so fashion is an assertion of individuality, especially in an era of affordable, mass-produced goods. Fashion is no longer just an easily-read semiotic of class, but reflects on the era, its mores, and the choices made by the individual wearer to create a self on display.

Of course, Baudelaire pointed out the significance of fashion back in 1846 when he identified the political and cultural meaning of the modern costume:

> N'est-il pas l'habit nécessaire de notre époque, souffrante et portent jusque sur ses épaules noires et maigres le symbole d'un deuil perpétuel? Remarquez bien que l'habit noir et la redingote ont non seulement leur beauté politique, qui est l'expression de l'égalité universelle, mais encore leur beauté poétique, qui est l'expression de l'âme publique; – une immense défilade de croque-morts, croque-morts politiques, croque-morts amoureux, croque-morts bourgeois. Nous célébrons tous quelque enterrement. (2: 494)

As bleak as the meaning of this fashion may be, it has its "beauty." In the *Salon de 1846*, Baudelaire also introduced his idea of beauty's duality:

> Toutes les beautés contiennent, comme tous les phénomènes possibles, quelque chose d'éternel et quelque chose de transitoire, – d'absolu et de particulier. La beauté absolue et éternelle n'existe pas, ou plutôt elle n'est qu'une abstraction écrémée à la surface générale des beautés diverses. L'élément particulier de chaque beauté vient des passions, et comme nous avons nos passions particulières, nous avons notre beauté. (2: 493)

But *Le Peintre de la vie moderne* gives the most extended attention to this idea of fashion as a transitory beauty that reveals a culture to itself, its "idea."

This semiotic and even "spiritual" function of fashion and ornament is readable in diverse cultures, as he insists in "Éloge du maquillage": "Je suis ainsi conduit à regarder la parure comme un des signes de la noblesse primitive de l'âme humaine. Les races que notre civilisation, confuse et pervertie, traite volontiers de sauvages, avec un orgueil et une fatuité tout à fait risibles, comprennent, aussi bien que l'enfant, la haute spiritualité de la toilette" (2: 716). His experience of the Universal Exhibition certainly may have contributed to his putting "primitive" culture as on the same aesthetic plane as French fine art; indeed, there were exhibits of the "sauvage," but the exhibition organizers excluded these from the "Beaux-arts" pavilion, as with the Chinese artifacts. Baudelaire clearly continues his rethinking of such categories here, and rejection of the nationalistic and ethnic "orgueil" that would think them in the first place. This sentiment appears again in his section on the dandy: "Le dandysme est le dernier éclat d'héroïsme dans les décadences; et le type du dandy retrouvé par le voyageur dans l'Amérique du Nord n'infirme en aucune façon cette idée : car rien n'empêche de supposer que les tribus que nous nommons *sauvages* soient les débris de grandes civilisations disparues" (2: 711-12). Here the equivalence between the denizens of the modern city – indeed, the tragic heroes of a civilization in decline – and the "savages" is explicit; both types are known through a marking, an ornament, a self- or cultural fashioning. To take Baudelaire's idea of object as signifier of cultural milieu and apply it here, we may know the culture through the dandy, civilized or "savage" – and further we may know the state of the culture, measured against other cultures. Here Baudelaire has gone so far as to contradict the strain of French nationalism that would view the state of the fine arts as evidence that French culture is at an apogee; he is quite clear that the dandy signals a culture in decline: "Le dandysme est un soleil couchant; comme l'astre qui décline, il est superbe, sans chaleur et plein de mélancolie" (2: 712).

Further, we might credit Baudelaire with the discovery of the meaning and value of popular culture, and the degree to which the distinction between the fine arts and popular spectacle is a false one. To argue this about a critic who repeatedly derided the popular taste for paintings by Horace Vernet and Ary Scheffer and expressed his wish that "les affaires d'art ne se traitent qu'entre aristocrats" may seem a bit perverse. Yet we may distinguish between what he saw as bad art, that after all was displayed year after year in the salons, and won prizes, with elements of popular culture whose very vulgarity was arresting. For instance, in decrying what he saw as the inferior work of landscape painters in the *Salon de 1859*, he expressed his preference for viewing dioramas "dont la magie brutale et énorme sait m'imposer une utile illusion" or theatre sets "où je trouve artistement exprimés et tragiquement concentrés mes rêves les plus chers." He concludes: "Ces choses, parce qu'elles sont fausses, sont infiniment plus près du vrai; tandis que la plupart de nos paysagistes sont des menteurs, justement parce qu'ils ont négligé de mentir" (2: 668). And so in " Éloge du maquillage, " the false visage, the made-up, signifies the truth of personal expression, the face as work of art, its exaggerated outlines an instance of the fusion of the ephemeral and the eternal– eyes surrounded by kohl, cheekbones defined by rouge:

> Le rouge et le noir représentent la vie, une vie surnaturelle et excessive ; ce cadre noir rend le regard plus profond et plus singulier, donne à l'œil une apparence plus décidée de fenêtre ouverte sur l'infini; le rouge, qui enflamme la pommette, augmente encore la clarté de la prunelle et ajoute à un beau visage féminin la passion mystérieuse de la prêtresse. (2: 717)

Rather than deriding popular taste, he has come to embrace it and interpret its exaggerations and excesses as signs of the culture's life and spirituality.

Thus, in *Le Peintre de la vie moderne*, he lays out a semiotics of modernity, a reading of fashions that attempts to get at the expressive "truths" of modern life. One often comes across the sentiment among scholars of Baudelaire that it was a shame that he did not choose a painter like Manet as the subject of this book, rather than the minor artist, Constantin Guys, who worked in a minor form.[17] But if, in fact, Baudelaire is seeking to analyze "la vie moderne" through Guys' works, in other words, everyday life during the Second Empire, then the choice of an artist who excels in "le croquis des moeurs," like

---

[17] Raser lists Henri Lemaitre, Pierre-Georges Castex, and Anne Coffin Hanson as among those who question this choice (Raser, *Poetics* 155, n. 2). But Compagnon surmises that Baudelaire passed over the more obvious painters of modern life, Courbet and Manet, because of he saw their approach as a positivist one, that is, one without imagination and spirituality (18).

Gavarni and Daumier, of whom he also speaks, is fitting. Such artists appeal to Baudelaire in that they carry out Balzac's project in *La Comédie Humaine*, depicting the Paris he evokes in the final section of the *Salon de 1846*: "La vie parisienne est féconde en sujets poétiques et merveilleux. Le merveilleux nous enveloppe et nous abreuve comme l'atmosphère; mais nous ne le voyons pas" (2: 496). As J.A. Hiddleston shows, Baudelaire is drawn to Guys' fecundity, both as the "painter of modern life" sketching Parisian subjects and in the way that the sketches themselves, their incompleteness in tracing their subjects, draw the viewer into the creative process to complete the scene using imagination and memory (212-15).[18] Baudelaire defines

---

[18] Paul de Man, in "Literary History and Literary Modernity," sees Baudelaire's interest in Guys who, in sketching, attempts to rapidly capture the moment, as an instance of the paradox of literary modernity: the desire to capture or dwell in presentness while writing itself requires duration: "At first, in the enumeration of the themes that the painter (or writer) will select, we again find the temptation of modernity to move outside art, its nostalgia for the immediacy, the facticity of entities that are in contact with the present and illustrate the heroic ability to ignore or to forget that this present contains the prospective self-knowledge of its end. The figure chosen can be more or less close to being aware of this: it can be the mere surface, the outer garment of the present, the unwitting defiance of death in the soldier's colorful coat, or it can be the philosophically conscious sense of time of the dandy. In each case, however, the 'subject' Baudelaire chose for a theme is preferred because it exists in the facticity, in the modernity, of a present that is ruled by experiences that lie outside language and escape from the successive temporality, the duration involved in writing" (158-59). De Man goes on to show the defeat of this move beyond writing and duration in his rendering of the movement of the carriage sketched by Guys, a sketching that Baudelaire describes as "stenography," a form of writing (160-61). Raser sees a critical trend of reading the essay as about something else, and confirms the legitimacy of this reading: "not simply does the essay mean something other than what it says, it does so systematically, or pathologically": "This displacement could even be called Baudelaire's aesthetics: his works include a purely superficial sensorial enjoyment, which is doubled by moral judgments" (*Poetics* 66). I will not argue with Raser's broad characterization of the mercurial quality of the essay, supported by critics who find even its subject of modernity to be undermined, at least, if not displaced. But the essay, if it does seek to specify "sensorial enjoyment" that folds into moral judgments, represents the thrust of Baudelaire's aesthetic trajectory throughout his career: rendering the sensual and seeing in this rendering a morality as it is a revelatory truth. I agree with Raser, but see this not as a "displacement", but as an aesthetic problem that Baudelaire seeks to solve again and again. Allegory that proceeds from description of the modern city and modern life is one prominent "solution." Raser points to the deictic in *Le Peintre de la vie moderne* as another instance of incessant and perhaps necessary displacement which is a general problem of art-critical discourse (68). To support this point, he discusses how the evocative

"le croquis des mœurs," itself a popular genre of art, as "la representation de la vie bourgeoise et les spectacles de la mode." The artist who interests him in this effort is "observateur, flâneur, philosophe" (2: 687), " homme du monde" (2: 689), Poe's observer in "The Man of the Crowd," one who has observed and even penetrated the "life" he sketches, but who is also a naïve, "homme-enfant" (2: 691) so that his vision remains fresh and "ivre". "Le croquis des moeurs" captures formally – as a rapidly executed sketch – and in its subjects "la vie moderne"; and fashion becomes a kind of art, seen aesthetically as "le goût de l'idéal" and as self-fashioning. The ideal viewer is alive in the moment and inhabits a "naïve" way of viewing.

This artist-observer is reminiscent of the "cosmopolitan" critic of the 1855 review. Indeed, Guys is cosmopolitan in the more commonplace sense as well. Baudelaire describes Guys as "par nature, très voyageur et très cosmopolite," as *"homme du monde,"* "citoyen spirituel de l'univers" (2: 689). Obviously Guys' job of supplying illustrations for an English newspaper of the Crimean conflict made him necessarily a traveler. Baudelaire devotes a section of *Le Peintre de la Vie Moderne* to "Les Annales de la Guerre." He is also fascinated by Guys' other travel drawings, of Turkey and Greece, which he describes in "Pompes et Solennités." Baudelaire develops his ideas about cosmopolitanism in at least two ways here: he contrasts this kind of art with that of the *"artiste"* – defined as his opposite, the narrow and parochial "spécialiste, homme attaché à sa palette comme le serf à la glèbe": "L'artiste vit très peu, ou même pas du tout, dans le monde moral et politique. Celui qui habite dans le quartier Bréda ignore ce qui se passe dans le faubourg Saint-Germain" (2: 689). Baudelaire's disdain for such an "artiste" contrasts his praise of Balzacian caricaturists who sketch both worlds and imply their interconnection.[19] This contrast replays the opposition posed in 1855 based in ways and the breadth of viewing: the cosmopolitan viewer

---

stanzas in "Les Phares" are reduced to a mere "cry to posterity" in the final three stanzas. In this, Raser argues, Baudelaire confronts the same problem as Hegel in the preface to his *Phenomenology*: "the failure of consciousness to base itself in the senses" (70). In my view, the experience of art ideally for Baudelaire is fully sensual and this sensuality informs consciousness; to turn this into writing, both deictically and in the materiality of the writing itself, is the constant challenge and self-imposed charge necessarily shared by the poet and the Baudelairean art critic.

[19] Baudelaire compares "peintres de moeurs" like Gavarni and Daumier to Balzac (2: 687).

versus the doctrinaire of absolute beauty. Baudelaire's famous definition of the aesthetic of modernity in *Le Peintre de la vie moderne*, in fact, expands his notion of contextually relative beauty and beauty as bizarre and *insolite* to the urban domestic scene. But he also treats the work of a "cosmopolitan" artist and viewer, a "translator" (2: 698) of scenes. Here we might ask: to what degree does Guys in Baudelaire's account fulfill the promise of the cosmopolitan spectator/critic of 1855? Does this artist evince a transformation of subjectivity in his works that illuminates foreign cultures as context, and shows an understanding of the "bizarre" as defined in each respective native culture?

Clearly, Baudelaire still sees a transformation of subjectivity, or even further, a chameleon self, as central to Guys' virtuosity in painting modern life. He is, in Baudelaire's words, a "kaléidoscope doué de conscience, qui, à chacun de ses mouvements, représente la vie multiple et la grâce mouvante de tous les éléments de la vie," "un moi insatiable de non-moi, qui, à chaque instant, le rend et l'exprime en images plus vivantes que la vie elle-même, toujours instable et fugitive" (2: 692). Does this chameleon self operate in non-european contexts or is it a phenomenon dependant on the *merveilleux* in the streets and boulevards of nineteenth-century Paris? More important to the notion of cosmopolitanism, is there a self-transformation that leads to a transformative understanding of the foreign culture?

Of course, Baudelaire's text is already once removed from the immediate experience of observing that Guys' drawings relate. Baudelaire is, in his own terms, translating a translation:

> M. G., traduisant fidèlement ses propres impressions, marquée avec une énergie instinctive les points culminants ou lumineux d'un objet (ils peuvent être culminants ou lumineux au point de vue dramatique), ou ses principales caractéristiques, quelquefois même avec une exagération utile pour la mémoire humaine ; et l'imagination du spectateur, subissant à son tour cette mnémonique si despotique, voit avec netteté l'impression produite par les choses sur l'esprit de M. G. Le spectateur est ici le traducteur d'une traduction toujours claire et enivrante. (2: 698)

As many others have pointed out, Baudelaire insists on the capacity of art, or at least, of the art he values, to create and draw on memory. Here exaggeration plays a role in assuring such an effect, a characteristic not unlike the "bizarre" in arresting attention and signifying the generation of meaning. We also see the common theme of the operation of the imagination for the spectator: as Hiddleston points out, the incompleteness of Guys' "ébauches parfaits" require an imagining beyond the work, as it were: "These drawings invite the spectator to fill the gaps, to create a story or narrative, possibly a moral lesson, a personality, a *legend*, from a gesture, attitude, bearing, or movement, which is why Baudelaire defines the art of this painter of modern life as 'cette traduction *legendaire* de la vie extérieure' (p. 698)" (217)[20] Baudelaire's concept of "translation" also entails a compounded instability: the scene draws on the individual imagination of the painter first, and then on the imagination and memories of the viewer. Hiddleston points out that the kind of reading proposed by Baudelaire for Guys' sketches "would involve not so much an act of identification of critic with artist, as an appropriation of the artist by the spectator-critic and the imposition of a replacement mental universe" (219), an aggressive imposition of the critic's imaginative apparatus that seems the obverse of the transformative reception of the object in the Universal Exhibition of 1855.

In a sense, we discover here the precariousness of a cosmopolitan sensibility defined in terms of the viewer's imaginative engagement. Baudelaire's readings of Guys' drawings are marked too often with an Orientalism that frames their subjects according to the Western commonplaces of the time, for instance, the signs of an Ottoman empire in decline. Gesture and body types indicate as much: in " Ramadhan à la mosquée de Tophane, Constantinople,"[21] Baudelaire finds "comme un soleil pale, l'ennui permanent du sultan défunt" and "des fonctionnaires turcs, véritables caricatures de décadence, écrasant leurs magnifiques chevaux sous le poids d'une obésité fantastique" (2: 704). More sinister and equivocal is his remark about Ahmed Pacha whose bachi-bouzouks participated in a massacre of Maronites in July

---

[20] Hiddleston goes on to argue that as critic Baudelaire wants to perform the artistic function of ordering and making permanent the random and transitory (213). But his theory of art as both eternal and transitory, if applied to the critic as artist, would imply that this critic, too, must render the unstable and fleeting, and so even the vision of order discerned or imposed on the art is impermanent and open to accidents that reveal its untruths. It is worth remembering that Baudelaire in *The Universal Exhibition -- 1855 – Fine Arts* is critical of his own earlier attempts to define a system that is ultimately upended by "un produit spontané, inattendu, de la vitalité universelle" (2: 577).

[21] Identified by Pichois, n. 2, 2: 1424.

1860 [22]: "Malgré l'ampleur de sa bedaine turque, Achmet-Pacha a, dans l'attitude et le visage, le grand air aristocratique qui appartient généralement aux races dominatrices" (2: 702). His paunch marks the enemy's body with the type of the luxurious Turk, while his expression and posture signify dominance and inspire fear.

But Baudelaire also draws attention to the relationship between the culture of the setting and of the figures in it, and to the relationships among figures from different cultures, again, constructed by and sometimes resisting the enveloping culture. About "Consécration d'un terrain funèbre à Scutari par l'évêque de Gibraltar," Baudelaire notes "[l]e caractère pittoresque de la scène, qui consiste dans le contraste de la nature orientale environnante avec les attitudes et les uniformes occidentaux des assistants, est rendu d'une manière saisissante, suggestive et grosse de rêveries" (2: 701); he finds that the soldiers and officers hold themselves like "*gentlemen*" whereas the priests remind him more of bailiffs. Contrast here induces "rêverie": stiff British heroism, emblematic of class and manners, jarringly out of place in "oriental" nature. He marvels at the Kurdish troops in "Kurdes à Scutari" – "troupes étranges dont l'aspect fait rêver à une invasion de hordes barbares," but considers the "bachi-bouzoucks" no less "singuliers" with European officers, Hungarian or Polish, "dont la physionomie de dandies tranche bizarrement sur le caractère baroquement oriental de leurs soldats" (2: 701). As the dandy is a mark of a culture in decline, so his impression implies the ultimate failure of the myth of European power and superiority. And, while his note of "barbarous hordes" relies on a cliché, it is worth recalling that "barbare" for Baudelaire is a positive quality. As Hiddleston notes, Baudelaire admires Corot and Guys for the "barbare" in their art, a capturing of the authentic first impression and rendering that in a way that is both synthetic and abbreviative (214). In other words, there is an energy in the "barbare" that is consonant with the modern aesthetic he is theorizing.

A mixture of cultural types draws his attention as well in "Ramadhan à la mosquée de Tophane, Constantinople": veiled Muslim women, indicated by "des regards curieusement féminins," in sumptuous, orientalized Louis XIV carriages, that is, doubly hidden from view, contrast " les femmes galantes, …, généralement composées de

---

[22] Pichois, n 1, 2: 1423.

Hongroises, de Valaques, de Juives, de Polonaises, de Grecques et d'Arméniennes; car, sous un gouvernement despotique, ce sont les races opprimées, et, parmi elles, celles surtout qui ont le plus à souffrir, qui fournissent le plus de sujets à la prostitution." He goes on to describe the divergence between nativism and hegemonic European culture in their dress:

> De ces femmes, les unes ont conservé le costume national, les vestes brodées, à manches courtes, l'écharpe tombante, les vastes pantalons, les babouches retroussées, les mousselines rayées ou lamées et tout le clinquant du pays natal ; les autres, et ce sont les plus nombreuses, ont adopté le signe principal de la civilisation, qui, pour une femme, est invariablement la crinoline, en gardant toute fois, dans un coin de leur ajustement, un léger souvenir caractéristique de l'Orient, si bien qu'elles ont l'air de Parisiennes qui auraient voulu se déguiser. (2: 704-705)

There is a curious cultural hierarchy here: the Ottomans are despots and clearly in control with signs of their imperial wealth in their French carriage that shields their women, partly, from view, but French culture is hegemonic both in their copying of Western signs of status and in the wearing of crinolines among the court's prostitutes. These women, Baudelaire makes clear, are victims, but are also capable of a degree of self-fashioning – signaling their native culture or appearing as quasi-Parisian through their dress. In this depiction of women, the Muslim women, represented by their glance, have an erotic allure that the detailing of the costumes and crinolines ironically dispels for the sexual workers. So while Baudelaire focuses on the intermingled cultural types in these drawings, he reads their relationships, often from the evidence of dress and gesture, as representing political and cultural frameworks of oppression and imposed hierarchies.

There is another figure in these representations of cultural contact: cultural misfit, the figure who does not belong. The trope of mismatch already appears the examples that I have mentioned; for instance, the contrast between the Hungarian or Polish bashi-bazouks, dandies as officers, and their "baroquely oriental" soldiers. But single figures appear as well: the German lady-in-waiting to the queen of Greece in "La fête commémorative de l'indépendance dans la cathédrale d'Athènes" – "la bizarrerie de sa physionomie aussi peu hellénique que possible" (2: 705) and significantly Guys himself: "Quel est ce cavalier, aux moustaches blanches, d'une physionomie se vivement dessinée, qui, la tête relevée, a l'air de humer la terrible poésie d'un champ de bataille, pendant que son cheval, flairant la terre, cherche son chemin entre les cadavres amoncelés, pieds en l'air, faces cris-pées, dans des attitudes étranges ? Au bas du dessin, dans un coin, se font lire ces mots : *Myself at Inkermann*" (2: 702). (Baudelaire also notes Guys' self-portrait in a drawing of the hospital at Péra, where he appears as a "visiteur au costume negligé" chatting with two sister of charity [2: 703].) Baudelaire's reading of Guys' self-insertion is im-portant: here Baudelaire sees Guys representing his own act of cultural interpretation and his assimilation of that experience: he is smelling, absorbing the alien "culture" which is, in this instance, war.

In reference to Baudelaire's use of "modernity" to designate "the ephemeral, the fugitive, the contingent," Compagnon observes: "Understood as a sense of the present, modernity cancels out any rela-tion to the past, conceived simply as a succession of individual moder-nities and of no value for discerning the 'character of present beauty'" (16). If we look at the admixture of cultural types represented in the present that Guys chooses, we see, as it were, a representation of the cancelling of tradition through cultural heterogeneity. It is the quality of modernity, the coming together of people and fashions from diffe-rent cultures, that effectively cancels the function of these traditions, that linger then only as style or fashion. One might speculate that Baudelaire is extending his theories of self-representation articulated in his comments on the dandy and in "Éloge du maquillage" to his understanding of foreign cultures or to moments of self-representation wrought of cultural contact. But given his cosmopolitan aesthetic of 1855 built around the notion of the bizarre, one might read this rela-tionship in reverse: that his attraction to other cultures, and his read-ings of these figures and their relationship to the contexts represented provided a framework for his diagnosis of Western modernity and for the idea of self as performance through gesture, fashion and toilette that he discerned both in the dandy and in the women of Paris.

Baudelaire alternates between commenting on the aesthetic features of Guys' drawings and on what they represent. Baudelaire as critic praises Guys' work on formal grounds; while noting his pen-chant and talent for depicting pageantry, Baudelaire remarks on his success in rendering space, perspective, and light (2: 705). Baudelaire finds that Guys' interest in soldiers as subjects is not enthusiasm for the military virtues etched in their faces and demeanors, but in the ornament of their uniforms (2: 707). This does not mean that Guys is concerned only with the rendering of gorgeous detail, with shine, sparkle, and texture; rather, pomp and ornament have meaning, and Baudelaire notes more than once the quality of exaggeration in his sketches, hence Guys' work promises a wealth of signification that Baudelaire gestures towards rather than spells out.

Finally, these drawings are representations and material evidence of what they represent: war and other occasions of cultural turmoil:

> En vérité, il est difficile à la simple plume de traduire ce poème fait de mille croquis, si vaste et si compliqué, et d'exprimer l'ivresse qui se dégage de tout ce pittoresque, douloureux souvent, mais jamais larmoyant, amassé sur quelques centaines de pages, dont les maculatures et les déchirures disent, à leur manière, le trouble et le tumulte au milieu desquels l'artiste y déposait ses souvenirs de la journée. Vers le soir, le courrier emportait vers Londres les notes et les dessins de M. G., et souvent celui-ci confiait ainsi à la poste plus de dix croquis improvisés sur papier pelure, que les graveurs et les abonnés du journal attendaient impatiemment. (2: 702-3)

Not only is he dealing with an abundance of images, but with the marks of their creation, the scars, as it were, of war correspondence – the coarse paper and evidence of erasures. (Clearly Baudelaire admires here the heroism of the artist as well as the beauty wrought of haste.) They are objects, bearing the marks of experience.

Susan Stanford Friedman has observed that modernity was discovered through the discovery of other cultures by the West: "modernity is often associated with the intensification of intercultural contact zones, whether produced through conquest, vast migrations of people (voluntary or forced), or relatively peaceful commercial traffic and technological or cultural exchange. Indeed, heightened hybridizations, jarring juxtapositions, and increasingly porous borders both characterize modernity and help bring it into being" (433). Undoubtedly one way in which this happened entailed the measurement of "civilization" through contrast with the so-called "primitive" of other cultures. As Rosalind Williams documents, eighteenth-century consumption habits of the elite validated a claim to "civilization," an idea that "referred both to a general social and political ideal and, more narrowly, to a comfortable way of life reserved for the upper classes" (38). In another tradition, coming out of Rousseau's noble savage, the "primitive" is valued above the "civilized"; within this tradition, Baudelaire reads laterally, finding significance in the ornaments of the "primitive," the soldier or the urban dandy, insisting on the "heroism" of each within his respective culture and their roles as cultural signifiers. As with his contemplation of the Chinese object, Baudelaire here discovers and insists on cultural relativism, and even when he employs ethnic or national stereotypes, he does not claim or assume French or Western cultural superiority.

The discovery of the "other" for Baudelaire is confirmation of cultural systems of signification. Such evidence frees him to assess fashion in all its temporality as having meaning beyond being simply a marker of the modern: "de dégager de la mode ce qu'elle peut contenir de poétique dans l'historique, de tirer l'éternel du transitoire" (2: 694). If fashion has meaning as an expression of the individual and the cultural, the individual uses fashion, ornament, make-up as means of self-fashioning that can only be read according to the cultural codes such marks would evade. It is an expression of individuality within the limits imposed by the dominant culture.

Thus, Baudelaire sees the possibility of a multiplicity of ways of being modern: in the dedication of *Le Spleen de Paris* to Arsène Houssaye, he corrects himself in describing his aim of sketching modern life – "plutôt d'*une* vie moderne." Fashion *is* the self on display, an opportunity to create with the self as medium: "Quel poète oserait, dans la peinture du plaisir cause par l'apparition d'une beauté, séparer la femme de son costume? " (2: 714). Or, more generally, "L'homme finit par ressembler à ce qu'il voudrait être" (2: 684). Popular tastes – fashion, ornament, and other means of self-presentation – work as a diagnostic of an era and an arena for aesthetic expression.

Conclusion

As disparate as the occasions for writing are in these essays spanning more than a decade from 1851 to 1863 – the publication of a volume of workers' "songs," the first Universal Exhibition in Paris, the work of a minor artist and newspaper illustrator — critical commonalities are apparent. Baudelaire is not only aware of the work's (image or text) embeddedness in its socio-historical context, but theorizes that relationship. From the workers' songs as symptoms of the state of the social body to the foreign object on display as an entry point in the imagining of its native context to Guys' "translations" of scenes, affected by his own memory of their impression upon him, which the spectator must then "translate,"— models of the relationship between the work and its context, if nothing else, become increasingly complex. As his aesthetic of the "bizarre" implies, Baudelaire comes to "see" that the heightened or exaggerated effect not only is essential to the work's beauty, but also to its "truth" in conveying the impression of the work on its viewer or reader and its power in conveying its socio-economic and cultural context. Art and poetry, indeed, have special cultural roles, but not as autonomous objects, revealing the aesthetic to aesthetes, in a strict *l'art pour l'art* modality, but rather as acute signifiers of their own historical milieu, albeit in need of especially perceptive "readers." The "bizarre" is "eternal" and "transitory," to use another famous Baudelairean aphorism about beauty: if art only *represented* without translation, without the impress of subjectivity, without heightening, then it would be merely historical. But the "bizarre" is such only in relationship to the context of which it is an exaggeration anchored in the historical; this heightening power *is* the constant, in other words, the eternal. It recasts the terms of Romanticism as an aspiration towards an ever-undefined ideal.

It is, perhaps, a small, but crucial step from art revealing its context (subject to interpretation, of course) to all artifacts doing the same. And so fashion is a critical object: "de dégager de la mode ce qu'elle peut contenir de poétique dans l'historique, de tirer l'éternel du transitoire" (2: 694). The critical sensibility that has come to understand art's "translation" of its context will also be able to read other artifacts, other objects. While it would be a mistake to conclude that Baudelaire ever gave up on art's special role and means of revealing a culture, to itself and to other cultures, in *Le Peintre de la vie moderne* he elevates other objects by suggesting they be interpreted within a similar hermeneutics. Always ready to skewer the *faux artiste*, Baudelaire deems the *art* of make-up, fashion, even military ornament worthy of the interpretive gaze and so, perhaps inadvertently, effaces their difference from "Art."

What is tricky about this aesthetics and its concomitant hermeneutics is the special role of the spectator/"reader"/interpreter. Undoubtedly, the subject-object relationship is at the heart of these processes, be it the transformative viewing of the 1855 Universal Exhibition or the more layered and indirect "translation of a translation" of *Le Peintre de la vie moderne*. If we consider, for simplicity's sake, the role of the spectator, we see how, with Baudelaire, spectatorship is anything but passive. (This is already obvious in his comments about the perception of color in *Le Salon de 1846*.) If, for a moment, we compare his theories of viewing or spectatorship with emerging theories of value in political economy, that put the consumer's relationship with the commodity in a central position, we might truly question how different this relationship is from that of the viewer. It is not, perhaps, the same as the critics' stance, that solitary traveler in nature whose sensibilities are open to perception of other cultures through the contemplation of a single object, who is able to perceive more fully and imaginatively than others. But consumer desire is not all that different from the desire induced in spaces of display, be they the salon or the industrial and universal exhibitions. By the same token, in Baudelaire's schema, we are all potentially critics and interpreters of the cultural object through which history takes form, and that object is everywhere.

V

Products of Desire in *Les Fleurs du mal*

Rappellerai-je encore cette série de petits poèmes de quelques strophes, qui sont des intermèdes galants ou rêveurs et qui ressemblent, les uns à des sculptures, les autres à des fleurs, d'autres à des bijoux, mais tous revêtus d'une couleur plus fine ou plus brillante que les couleurs de la Chine et de l'Inde, et tous d'une coupe plus pure et plus décidée que des objets de marbre ou de cristal ? Quiconque aime la poésie les sait par cœur.
– Baudelaire, "Théophile Gautier [I]" (1859)

In the following description of a Parisian salon, Gautier gives drastic expression to the integration of the individual into the interior: "The eye, entranced, is led to the groups of ladies who, fluttering their fans, listen to the talkers half-reclining. Their eyes are sparkling like diamonds; their shoulders glisten like satin; and their lips open up like flowers." (Artificial things come forth!) *Paris et le Parisiens au XIXe siècle* (Paris, 1856), p. iv (Théophile Gautier, "Introduction").
– Walter Benjamin, *The Arcades Project*

Baudelaire's praise of Gautier's *Émaux et camées* in the first passage and Gautier's evocation of a Paris salon in the second, collected by Walter Benjamin for *The Arcades Project*, both appraise their objects with a connoisseur's eye, a connoisseur, that is, of luxury goods whose color, whose crystalline cut may be familiar from the displays at exhibitions that both poets visited and covered in essays and reviews. As Benjamin notes, the individual is drawn into and becomes a piece with the interior in Gautier's description. In Baudelaire's comment, poems take shape and become vivid through an imaginary of things. Luxury products, desired objects sparkle, gleam, entice: poetry aspires to the condition of a bright, sensual world of objects. Indeed, Baudelaire's own great work is a collection of "flowers."

The gaze in Gautier's passage transforms women, or parts of their bodies, into such luxury items and flowers where scent, color, and sensual form combine. As we saw in the coverage of the industrial exhibitions (chapter two), fascination with material objects, especially the qualities of luxury goods, grew from such spectator practices, themselves informed to some degree by reviewers' rhetoric and vocabulary. Thus not only is the display of worldly goods prominent in urban spectacular life, but also they provide tropes for the beauties of bodies and poetry. Despite a sense that poetry of all the arts should be spiritual and immaterial among poets like Baudelaire, the lure of gorgeousness, the imaginary of sensual luxury, seems to pull in quite the opposite direction.

Such linkages between the poetic and the realm of material goods in the nineteenth century are familiar from Walter Benjamin's seminal study of Baudelaire, *Charles Baudelaire: A Lyric Poet in the Era of High Capitalism,* and from the larger work adumbrated in *The Arcades Projects* with sections or "convolutes" devoted to "Arcades, *Magasins de Nouveautés*, Sales Clerks," "Fashion," "Exhibitions, Advertising, Grandville," "The Collector," "The Interior, the Trace," as well as "Baudelaire" and "Literary History, Hugo." In her chapter on Walter Benjamin in *Mother Tongues*, Barbara Johnson takes up the consequences of Benjamin's approach for understanding the subject-object relationship. In her analysis of his debate with Theodor Adorno over Marxist praxis, documented in their correspondence in the 1930s, she characterizes Adorno's Marxism as a metadiscourse with explanatory power, while finding that Benjamin draws attention to the historical character of Marxism itself, that is, how it expresses the milieu in which it arose and how it shares expressive features with the material products of its time (113). Benjamin's focus is on the dialectic between subjects and objects (115), including that between the metadiscourse, as it were, and its objects that were part of the very fashioning of that heuristic system. She defends his dialectical method against the charge that he takes the things of the world themselves as object, a "fallacy of misplaced concreteness," or a "fetishism," contending that instead he "treat[s] *the world itself* as a fallacy of misplaced concreteness" (113). In other words, "[d]ialectical history is a history of the interaction between objects and subjects" (115).

If Benjamin's dialectical method does undermine the a priori stability of the Marxist metadiscourse in order to focus on the subject-object relationship as one of mutual construction, this approach reflects, or at least suits the desires and anxieties of his principal poetic subject (or object of analysis), Baudelaire.[1] Undoubtedly these desires and anxieties were informed by his experience of urban modernity, as Benjamin's own study so brilliantly shows. In Baude-laire's unceasing attempts to mold and articulate a new aesthetic, we find an arena for inquiry into subject-object dynamics. He sought an aesthetic literally informed by viewing, that is, by his activity as an art critic, yet his own medium, of course, was words. Such theorizing was also driven by his sense of the false and the faulty in the dominant poetic theories of his day. Afraid to lose the "real" in neoplatonic abstractions, Baudelaire endeavors to use language to produce a "real-ity" as vivid as the world, visionary or splenetic, and the works of art that inspired him. In doing so, he enacts a dialectic of interrogation: of neoplatonic discourse and its objects, of *l'art pour l'art* and its poetic products, and of the creative personality and the realm of the per-ceived, writing with a self-consciousness as extreme as any seen even in the recent throes of postmodernism.

This chapter concerns Baudelaire's interest in making poetry as "real" as things through its evocative powers without making it inert, or reified in the Marxist sense. From the beginning of his career as a poet, painting – the phenomenal realm of color and visual images – serves as a model for this dynamic creativity, while sculpture is less

---

[1] Johnson, too, points to the affinity between Benjamin and his poet-subject, but with a more psychological focus. Playing Benjamin's understanding of the poet's personality off Sartre's, she emphasizes the positive relationship between alienation and productivity:

> The immense productivity of Baudelaire consists of creating a psychology that doesn't have health and well-being as its end, but is rather alienated irremediably. Instead of claiming, as Adorno did of Benjamin while editing Benjamin's correspondence, that he was productive "in spite of self-alienation," Benjamin would claim that Baudelaire (and indeed Benjamin) was productive because of it. Or rather—that it was that alienation itself that became productive, often against the express wishes of the author. (98)

Here Johnson is referring not only to existential alienation à la Sartre, but more importantly to the Marxist notion and its relationship to reification in Benjamin, or that which is *dingfest*, a keyword in Johnson's reading of Benjamin's project.

congenial given its association with a neoclassical aesthetic; my discussion begins with poems that explore these alternatives to give a sense of the profile of creativity that inspired him, and those he rejected. I then turn to several poems in *Les Fleurs du mal* in which his desire to incorporate the sensate into his verse appears in the form of erotic desire and results in the transformation of these objects of desire into things through his tropes for women and their body parts. In effect, the impetus for intimate relationships shifts from bodily desire to a different sense of possession, that is, consuming or surrounding oneself with luxurious things. To contextualize these remade relationships, I draw on Jacques Rancière's understanding of the productivity embodied in word and figure in the nineteenth-century "aesthetic regime," a making-real or producing of the nineteenth-century world, through art and literature that Baudelaire's aspirations and career exemplify.

Artist as Laborer: "Le Mauvais Moine"

Baudelaire's interest in the visual arts as a model for his own art is evident early in his poetic career. As opposed to Romantic notions of creative genius as a sort of spontaneous generation, we find in his poetry from the 1840's models of creativity based in observation of painting consonant with the spectacular quality of everyday life in Paris, "capital of the nineteenth century," in Walter Benjamin's title. Certainly Baudelaire's work as an art critic plays a role in such modeling, yet a close examination of one of the earliest poems of *Les Fleurs du mal*, "Le Mauvais Moine," reveals a complex of tensions – locating the aesthetic within the ascetic, creativity in frescoes of Death, and work or labor in expressing or rendering the spectacle. Composed probably in 1842 or 1843,[2] and thus one of the earliest poems in *Les Fleurs du mal*, this poem is strategically placed in the collection as one answer to poetic complaints about obstacles to creativity in the present day: it follows "La Muse malade" which invokes a near mad, although erotic muse of modernity, and "La Muse vénale," in which the poet laments the exigencies of market culture, which force the artist to debase his or her work in order to sell it. In contrast with these failed muses, visual art is muse and model of creativity in "Le

---

[2] See Claude Pichois, "Notes et Variantes," Baudelaire 1: 856.

Mauvais Moine." Of course, the speaker's admiration for what critics have identified as a fourteenth-century Pisan fresco[3] depicting Death in a cloistered monastery may well betray a longing to retreat from modernity and the market. But the imagining of the creative process as both work and the expression of spectacle intimates a distinctly modern conception of that creativity.[4] The poem exhibits tensions about work and spectacle similar to those at play in the contemporary debate over value in political economy: between the labor theory of value and more consumption-oriented theories in which commodity desire, inspired by display, has a central role, as discussed in chapter one. Such competing theories imply divergent models for producing subjectivity: as a worker or as a consumer of images.

Le mauvais moine

Les cloîtres anciens sur leurs grandes murailles
Étalaient en tableaux la sainte Vérité,
Dont l'effet, réchauffant les pieuses entrailles,
Tempérait la froideur de leur austérité.

En ces temps où du Christ florissaient les semailles,
Plus d'un illustre moine, aujourd'hui peu cité,
Prenant pour atelier le champ des funérailles,
Glorifiait la Mort avec simplicité.

---

[3] According to Pichois, Jean Prévost identified the fresco as "The Triumph of Death," one of the frescoes of the Campo Santo in Pisa, attributed in Baudelaire's time to Andrea Orcagna and now attributed to Francesco Traini. This first attribution appears in Giorgio Vasari's *Lives of Painters*; a translation by Léopold Leclanché of volume one was published in Paris in 1839 (1: 857).

[4] Benjamin stresses Baudelaire's sense of writing as work and documents sources confirming the effort that Baudelaire put into writing poetry (*Charles Baudelaire 67*). This effort, in Benjamin's reading of Baudelaire's modernity, distinguishes the hero of Modernism from that of Romanticism: "The hero is the true subject of modernism. In other words, it takes a heroic constitution to live modernism. That was also Balzac's opinion. With their belief, Balzac and Baudelaire are in opposition to Romanticism. They transfigure passions and resolution; the Romanticists transfigure renunciation and surrender" (74). Benjamin famously reads the figure of the fencer as Baudelaire's representation of the heroic worker in verse and art and draws on Marx to note that "overtaxing of the productive person in the name of a principle, the principle of creativity" – "applies equally to intellectual and manual labour," linking the bohemian and working classes (71).

— Mon âme est un tombeau que, mauvais cénobite,
Depuis l'éternité je parcours et j'habite;
Rien n'embellit les murs de ce cloître odieux.

Ô moine fainéant! quand saurai-je donc faire
Du spectacle vivant de ma triste misère
Le travail de mes mains et l'amour de mes yeux?

On the one hand, the point to the poem may be simply summarized: if now-forgotten monks could paint death in such an inspiring fashion, why can't I, the poet, who lives Death, paint as well? One simple answer would be the poet's loss of piety, that his soul is dead, a tomb, unlike the "pieuses entrailles" of the monks.[5] He falters, then, first, in his spirituality before the spectacle of Truth (his presumably cold soul), and second, in his creativity (the unadorned walls of his soul/tomb). He blames himself for laziness, for being the "bad monk." Yet to read the poem as a lament over a loss of faith would be mistaken, for the poet's primary concern here, expressed in the final tercet, is creativity. Further, the poet as viewer of these frescoes both imagines and replicates the experience of these pious souls, and his soul as tomb is analogous to the cloisters in which Death is depicted. In effect, the poem offers a quite positive map for creativity. The poet has his subject (his death-like existence), a model (the frescoes), and a weak obstacle to productivity (laziness; "fainéantise," literally "do-nothingness"). Although to declare that his soul is a tomb, a "cloître odieux," might seem to be a way to suggest artistic sterility, within the context of the poem, cloisters are the place of creativity, their walls the equivalent of the empty canvas. Further, death is positively associated with creativity, since it is the depiction of death that warms and inspires. All he needs to do is to work ("[l]e travail de mes mains") and see ("l'amour de mes yeux") to fashion and judge his own creation. Or, to put it in terms of a dual economic subjectivity, he already enjoys the consumption of images – in fact, is in love with such images, and so berates himself for his failure to produce.

---

[5] Mario Richter, in a much darker reading than my own, one which emphasizes the ennui figured in the poet's soul as empty tomb, also finds no nostalgia for a more pious age, but rather sarcasm and irony in the depiction of monastic life. See Richter 99-117, especially 108-109.

As noted earlier, Rancière, in his critique of theories of modernism, outlines a "distribution of the sensible"6 ("le partage du sensible") that gives literary language a privileged role since Romanticism:

> By declaring that the principle of poetry is not to be found in fiction but in a certain arrangement of the signs of language, the Romantic Age blurred the dividing line that isolated art from the jurisdiction of statements or images, as well as the dividing line that separated the logic of facts from the logic of stories. It is not the case, as is sometimes said, that it consecrated the 'autotelism' of language, separated from reality. It is the exact opposite. The Romantic Age actually plunged language into the materiality of the traits by which the historical and social world becomes visible to itself, be it in the form of the silent language of things or the coded language of images. (*Politics of Aesthetics* 36)

If Rancière's theory is correct, Baudelaire's famous theory of *correspondances* comes to mind as one model of this making-material through language, the idea that an architecture of relationship among the stimulation of the different senses – the perception of color, scent, and sound – is meaningful and waiting to be read by the observer, an echoing that the poem replicates in its own resonances. (See "Correspondances" 1:11.) One can speak of Baudelaire's theory as "partage" – sharing and division – of the sensible in that it is based in the universality of the senses, yet experience entails an acute sensitivity to the synaesthetic interplay. Baudelaire's color theory, which relies on analogies with melody and musical harmony, is another early instance in his thought of how relationships among the senses produce a resonant and complexly structured aesthetic experience. But, a true disciple of Balzac (who is a key figure in Rancière's theory of the aesthetic regime), Baudelaire is fascinated with the language of things and the coding of images beyond the temple of Nature, or to borrow Rancière's words, "the potential for meaning inherent in everything silent and the proliferation of modes of speech and levels of meaning"

---

[6] Rancière defines the "distribution of the sensible" as "The system of self-evident facts of sense perception that simultaneously discloses the existences of something in common and the delimitations that define the respective parts and positions within it. A distribution of the sensible therefore establishes at one and the same time something common that is shared and exclusive parts. This apportionment of parts and positions is based on a distribution of spaces, times, and forms of activity that determines the very manner in which something in common lends itself to participation and in what way various individuals have a part in this distribution." (*Politics of Aesthetics* 12)

(37). The world of fact and material objects is a system of signs like literature; literature produces the models for reading these worlds, thereby producing the means of writing and comprehending history. Indeed, with Balzac as exemplar, Rancière has a broader point: that what he calls the "aesthetic regime" made fact-based and fiction-based logics or discourses interdependent, indeed, giving priority to fiction.[7]

If Rancière is correct that in the "aesthetic regime" the historical and social world became visible through literary language, then we see the attraction of allegory for Baudelaire: the model here is literally the coded language of images, painted meanings. The poem presents the means for replicating that creativity in "travail," labor, an idiom that the artist and poet share with workers, here represented by an idyll of workers in the fields. In later poems, like "Hymne à la beauté," Baudelaire creates his own medieval allegory, with Beauty stepping on the dead, bedecked in jewelry that signifies Horror, the trinket of Death dancing "amoureusement" on her breast. The image is vividly detailed, and yet saturated with signification, warnings against the adoration of Beauty in one's intimate relationships and as an artistic aim.

The connection between artistic creativity and labor is a theme that Rancière takes up, rejecting, indeed ridiculing the "lazy and absurd schema that contrasts the aesthetic cult of art for art's sake with

---

[7] In *Genres of the Credit Economy*, Poovey, in analyzing the growth of generic distinctions between "imaginative" and economic writing in the nineteenth century, seems to argue the opposite: that the Romantics indeed did enshrine the idea of textual "organic unity" that eventually evolved into the New Critics' autonomous text. She posits a fact/fiction continuum in the seventeenth and eighteenth centuries that allowed an indistinction between imaginative and economic writing that the emergence of the novel began to break down. The reasons for this are Bourdievian: that imaginative writing must gain prestige by distinguishing its value from that of the market, while the institutions that supported economic writing prized ever greater abstraction especially after the *Wealth of Nations* and into the nineteenth century as economic writing fashioned its own grounds for validity. Poovey acknowledges that this analysis runs counter to much recent economic criticism of literature, and she hardly uses "fact" naively, having written her own ground-breaking history of the idea of "fact." With her focus on genres of writing linked to contemporary understandings of "fact," she is, perhaps, using the terms in a strict historical sense, whereas Rancière is interested in problematizing the separation of the aesthetic agenda from the experience of daily life that he sees as a distortion created by the later enshrinement of artistic autonomy. In the end, Rancière is less interested in the textual than Poovey, but would describe instead how the textual (fiction) shaped lived experience in Balzac's time. See Poovey, *Genres*, especially 121-23; 166-169.

the rising power of industrial labour" (45).[8] He constructs an alternative relationship between art and work by starting with Plato's condemnation of the poet as "mimetician" who "does two things at once" which is also a violation of the privacy of labor in that artistic creation is produced for the community, for display in one form or another. In other words, labor is relegated to a private space, and we might even, to adopt a reading from classical political economy, see the worker as the owner of his or her labor. Artistic labor, even if it is paid for privately, is meant for the public sphere through display, performance, or publication. (Curiously, from this point of view, commodity display, in the industrial or universal exhibitions, for instance, is similarly ambivalent, positioned between private owner-ship and public delectation.) Rancière concludes: "Hence artistic prac-tice is not the outside of work but its displaced form of visibility" (43).

If the mimetician is banned from the Republic for this duplica-tion, a violation of the division of labor, the "aesthetic regime of the arts disrupts this apportionment of spaces," according to Rancière. In Schiller, the "'aesthetic' state, by suspending the opposition between active understanding and passive sensibility, aims at breaking down – with an idea of art – an idea of society based on the opposition between those who think and decide and those who are doomed to material tasks" (44). Hence, labor takes on a more positive value in the aesthetic regime – as part of that which defines the human. Art, then, has a special role to play: "production asserts itself as the prin-ciple behind a new distribution of the sensible insofar as it unites, in one and the same concept, terms that are traditionally opposed: the activity of manufacturing and visibility. Manufacturing meant inhabit-ing the private and lowly space-time of labour for sustenance. Pro-ducing unites the act of manufacturing with the act of bringing to light, the act of defining a new relationship between *making* and *seeing*. Art anticipates work because it carries out its principle: the transformation of sensible matter into the community's self-presen-tation" (44). In other words, art's labor is the production of public

---

[8] Gallagher offers a more nuanced and complicated picture of, at least, the British Romantics' representation of the relationship between their work and industrial labor: "The Romantics, …, defended literary labor in two, incommensurate ways: (1) they presented it as an idealized, perhaps utopian, contrast to the economists' miserable but 'productive' labor, and (2) they stressed that they felt as alienated in their work, as jeopardized or engulfed in suffering, as any productive worker" (28).

thought for the community. Further, viewing itself is active, a positive form of labor.

If we look at one of the poems preceding "Le Mauvais Moine" in *Les Fleurs du mal*, "La Muse vénale," we find a negative depiction of artistic labor in a market economy. The Muse, although lover of palaces, feels want and is thus compelled to work, despite art's spiritual aspirations: "Sentant ta bourse à sec autant que ton palais/ Récolteras-tu l'or des voûtes azurées?" The Muse/Poet must produce works that fit a requisite mold: "Il te faut, pour gagner ton pain de chaque soir,/ Comme un enfant de chœur, jouer de l'encensoir,/ Chanter des *Te Deum* auxquels tu ne crois guère." The Muse/Poet is also compared to a starving performer who must display his charms to amuse the crowd : "saltimbanque à jeun, étaler tes appas/ Et ton rire trempé de pleurs qu'on ne voit pas, /Pour faire épanouir la rate du vulgaire" (1: 15). Display or publication is part of humiliation, because the performer must cater to vulgar tastes, playing to the public's appetite for bad art. Yet acknowledgement of the ennui of the vulgar public itself is important; such ennui is a sign of discontent, and the impoverished poet, compelled to labor for his daily bread, shares this with the poor crowd he entertains. There is an implied analogy: If the poet is forced by necessity to create "bad" art, so compulsion in manufacturing, for instance, produces not only a tedious occupation, but poor products, although they may distract momentarily those with bad taste.

If we return for a moment to the artist's doubleness denounced by Plato, in Rancière's reading, which is "suspended" in Romanticism's vision of work as "shared effectivity of thought and community" (44), Baudelaire shows us yet another wrinkle in this production which includes work and display in "Le Mauvais Moine." For the modern artist, viewing or spectacle precedes as well as results from the work of production. But this first viewing takes place in an interior theatre, and so the creative artist anticipates the part of the public in a sort of proleptic reflexivity.

Indeed, the poet is the theatre in two respects: where the "spectacle vivant de ma triste misère" is projected mentally and as the empty tomb with space for art. The impasse in the poem to creativity is the missing transition from seeing the mental "spectacle" to making that spectacle into ornament for the "walls" of his soul, the making material of the affective visual. (Of course, the poem itself is the self-evident product of the overcoming of that impasse, the evidence of creative work.) This figurative shrinking of the art space from the monastery's walls to the poet's mind points to an important difference between the world of the cloister and that of the modern poet: there is nostalgia for the collective production of monks in this contrast with both the subject (death) and place of art internalized within the modern individual. No doubt such nostalgia for community also adds luster to labor in these idealized representations in contrast with the immaterial and solitary production of the modern poet.

The casting of the creative subject figuratively as a place is not unique to "Le Mauvais Moine," but appears repeatedly in Baudelaire's most famous poem about art and artists, "Les Phares." Here Rubens is a "fleuve," a "jardin," Leonardo a mirror reflecting a place "à l'ombre/ Des glaciers et des pins qui ferment leur pays," Rembrandt a hospital, Michelangelo, a "lieu vague," Watteau, a carnival, Delacroix, a lake of blood (1: 13-14). Certainly these tropes work metonymically, suggesting the atmospheres of the paintings which in turn signify the artists, yet Baudelaire's return again and again to this equivalence of place and artist implies, at least, an indistinction between creative personality and creation, or, to take this identity further, an expansion of subjectivity into place and atmosphere, or a diminution of oeuvre to personality. Given Baudelaire's definition of the art he admired as "intimité, spiritualité, couleur, aspiration vers l'infini" (*Salon de 1846* 2: 421) the former may represent the "ideal" for the creative subject with the latter its splenetic and narcissistic inversion.

Such ambiguities between human subject and place appear elsewhere in the "Le Mauvais Moine." For instance, in the first quatrain, the effect of the frescoes, "réchauffant les pieuses entrailles,/Tempérait la froideur de leur austérité," temper the cold of the austerity of those monks with their pious entrails, or is it the cold of the austere walls? The antecedent of "leur" is ambiguous, leading to a confusion of person/viewer with place/structure. Another telling ambiguity occurs in the second quatrain: monks "[p]renant pour atelier le champ des funerailles" may be choosing a field of subjects, concerning death, or their studio is a tomb, the austere cloisters. While this second reading at first may seem less likely, the comparison of the poet's soul to a tomb without paintings makes it seem as plausible as the first. In other words, the studio, the place of production, is both the subject, that is, fitting inspiration, and the actual place of painting, the holy walls embellished with the allegory of death. Both subject and place are crucial to creation; the poet embodies subject – death, and place – a tomb.

To return, for a moment, to the labor theory of value, in this poem, as the poet castigates himself for his laziness, there is an implication that the value of the frescoes may be measured as products of labor, a reading that the figures of sowing and fields support. And yet the poet in the present of the poem is a consumer of images; it is that experience that gives them their heuristic value as well as visual delight ("l'amour de mes yeux"); in other words, the subjective consumption of art is also a measure of its value.

> Chaque secte a eu sa devise; Smith aura aussi la sienne, le travail, c'est-à-dire l'action de l'homme sur la nature. Des ce moment, le travail prendra sur ce globe le rang qui lui appartient ; il deviendra l'honneur et la noblesse des peuples modernes."
> – Louis Reybaud, "Économistes contemporains. M. Rossi. *Cours d'Économie Politique*," *Revue des Deux Mondes*, 15 August 1844.

Work, or labor, typifies the modern and yet it is Biblical, Adamite, in its meaning and value, emblematic of who man is after the fall, and defines his relation to nature, his role as actor.[9] I am leaning heavily on Baudelaire's use of "travail" here, yet it is, after all, half of the answer to artistic sterility in the poem (the other, inspiration from consuming images), and connotes the crucial relationship between the artist acting and the field of production. Within the discourse of theories of value, it is also modern – an umbrella term, linking agricultural to industrial production. Here its connotation is entirely positive, while sympathy for modern laborers, their miseries, and acknowledgement of a shared fate is increasingly a motif in Baudelaire's later poetry, for instance, in the urban panoramas of "Le Crépuscule du soir" and "Le Crépuscule du matin" of the "Tableaux parisiens" of *Les Fleurs du mal*.

---

[9] See Sewell on the heightened public fascination with labor in the 1840s in France, which was not without its paradoxes: "Labor was praised as never before, hailed as the source of all order in the human world; yet at the same time, men who lived by labor were increasingly portrayed as morally and physically debilitated, as threatened by complete bestiality and degradation" (222). Clearly Baudelaire's invocation of "travail" relies on the former rhetorical strain, the idealizing impulse. Gallagher points to the association of pain with "labour" in British political economy as opposed to the more neutral "work" (58-59).

Baudelaire's "Le Mauvais Moine" helps us see the special relationship between ideas of labor and of creative production in the nineteenth century. While Rancière demonstrates the importance of the new way of thinking about artistic production for the valorization of labor, Baudelaire's poem supports this notion by tracing a creative process that absolutely depends on "travail." But creativity also depends on preconception, described as a spectacle in the mind, whose realization not only requires labor but also results in communal or public display. At the same time the poem marks how production is sadly individual, in contrast with the communal production of the images that inspire the poet. Symptomatic of this sense of loss and solitude is the imagining of the artist as place, metaphorically and in the poem's minor ambiguities, a lyrical overcoming of the conscription to solitude. The distinction between the artist and work is tenuous, yet the roles of the artist in production are multiple: seer, laborer, and consumer of his own product, that is, images. Of course, imagining artistic production as a special instance of industrial labor obscures a crucial difference: the division of labor that gives the capitalist economy its efficiency. Hence the growing importance of the ideology of consumption as a displaced realization of labor's creativity for workers; the fantasies of self-expression through interior décor fed by the reviews of the industrial exhibition are one symptom of this displacement.

If "Le Mauvais Moine" reflects Baudelaire's desire to replicate the creativity he saw in the visual arts, "Les Phares," composed at about the same time as his essay on the Universal Exhibition of 1855, concerns less the process of creativity than the creative products and their effect on the viewer. Putting the poem in context of his comments on the power of art in the essay on the Universal Exhibition helps us see how he has extended and refined his earlier aesthetic that drew on painting for inspiration.

Les Phares

Rubens, fleuve d'oubli, jardin de la paresse,
Oreiller de chair fraîche où l'on ne peut aimer,
Mais où la vie afflue et s'agite sans cesse,
Comme l'air dans le ciel et la mer dans la mer;

Léonard de Vinci, miroir profond et sombre,
Où des anges charmants, avec un doux souris

Tout chargé de mystère, apparaissent à l'ombre
Des glaciers et des pins qui ferment leur pays;

Rembrandt, triste hôpital tout rempli de murmures,
Et d'un grand crucifix décoré seulement,
Où la prière en pleurs s'exhale des ordures,
Et d'un rayon d'hiver traversé brusquement;

Michel-Ange, lieu vague où l'on voit des Hercules
Se mêler à des Christs, et se lever tout droits
Des fantômes puissants qui dans les crépuscules
Déchirent leur suaire en étirant leurs doigts;

Colères de boxeur, impudences de faune,
Toi qui sus ramasser la beauté des goujats,
Grand coeur gonflé d'orgueil, homme débile et jaune,
Puget, mélancolique empereur des forçats;

Watteau, ce carnaval où bien des coeurs illustres,
Comme des papillons, errent en flamboyant,
Décors frais et légers éclairés par des lustres
Qui versent la folie à ce bal tournoyant;

Goya, cauchemar plein de choses inconnues,
De foetus qu'on fait cuire au milieu des sabbats,
De vieilles au miroir et d'enfants toutes nues,
Pour tenter les démons ajustant bien leurs bas;

Delacroix, lac de sang hanté des mauvais anges,
Ombragé par un bois de sapins toujours vert,
Où, sous un ciel chagrin, des fanfares étranges
Passent, comme un soupir étouffé de Weber;

Ces malédictions, ces blasphèmes, ces plaintes,
Ces extases, ces cris, ces pleurs, ces Te Deum,
Sont un écho redit par mille labyrinthes;
C'est pour les coeurs mortels un divin opium!

C'est un cri répété par mille sentinelles,
Un ordre renvoyé par mille porte-voix;
C'est un phare allumé sur mille citadelles,
Un appel de chasseurs perdus dans les grands bois!

Car c'est vraiment, Seigneur, le meilleur témoignage
Que nous puissions donner de notre dignité
Que cet ardent sanglot qui roule d'âge en âge
Et vient mourir au bord de votre éternité!

To begin with the ending, the final three quatrains of the poem, its *Te Deum*, we find the power of the paintings in their character as prayers of all kinds, sharing in common an intensity despite the diversity of postures towards the deity ("malédictions," "blasphèmes," "plaintes," "extases," "cris," "pleurs"). This strain of metaphor indicates their figurative roles as speaking pictures and their social roles as illustrations of human suffering. How does art produce such dramatic effects? In his section on Delacroix in "Exposition Universelle – 1855 – Beaux Arts," Baudelaire represents effective (and affective) art as nearly an assault on the viewer, as an object turned subject. He quotes a line from a poem by Gautier, "Et le tableau quitté *nous* tourmente et *nous* suit," substituting "nous" for "les" (n. 5, 2: 1376), to describe the impact of Delacroix's Shakespearean paintings like "Hamlet" and "Adieux de Roméo et Juliette" (2: 593). Later in this section, he develops this idea further and explicates his own quatrain on Delacroix from "Les Phares":

Par le premier et rapide coup d'œil jeté sur l'ensemble de ces tableaux, et par leur examen minutieux et attentif, sont constatées plusieurs vérités irréfutables. D'abord il faut remarquer, et c'est très important, que, vu à une distance trop grande pour analyser ou même comprendre le sujet, un tableau de Delacroix a déjà produit sur l'âme une impression riche, heureuse ou mélancolique. On dirait que cette peinture, comme les sorciers et les magnétiseurs, projette sa pensée à distance. Ce singulier phénomène tient à la puissance du coloriste, à l'accord parfait des tons, et à l'harmonie (préétablie dans le cerveau du peintre) entre la couleur et le sujet. Il semble que cette couleur, qu'on me pardonne ces subterfuges de langage pour exprimer des idées fort délicates, pense par elle-même, indépendamment des objets qu'elle habille. Puis ces admirables accords de sa couleur font souvent rêver d'harmonie et de mélodie, et l'impression qu'on emporte de ses tableaux est souvent quasi musicale. Un poète a essayé d'exprimer ces sensations subtiles dans des vers dont la sincérité peut faire passer la bizarrerie :

> Delacroix, lac de sang hanté des mauvais anges,
> Ombragé par un bois de sapins toujours vert,
> Où, sous un ciel chagrin, des fanfares étranges
> Passent, comme un soupir étouffé de Weber.

Lac de sang : le rouge ; — *hanté des mauvais anges* : surnaturalisme ; — *un bois toujours vert* : le vert, complémentaire du rouge ; — *un ciel chagrin* : les fonds tumultueux et orageux de ses tableaux ; — *les fanfares et Weber* : idées et musique romantique que réveillent les harmonies de sa couleur. (2 : 594-95)

Baudelaire supports his concept of the active power of art, comparable to the projection of thought of sorcerers and mesmerists, with a somewhat cut-and-dried exegesis of his own verse meant to convey these sensations. His reading points to how the effects of color contrast create the paradox of stormy harmony, reminiscent of how he describes Delacroix's use of red and green in *Le Salon de 1846* as "cet hymne terrible à la douleur" (2: 436), how these effects follow the viewer like music, drawing on the musical analogy that is one of the central ideas of "De la couleur," and how these sensory effects combine with evocation of the supernatural. Baudelaire's reading of his own verse is piecemeal and refers to different registers of meaning: the effects of color rely on a formal architecture of contrast, while the supernatural is literally represented as a subject in the painting. (His comments on the treatment of the sky, the stormy base note and the analogy of Weber's music, are more synthetic.) Yet this reading again gives us a sense of Baudelaire's aim of describing the sensations of art that begin with the material, enhanced by the work of our perceptual apparatus, but transcend mere materiality: "cette couleur … pense par elle-même." He understands art to hold not only active powers but supernatural ones – an art of conjuring, as it were. Earlier in the essay, he states that "La peinture est une évocation, une opération magique" (2: 580) and that we should avoid the pedantry and puerility of discussing the magician's formulas. Of course, in this later section, he is reading his own verse as a deciphering of the formula – of complementary colors and their harmonic analogies. At another point in the essay he compares the effects of Delacroix's painting to those of opium, with Poe as his hallucinogenic authority: "Edgar Poe dit, je ne sais plus où, que le résultat de l'opium pour les sens est de revêtir la nature entière d'un intérêt surnaturel qui donne à chaque objet un sens plus profond, plus volontaire, plus despotique" (2: 596). Again an enhancement of the relationship of the viewer with things, this time a transformation that gives things depth, will, and power.

As noted in the previous chapter, in the first part of his essay on the Universal Exhibition, Baudelaire invokes Balzac's remarks on the power of painting to spur the imagination. I quote the passage more fully here:

> On raconte que Balzac (qui n'écouterait avec respect toutes les anecdotes, si petites qu'elles soient, qui se rapportent à ce grand génie?), se trouvant un jour en face d'un beau tableau, un tableau d'hiver, tout mélancolique et chargé

de frimas, clairsemé de cabanes et de paysans chétifs, – après avoir contemplé une maisonnette d'où montait une maigre fumée, s'écria : "Que c'est beau ! Mais que font-ils dans cette cabane ? à quoi pensent-ils, quels sont leurs chagrins ? les récoltes ont-elles été bonnes ? *ils ont sans doute des échéances à payer ?*"

Rira qui voudra de M. de Balzac. J'ignore quel est le peintre qui a eu l'honneur de faire vibrer, conjecturer et s'inquiéter l'âme du grand romancier, mais je pense qu'il nous a donné ainsi, avec son adorable naïveté, une excellente leçon de critique. Il m'arrivera souvent d'apprécier un tableau uniquement par la somme d'idées ou de rêveries qu'il apportera dans mon esprit. (2: 579)

Rancière insists on the role of the realist novel in representing things as signs, and Balzac's works are among his prime examples: "[The] principle [of the so-called realistic novel] was not reproducing facts as they are, as critics claimed. It was displaying the so-called world of prosaic activities as a huge poem – a huge fabric of signs and traces, of obscure signs that had to be displayed, unfolded and deciphered" ("Politics of Literature" 18-19).[10] If we apply Rancière's point to the anecdote related by Baudelaire, then Balzac's questions have to do with reading the scene represented for signs that reveal its story, a meaning that includes indices of the economic welfare of the inhabitants of the hut – *"ils ont sans doute des échéances à payer?"* Of course, Baudelaire's primary point is that the strength of the painting lies in its capacity to act on the viewer, to arouse Balzac's imagination, to generate conjecture and concern: "faire vibrer, conjecturer et s'inquiéter l'âme." "Les Phares" celebrates this evocative power – the power to create an atmosphere saturated with latent meaning, to convey the presence of mystery as well as hints of story, all of which may tell of human anxieties, sorrows, and joys, hence a moral. His exegesis of his own poem reveals his faith in the perceived material – the basic elements of color contrast, for instance – to build a structure of complex sensation, evocation, and sympathetic meaning or signification. But, as reported, the remark also highlights – in italics – that the economic haunts the aesthetic experience, that the viewer with the greatest imaginative powers is able to read economic signs as well.

---

[10] In his essay Rancière draws on a more obvious example from Balzac, the antique shop of *The Wild Ass's Skin* that Raphael, the protagonist, views as "an endless poem" ("Politics of Literature" 19).

Fatal Beauties

While both analyzing and extolling the expressive capacities of painting in his poetry and criticism, Baudelaire is more ambivalent about another category of visual art: sculpture. This ambivalence, I will argue, has to do with his questioning and eventually rejecting the legacy of neoclassicism, still hegemonic in academic art, as he develops his own aesthetic theory.

Neoplatonic notions of ideal beauty present more of a dilemma for him; they represent an ideal which he sought in order to transcend the mere materiality of the sensual, yet they are a legacy of neo-classicism and, in the shedding of the material, they threaten a sterile aesthetic of abstraction. Michel Brix astutely situates this dilemma within contemporary debates about beauty, arguing that Baudelaire comes out of a second Romantic tradition, following Stendhal, in op-posing the Platonist idea of a single, absolute Beauty inextricably tied to the Good and the True, imported to France by Germaine de Staël and adopted by the influential philosopher, Cousin. Like Stendhal, Baudelaire favors instead a relative notion of beauty and develops an aesthetic based on sense experience as expressive of feelings and the moral. Drawing on his criticism and correspondence, Brix demon-strates how the sense of the beautiful for Baudelaire arises from feel-ings within the subjective viewer, and has symbolic value in cor-respondences between a moral and material world that are volatile and transitory rather than fixed and eternal.

As noted in the previous chapter, Baudelaire's aesthetic of modernity, articulated in "De l'héroïsme de la vie moderne" of *Le Salon de 1846*, famously rewrites the doctrine of the immortality of beauty by proposing a twofold nature:

> La beauté absolue et éternelle n'existe pas, ou plutôt elle n'est qu'une abstraction écrémée à la surface générale des beautés diverses. L'élément particulier de chaque beauté vient des passions, et comme nous avons nos passions particulières, nous avons notre beauté. (2: 493)

While not rejecting "la beauté absolue et éternelle," Baudelaire im-plies that it is incomplete in that it is literally an abstraction of diverse particular beauties and thereby an abstract generality. This famous passage is part of an argument with the conventional wisdom of the time that French painting was in a state of decadence, that the great tradition was a thing of the past that present art could not match. Instead Baudelaire places the blame for any decadence squarely on the upholders of tradition who persist in using antique subject matter as part of their effort to paint on a par with art from a past golden age. That he critiques a classical model hardly seems revolutionary in 1846 after decades of Romantic polemic against the classical. But his emphasis on the particular grows into the cosmopolitan aesthetic of 1855, where the relative beauties of the "universal" are discovered in the particular of the exotic object. This definition of beauty is another instance of the harmonizing impulse of his aesthetic at this time, as he balances the eternal and abstract ideal against the transitory and particular.[11] But if we look to poems like "La Beauté" for an argument in verse about immortal beauty as an ideal, we find a less pacific stance, for such beauty provokes him both as an artist and a lover:[12]

> Je suis belle, ô mortels ! comme un rêve de pierre,
> Et mon sein, où chacun s'est meurtri tour à tour,
> Est fait pour inspirer au poète un amour
> Eternel et muet ainsi que la matière.
> Je trône dans l'azur comme un sphinx incompris;
> J'unis un coeur de neige à la blancheur des cygnes;
> Je hais le mouvement qui déplace les lignes,
> Et jamais je ne pleure et jamais je ne ris.
> Les poètes, devant mes grandes attitudes,
> Que j'ai l'air d'emprunter aux plus fiers monuments,
> Consumeront leurs jours en d'austères études;
> Car j'ai, pour fasciner ces dociles amants,
> De purs miroirs qui font toutes choses plus belles:
> Mes yeux, mes larges yeux aux clartés éternelles !

In this *agon* over ideal Beauty, we see the extent to which Platonic or classical ideals remain a temptation. Baudelaire flirts with the ideal of "pure art" through such conventional motifs as white swans, snow, and marble, images that anticipate *la poésie pure* of Stéphane Mallarmé, and that many critics in the past have taken as evidence of the influence of le Parnasse, Gautier's own poetic school. But more re-

---

[11] Pierre Lapaire points to Baudelaire's generally binary aesthetic and the power of limiting groupings to two terms, as seen in the many catachreses and oxymorons in Baudelaire's writing. In other words, with Baudelaire, the drive to harmonize oppositions does not create an effect of unity, but rather a more powerful contrast (282-83).

[12] Brix finds this theme in two other poems from *Les Fleurs du mal*: "Les Plaintes d'un Icare" (1868 edition) and "La Mort des artistes" (5).

cently readers have argued an ironic presentation of the Parnassian ideal.[13] Indeed, the icy, unchanging beauty of the speaker is ultimately sterile for poetry, for, as muse, she silences the poets: "mon sein, où chacun s'est meurtri tour à tour,/ Est fait pour inspirer au poète un amour/ Eternel et muet ainsi que la matière." That her beauty is sculptural is also significant: with the academic neoclassical tradition dominating "almost all the theoretical writing on sculpture and almost all the sculpture exhibited at the Salons" (Millard 15), statues served as the literal embodiment of this ideal. Baudelaire sums up his attitude towards sculpture in the 1840's in the section of *Le Salon de 1846*, "Pourquoi la sculpture est ennuyeuse." Sculpture is "[b]rutale et positive comme la nature," and thus appeals to what he sees as a more primitive sensibility whereas painting has a "mystère singulier qui ne se touche pas avec les doigts" and which requires "une initiation particulière" (2: 487). Pichois in his notes to the Pléiade edition hazards that the poem could have been composed as early as the 1840s (1: 872). If so, the poem may be read as support for this idea that the model of sculptural beauty leads to an impasse for the imagination as opposed to colorist and evocative Romantic painting. In other words, if sculptural beauty is material and positive, despite its association with the abstract and ideal beauty of neoclassicism, it dulls the imaginative powers of the viewer, while the appeal of painting, in its very different materiality and mode of representation, draws on the viewer's imagination and openness to transcendent networks of meaning, putting in play a dynamic exchange between viewer and object.

Neoclassicism was rooted in neoplatonic theory, and Baudelaire does not neglect the spiritual aspirations of neoplatonic art in this poem. But "La Beauté" suggests the conundrum for the artist in such aspirations. Perhaps the most neoplatonic moment of "La Beauté" lies in the final image of the allegory's eyes: "De purs miroirs qui font toutes choses plus belles:/Mes yeux, mes larges yeux aux clartés éternelles." While the platonic idea of beauty cannot by definition be

---

[13] See Pichois, notes, 1: 871, and Francis Heck (85-87) for summaries of readings of "La Beauté" as the articulation of a Parnassian aesthetic. The irony in Baudelaire's presentation of this ideal is argued by Heck and Paul Allen Miller. Heck locates particular lines in poetry by Leconte de Lisle that Baudelaire seems to echo and subtly mock. Miller reads the sonnet within a dialogic relationship of "mutual overdetermination" (327) with the poems that follow it in *Les Fleurs du mal*, "L'Idéale" and "La Géante," to demonstrate the instability of any single aesthetic system in these poems about beauty and its antitheses.

embodied, these eyes, in the latter instance, seem to serve as its index with their eternal brightness, "clartés éternelles." But as mirrors (art) they heighten, indeed, exaggerate beauty and thus deceive while blocking the viewer's gaze into beauty's soul, to follow the old trope. So not only is this Beauty cold, dispassionate, and dangerous to these poor masochistic poets, but she is also impenetrable, physically certainly, but more to the point spiritually or morally. The nature of the speaker has been a point of dispute in some recent readings of the poem: Is she a statue, a woman, or as Judith Ryan suggests, an artist's model?[14] If we read the poem as an allegory of an ideal, that the speaker is an abstraction, "Beauty," this question is less crucial for these lines then describe what this kind of classical beauty does: It lures artists and poets into a self-deluding perception and an impossible mimesis – "aux clartés éternelles." That these eyes are made to fascinate her lovers, the poets, suggests the folly of wor-shipping this version of beauty, although this deception may be at the heart of her allure. The artist or poet sees himself mirrored in her eyes, suggesting a blurring between artist and creation: through Beauty he sees his own capacity to create beauty, a beauty in and of itself. In other words, he is both defeated by the aspiration towards a beauty closed to him and caught up in a self-defeating narcissism.

Reading the poem as a warning against a Platonist or Parnassian aesthetic whose abstract character renders any embodiment an instance of the mute material, a warning against the obsession with the ideal of beauty for beauty's sake as a creative impasse, situates it within Baudelaire's ongoing concern with articulating a new aesthetic. Beauty's attributes here differ markedly from Beauty in "Hymne à la beauté," published in 1860. In the later poem beauty is characterized by color, movement, scent, and hot sensuality. For instance, the second quatrain begins with a description of her eyes: "Tu contiens dans ton oeil le couchant et l'aurore" – a reference, yes, to their sublimity, but also to the spectrum of the crepuscular palette, the hues of dawn and dusk. Unlike the stone-cold subject of "La Beauté," she exudes perfumes "comme un soir orageux" and moves rhythmically. She is as dangerous and powerful as the muse of "La Beauté," but the danger is not a narcissistic and empty sterility, but rather the pos-sibility of damnation, a frequent concern of Baudelaire's in his drive

---

[14] See Ryan 1134 for a summary of this debate and her reading.

towards a sensualist aesthetic and invocations of death. In fact, this poem strikes at the heart of that dilemma: whether such a full sensory experience as that proffered by beauty (or art) is heavenly or damnable. The poem refuses to represent beauty itself as, by definition, a moral good; rather, it is ambivalent: "ton regard, infernal et divin,/Verse confusément le bienfait et le crime." His final answer is that if Beauty makes life endurable, "Qu'importe?" For all the de-tailing of sensory experience, this poem does not mention "matière," as does "La Beauté." This omission is telling: that Baudelaire assigns a potential for transcendence to the sensual materiality of this beauty that the dead matter of classical beauty, whose material embodiment is sculpture, lacks. This sensual beauty comes from elsewhere: "Viens-tu du ciel profond ou sors-tu de l'abîme." There is also little ambiguity in this poem about the subject: Beauty here is a woman, even though she shares features with Romantic painting. While we may read his *agon* with Beauty in "La Beauté" as an *agon* with a particular aesthetic, as I am arguing, we should also keep in mind the many other ways in which art has framed feminine beauty and relied on feminine beauty in framing aesthetic ideals. That is not to neglect Baudelaire's aesthetic concerns and preferences, but to seek to understand how such preoccupation with art's beauties sets up his representations of women and vice versa.

The sublime of Beauty's eyes in "Hymne à la beauté," – the eye that encompasses sunset and dawn, whose glance is infernal and divine – sets up a dialectic with the hypothetical speaker/viewer in contrast with the closed-off gaze of "La Beauté." In the latter poem, the trope of eyes as deceptive mirrors, reflecting the eternal, all things, or the image of the beaten-down artist, is its most indeterminate moment. Motifs of eyes, the gaze, and the glance in *Les Fleurs du mal* are central to Benjamin's reading of modernity in Baudelaire. In "On Some Motifs in Baudelaire" he predicates the aura on the return of the glance, and thus blank eyes are a symptom of the disintegration of the aura: "The deeper the remoteness which a glance has to overcome, the stronger will be the spell that is apt to emanate from the gaze. In eyes that look at us with a mirrorlike blankness the remoteness remains complete" (*Illuminations* 190). So, beyond a sign of the poet's frustra-tion with neoplatonic ideals and neoclassical models of beauty, the eyes in "La Beauté" may be read within a larger thematic of moder-nity in which vision is dominant for different reasons: to follow

Benjamin's lead, because of the emerging society of the spectacle, the urban consciousness shaped by experience of the arcades, the crowds, and later the boulevards. At the same time, Baudelaire has insisted on art as an experience of all five senses, and so his aesthetic aims come up against a tendency for the visual to define experience in the emerging culture and in the reigning aesthetics. It is of course striking that in *Le Salon de 1846* that he fashions an aesthetic from viewing that he insists transcends the visual. But the dominance of vision is in many ways overdetermined: by the reigning neoplatonic aesthetic philosophy of Cousin, France's most influential philosopher, that Baudelaire attacks, by the practice of viewing and writing about viewing that is the occupation of the art critic, by the general prominence of metaphors of vision in Romantic philosophy and poetry, and finally and perhaps most tellingly, by the experience of modernity that Baudelaire, then Benjamin in suit theorizes. Baudelaire's own aesthetic trajectory is caught in this paradox: painting serves as the creative model par excellence for his poetry yet his desire for a more than visual aesthetic experience, one replete with music, sensation, scent, repeatedly informs the figures and tropes of *Les Fleurs du mal*.

The poem that Benjamin has made famous as reflective of the urban experience of beauty and eros, "love at last sight," is "A Une Passante." Its details reflect Baudelaire's aesthetic, the fusion of the eternal and the transitory:

> La rue assourdissante autour de moi hurlait.
> Longue, mince, en grand deuil, douleur majestueuse,
> Une femme passa, d'une main fastueuse
> Soulevant, balançant le feston et l'ourlet;
>
> Agile et noble, avec sa jambe de statue.
> Moi, je buvais, crispé comme un extravagant,
> Dans son œil, ciel livide où germe l'ouragan,
> La douceur qui fascine et le plaisir qui tue.
>
> Un éclair... puis la nuit ! – Fugitive beauté
> Dont le regard m'a fait soudainement renaître,
> Ne te verrai-je plus que dans l'éternité ?
>
> Ailleurs, bien loin d'ici ! trop tard ! jamais peut-être !
> Car j'ignore où tu fuis, tu ne sais où je vais,
> Ô toi que j'eusse aimée, ô toi qui le savais!

This woman, unlike the allegory of Beauty, stirs passion. She combines the eternal and the transitory in that she is both sculpture and fashion: sculpture in "sa jambe de statue" and fashion with her "festoon" and "l'ourlet" (scallop and hem) despite her mourning dress, and her gesture, how she holds her skirt with "une main fastueuse". Beryl Schlossman, noting that the gaze petrifies both subject and object, links the breaking up of her image into pieces to an allegorization: "The woman's form is nearly dissolved in an allegorical process. It seems to capture her for a musical instant of *rallentando*, to fetishize or cut her into pieces in the description, and to anticipate her disappearance in the abstractions of her mourning and her beauty" (1020). Her eye is sublime, by token of the analogy to a nascent hurricane, but moreover in the negative pleasure it causes: its sweetness and pleasure that kill, a doubly-determined sublime. In a single glance, she is more receptive or open than the reflective mirrors that are the eyes of classical beauty and herein also lies the draw of the modern, that she is imagined as open to passion, although lost in the rush of the modern street, and that this passion is limned in terms of the sublime. Pace Lyotard, her eyes are an instance of the sublime as the failure of representation, but the process is not limited to a deceptive and self-perpetuating reflection, as in "La Beauté."

Schlossman, reading the poem within the framework of Benjamin's reading, locates a loss of Aura in this moment of desire and renunciation: "The moment of the gaze is complex: the Poet figure falls in love at first sight, but his gaze remains the gaze of the Allegorist who observes the ruin of the Aura" (1029). We have already discussed the "mirrorlike blankness" (to use Benjamin's phrase) of Beauty's eyes, a motif that Benjamin associates with the decline of the aura. Eyes that are seen as jewels, or agates likewise fail to return the gaze.[15] Benjamin's understanding of this failure of reciprocation that induces longing depends on his theory of the aura as a projection of such reciprocity onto an object: "Experience of the aura ... rests on the transposition of a response common in human relationship to the

---

[15] Elissa Marder points out that in the rare occurrence of a woman's speaking, hence seeing, eyes in "Sonnet d'Automne" the poet asks her to be quiet: "we understand that these eyes see because they are endowed with speech. By speaking, they see him, they read 'the infernal secret' in his heart; in their clear lucidity they show the poet (and the reader) that they know that he knows that he only permits these woman's eyes to speak at all so that he can tell them to shut up" (19).

relationship between the inanimate or natural object and man. The person we look at, or who feels he is being looked at, looks at us in turn. To perceive the aura of an object we look at means to invest it with the ability to look at us in return" (*Illuminations* 188). In a note, Benjamin goes on to explain that "[t]his endowment is a wellspring of poetry. Wherever a human being, an animal, or an inanimate object thus endowed by the poet lifts up its eyes, it draws him into the distance. The gaze of nature thus awakened dreams and pulls the poet after its dream" (200).

What is disturbing in the poet's gaze as Benjamin describes it is the projection of the aura onto women and objects without distinction, as if they have the same ontological status as objects of desire. With Baudelaire, inanimate objects are imagined as returning the gaze while the eyes of most female figures in *Les Fleurs du mal* do not. The implied irony here is that in modernity things are invested (fantastically) with the capacity to engage in a relationship with the (here male) subject, while women are figured physically – in their eyes – as lacking such a capacity, as falling away from the human. A further question arises: one sign of the disintegration of the aura in Baudelaire are eyes who "have lost their ability to look," yet Benjamin notes that they hold a certain "charm" nonetheless whose strength is tied to the degree of remoteness engendered by these blank looks: "The deeper the remoteness which a glance has to overcome, the stronger will be the spell that is apt to emanate from the gaze" (190). It is remoteness or "distance" from the object that helps create the aura around natural objects or art according to Benjamin in "The Work of Art in the Age of Mechanical Reproduction" (*Illuminations* 222-23), and thus unseeing feminine eyes and works of art share a like dynamic.

But if we return to those motifs in Baudelaire, there is undoubtedly an affective difference between the auratic experience of art and nature and the disintegration of the auratic around feminine figures who nonetheless draw in and enchant the poet. These latter encounters are part of "modern life," but I would like to suggest that it is not modernity itself that dissolves the auratic, but instead the vestiges of an older aesthetic, a remnant of the premodern. One way to read the disintegration of the aura in "A une passante" as Schlossman demonstrates is to read the erotic spell within a Modern thematic of Death (she wears mourning and black is the color of modern dress) and the City (1018). Benjamin's own reading emphasizes the scourge of modernity in this brief encounter, "the stigmata which life in a metropolis inflicts upon love" (169). But the unseeing eyes are different from the veiled glance of the widow: her glance may be fleeting, but the eyes of "La Beauté" lack the ability even to look. At the same time the widow of "A une passante" with "sa jambe de statue" – her statue-leg – is threatened by a like transformation into the inert. We see here the tendency of Baudelaire to turn the woman into something of great value, but inorganic: into a statue, or, her eyes into gems, or mirrors. Is modernity to blame for increasing the desire to capture the ephemeral, to halt the transient? Perhaps. But this poem is also at some level an interrogation of Baudelaire's own duality of the eternal and transitory, the desire to arrest the Other in a moment's encounter that can turn modern beauty into dull, motionless matter. In other words, because of the valence of the eternal, even the modern is threatened and in a position to become as dead and superannuated as the antique.[16] In contrast, Romantic painting – which defines the Modern according to *Le Salon de 1846* – not only speaks to the viewer, but pursues him; it is in effect hyper-animated, super-auratic.

Or to consider Baudelaire's aesthetic from another perspective: John MacKay compares the *passante* to the statue of Juno Ludovisi of Schiller's description of the aesthetic encounter that Rancière has deemed the "original scene" of aesthetics. But MacKay finds the *passante* wanting in this regard: "the 'flash' experience recounted by the poet can hardly be called a new sensorium: it seems too temporary, too discontinuous, too detached from time and space to carry any promise of 'a new world'" (citing Schiller) (130). The comparison is illuminating, but in quite another way. The aesthetic experience described by Schiller is free of desire; Baudelaire's is not. It is the tension between his immediate erotic response and his countervailing

---

[16] Peter Osborne makes a similar point about Baudelaire's aesthetic of modernity in general: "Modernity in art, for Baudelaire, is a 'distillation' or 'purification' of the beautiful feeling of transitoriness, a distillation of the beauty of time from life into art, which thereby, paradoxically, effects its *eternalization*. As Walter Benjamin showed, there is a dialectic of the transitory and the eternal at work in Baudelaire's thought (they turn into each other), which extends considerably beyond Baudelaire's self-understanding" (168-69). Osborne's move to understand the aesthetic in Baudelaire as a "distillation or purification" is, I think, to apply other notions of the aesthetic that Baudelaire himself questions to his own. Rather in these lines Baudelaire reveals himself as cognizant of the possibility of ossifying, and hence destroying modern beauty by seeking to capture it, to make it "eternal," arresting its, or *her* transit.

urge to imagine her as an aesthetic object, a statue, something enduring, that results in her piecemeal representation. The availability of this sensorium, however, is symptomatic of modernity: her beauty in passing is open for all, for the crowd, to view.

Baudelaire's practice of metamorphosing the feminine figuratively into hard, rigid objects, whole or piecemeal, appears frequently in *Les Fleurs du mal*.[17] At times his poems seem to enact the danger of turning the object of desire into precious goods, that such an aestheticization ends in sterility. The sonnet, "Avec ses vêtements ondoyants et nacrés," is a good example: here the eyes appear as the touchstone or first sign of the desired woman's inorganic nature:

> Avec ses vêtements ondoyants et nacrés,
> Même quand elle marche on croirait qu'elle danse,
> Comme ces longs serpents que les jongleurs sacrés
> Au bout de leurs bâtons agitent en cadence.
> Comme le sable morne et l'azur des déserts,
> Insensibles tous deux à l'humaine souffrance
> Comme les longs réseaux de la houle des mers
> Elle se développe avec indifférence.
> Ses yeux polis sont faits de minéraux charmants,
> Et dans cette nature étrange et symbolique
> Où l'ange inviolé se mêle au sphinx antique,
> Où tout n'est qu'or, acier, lumière et diamants,
> Resplendit à jamais, comme un astre inutile,
> La froide majesté de la femme stérile.

In this sonnet, the first quatrain is all about movement, indeed, the art and beauty of her walking as dance, yet the tercets, beginning with the image of her polished eyes, made of "charming minerals," describe her in terms of brilliant hardness. The poem builds an oxymoron of undulating rigidity and her nature "[o]ù l'ange inviolé se mêle au sphinx antique," suggests again her status as statuary, the indistinction between woman and sculpture that underlies the problematic of "La Beauté." By rhyming "inutile" with "stérile," the poet devalues her beauty by associating it sneeringly with her lack of procreativity. Yet her aura is dazzling, and defined by material goods of durability and value: gold, steel, diamonds. This image invokes and critiques a paradox of value: that the useless may be the most desired.

---

[17] Benjamin speaks of the "capacity to become rigid" in Baudelaire's writings as "a kind of mimesis of death" (*Charles Baudelaire* 83).

In light of Baudelaire's tendency to render inert parts of women's bodies in his poems, his choice of a literally dismembered body as subject in "Une Martyre" may simply be an extreme case of this pattern. Debarati Sanyal's insightful reading of this poem inspired by a painting of a beheaded woman takes up problems of viewing, of reading, and of commodification: in this poem, and others, "the self-reflexive features of aesthetic modernism open up a critique of the material conditions of urban modernity" (105). In line with her general argument that violence in Baudelaire constitutes a critique and an opposition to power through contestatory and complicit positions enacted through irony and ambiguity (10), she finds in this poem a poet-witness, who identifies with both the victim and the criminal, and "enlists the reader's participation and complicity in the voyeuristic reading of the crime scene: as detective, as empathic dandy and aesthete, as prurient voyeur and avid *faits divers* reader, as moralist and finally, as both courtroom prosecutor *and* criminal lover." In this reading, the gaze in the poem allegorizes and commodifies the murdered woman, and so Sanyal concludes that the poem presents reading itself as a violent act, constituting a relationship between detective and criminal, the executioner and his victim, and the poet and reader. In other words, the female body here "has been produced through the interwoven violence of allegorization, prostitution, commodity production, and textual – as well as visual – consumption" (111). This insight is relevant to less literally violent depictions of women in Baudelaire, as his "readings" of them often demonstrate how viewing dismembers and transfixes, how allegory deadens in its insistence on meaning, how metaphor may transform people into things, a poetic reification.

One reservation, however: Sanyal, in her reading, takes the use of the verb, *étaler*, as evidence that the body is commodified (108). But public display is not only a feature of the marketplace, but also of the Salon and museum, that is, of the experience of art. In other words, in nineteenth-century Paris, the assessing gaze may be commercial or aesthetic, or most tellingly both – perhaps inextricably. As Sanyal points out, here it is also erotic and readerly. Yet without allegory, metaphor, and reading itself, how can the poet/viewer make meaning at all? Perhaps more to the point is to interrogate how an ontology of display shapes those readings, those understandings, those reifications.

The Voyage Poems: Women as Souvenirs

> Within the development of culture under an exchange economy, the search for authentic experience and, correlatively, the search for the authentic object become critical. As experience is increasingly mediated and abstracted, the lived relation of the body to the phenomenological world is replaced by a nostalgic myth of contact and presence. "Authentic" experience becomes both elusive and allusive as it is placed beyond the horizon of present lived experience, the beyond in which the antique, the pastoral, the exotic, and other fictive domains are articulated. In this process of distancing, the memory of the body is replaced by the memory of the object, a memory standing outside the self and thus presenting both a surplus and lack of significance. The experience of the object lies outside the body's experience – it is saturated with meanings that will never be fully revealed to us. Furthermore, the seriality of mechanical modes of production leads us to perceive that outside as a singular and authentic context of which the object is only a trace.
> – Susan Stewart, *On Longing,* concerning the souvenir

While much has been written on prostitutes in Baudelaire, with the *flâneur* and poet likewise occupying the position of women of the streets, I will not take up this most evident motif of commodification and objectification of women in exploring their depiction in relationship with things. No doubt the presence of prostitutes in the streets of nineteenth-century Paris suggested a figure for cultural critique,[18] but focusing too heavily on this role can produce a one-dimensional critique of capitalism that elides a more complex and multivalent understanding of how women are represented in Baudelaire's modernity. By the same token, Baudelaire's frequent tropological objectification of women – turning them into literal objects through metaphor – no doubt sheds light on his insistent misogyny, but it also opens a window onto the desire for objects mingled with sexual desire. In other words, Baudelaire's association of luxury goods with his desire for women reveals a fascination with the goods themselves and their promise to stimulate an imaginary including travel across time and space, like that of the ideal viewer of the industrial, then uni-

---

[18] Sanyal's own interest in prostitution as a general cultural archetype is part of the background for her reading of "Une Martyre": she finds that "poetic prostitution becomes a metaphor for the semiotic exchanges of allegory and commodity production, a heuristic tool for investigating the tension between body and form within interlocking processes of representation" (102). For works like "Les Foules" where the flaneur-poet gives himself gleefully to the crowd this is a productive approach.

versal exhibitions. Consumption activity was presented by reviewers of the exhibitions as a way of creating one's own world; hence Baudelaire and his contemporaries were not only confronted with a new world of goods, but with goods that could deliver a world. Baudelaire's frequent use of the trope of the ship is a case in point. He invokes a centuries-old motif of ships laden with exotic goods, and as many critics have pointed out, the ship also carries for him memories of his voyage east when a young man, the promise of escape and the rocking, lulling motion that has both sexual and childhood associations, as in this passage from *Fusées*:

> Ces beaux et grands navires, imperceptiblement balancés (dandinés) sur les eaux tranquilles, ces robustes navires, a l'air désœuvré et nostalgique, ne nous dissent-ils pas dans une langue muette: Quand partons-nous pour le Bonheur? (1: 655)[19]

The ship speaks in its mute language of promise, a signifying objecthood.

In "Le beau navire," the trope of woman as ship is central. Pichois notes that the Crépet-Blin edition locates the image of the woman/ ship in passages in Ronsard's *Discours à très illustre et vertueuse princesse Marie Stuart, reine d'Écosse* and Milton's *Samson Agonistes* (1:926-27). But another well-known example of this trope from Shakespeare's *A Midsummer Night's Dream* offers a suggestive contrast to Baudelaire's use. The queen of fairies, Titania, addresses Oberon, her former consort, who "begs" of her "a little changeling boy/ To be my henchman":

> Set your heart at rest;
> The fairy land buys not the child of me.
> His mother was a vot'ress of my order,
> And in the spiced Indian air, by night,
> Full often hath she gossip'd by my side,
> And sat with me on Neptune's yellow sands,
> Marking th' embarked traders on the flood;
> When we have laugh'd to see the sails conceive
> And grow big-bellied with the wanton wind;

---

[19] See Benjamin's reading of the allure of rocking ships for Baudelaire : "In the ships, nonchalance is combined with readiness for the utmost exertion of energy." This "constellation" is an allegory for the combination of "greatness and indolence" in people that typifies modernism: "the high seas beckon to him in vain, for his life is under an ill star. Modernism turns out to be his doom" (*Charles Baudelaire* 95).

> Which she, with pretty and with swimming gait,
> Following (her womb then rich with my young squire)
> Would imitate, and sail upon the land
> To fetch me trifles, and return again,
> As from a voyage, rich with merchandise.
> But she, being mortal, of that boy did die,
> And for her sake do I rear up her boy;
> And for her sake I will not part with him.
> II.i.ll. 122-37

Titania's votaress plays well her role as merchant ship, transporting "trifles" for her mistress, in imitation of the ships that she and Titania "mark." But her most essential cargo she carried in her womb, and that Titania will not "sell." The boy is a "good" representing and substituting for his mother (for through death and birth there was a replacement and exchange) and it is the fairy queen's affection and loyalty to his mother that marks him as an unmarketable possession. Woman as ship is trivially represented as the carrier of merchandise ("trifles") but corporeally and ultimately tragically represented as the carrier of the child.

In contrast, in "Le beau navire," the woman addressed is figured as a body packed with goods. In detailing the separate beauties of her features, in the tradition of the Renaissance *blazon* poem, the speaker re-creates her as a ship, transforming the object of his desire into an object:

> Je veux te raconter, ô molle enchanteresse!
> Les diverses beautés qui parent ta jeunesse;
>   Je veux te peindre ta beauté,
> Où l'enfance s'allie à la maturité.
>
> Quand tu vas balayant l'air de ta jupe large,
> Tu fais l'effet d'un beau vaisseau qui prend le large,
>   Chargé de toile, et va roulant
> Suivant un rythme doux, et paresseux, et lent.

In this initial image of ship, its slow movement suggests the weight of cargo, and her skirt, a wind-filled sail, as in Shakespeare's image although the ballooning of the votaress' dress is a sign of her pregnancy. In Baudelaire's poem a second quite separate image of stored goods appears to evoke her breasts:

> Ta gorge qui s'avance et qui pousse la moire,

Ta gorge triomphante est une belle armoire
            Dont les panneaux bombés et clairs
Comme les boucliers accrochent des éclairs;

Boucliers provocants, armés de pointes roses!
Armoire à doux secrets, pleine de bonnes choses,
            De vins, de parfums, de liqueurs
Qui feraient délirer les cerveaux et les cœurs!

What cargo does Baudelaire's beloved carry? The fullness of her body
suggests a well-supplied cupboard – full of wines, perfumes, and
liqueurs – and so erotic desire is figured as desire for a particular category of goods, literally intoxicants. He would drink her up, in other
words. Consumption here appears in both senses: to drink or drink in
(perfume) and to own a fully supplied cupboard of intoxicating
liquids, a step beyond the "elixir" of "Sed non satiata," drunk from her
mouth. If her chest is an armoire, catching light like a shield, this
desire for goods, aside from the obvious erotic flattery, suggests the
violence of her breast opened up. Military metaphors reinforce this
sense of combat, that her body would be a worthy foe, an obstacle to
his plunder (playing with the echo of "armée" in "armoire"). That his
desire takes this form makes it concrete and adds to the objectification
of the woman: her charms are pictured as bottled. That his desire for
her is transformed into a desire for goods that intoxicate suggests both
the secret and secure place of these charms and the violence of his
penetration.

Without disregarding the implied violence and misogyny of this
group of images, we should note that in describing her breasts, the
detail and delineation grows as she becomes figured as an armoire
rather than a woman, except for the erotic detail of her pink nipples. In
a way, erotic desire is not only figured as but also transformed into the
desire for a wealth of goods, a full pantry, as it were, of intoxicants. It
is as if she is not real enough until she is represented as something
solid and unmoving. As in "A une passante" and more literally in
"Une Martyre," this looking and describing borders on dismember-
ment as parts of the feminine body become things. Looking at this
motif within Baudelaire's articulated aesthetics, we see the desire for
fully sensate materiality, and the threat *and* promise of fixity, unlike
Shakespeare's image of movement and change.

Yet further transformation of her body in "Le beau navire" takes
an even more hallucinatory form: her legs as two witches, stirring a

love potion in a deep vase (suggestive of her sexuality if oddly
misplaced), her arms as powerful snakes, adding to the play of dark
and light, mystery and luster:

> Tes nobles jambes, sous les volants qu'elles chassent,
> Tourmentent les désirs obscurs et les agacent,
> Comme deux sorcières qui font
> Tourner un philtre noir dans un vase profond.
>
> Tes bras, qui se joueraient des précoces hercules,
> Sont des boas luisants les solides émules,
> Faits pour serrer obstinément,
> Comme pour l'imprimer dans ton cœur, ton amant.
>
> Sur ton cou large et rond, sur tes épaules grasses,
> Ta tête se pavane avec d'étranges grâces;
> D'un air placide et triomphant
> Tu passes ton chemin, majestueuse enfant.

Much is disconcerting about these figurative moves: is her body's
power in its stiffness, its potency, or its sinuosity? When the poetic
gaze suggests what may be beneath the surface, is this merely a
fantasy of disrobing, or a dissection? And why, when she is *opened
up*, as it were, do we find things, themselves intoxicating and vague?
In a way, we see here the configuration of his desire: to reveal the
sources of her power by seeing her inner workings as well as the
erotic charge of imagining her undressed. But to turn her interior into
vessels of intoxication and magical spells is also to insist on a
materiality, yet one potent with the capacity to transform the state of
mind of the viewing, desiring subject.[20] While this portrait of his
beloved has little to do with mimesis, its figures evoke the concrete
and particular, the "thingness" of experience in metamorphosis.

In Baudelaire's well-known love poem, "La Chevelure," the
woman becomes the vehicle of voyage differently: sensual contact
with her transports him. Here the full sensual panoply is highlighted –
smell, touch, taste, sound – as if to avoid the barriers to access, the
distance and failure of exchange that viewing alone may entail. Here,

---

[20] Victor Brombert reads the desire for intoxication in this poem and in "La
Chevelure" as examples of Baudelaire's association of intoxication with creativity and
the conflicting will of the artist to control the inebriating experience. Such a desire to
create art, of course, does not mitigate the representation of other desires in the
enjoyment of material goods.

too materiality takes on a more positive connotation: the fullness of
her hair, its scent, as opposed to the "rêve de pierre" of "La Beauté."

La Chevelure

Ô toison, moutonnant jusque sur l'encolure!
Ô boucles! Ô parfum chargé de nonchaloir!
Extase! Pour peupler ce soir l'alcôve obscure
Des souvenirs dormant dans cette chevelure,
Je la veux agiter dans l'air comme un mouchoir!

La langoureuse Asie et la brûlante Afrique,
Tout un monde lointain, absent, presque défunt,
Vit dans tes profondeurs, forêt aromatique!
Comme d'autres esprits voguent sur la musique,
Le mien, ô mon amour! nage sur ton parfum.

J'irai là-bas où l'arbre et l'homme, pleins de sève,
Se pâment longuement sous l'ardeur des climats;
Fortes tresses, soyez la houle qui m'enlève!
Tu contiens, mer d'ébène, un éblouissant rêve
De voiles, de rameurs, de flammes et de mâts:

Un port retentissant où mon âme peut boire
À grands flots le parfum, le son et la couleur
Où les vaisseaux, glissant dans l'or et dans la moire
Ouvrent leurs vastes bras pour embrasser la gloire
D'un ciel pur où frémit l'éternelle chaleur.

Je plongerai ma tête amoureuse d'ivresse
Dans ce noir océan où l'autre est enfermé;
Et mon esprit subtil que le roulis caresse
Saura vous retrouver, ô féconde paresse,
Infinis bercements du loisir embaumé!

Cheveux bleus, pavillon de ténèbres tendues
Vous me rendez l'azur du ciel immense et rond;
Sur les bords duvetés de vos mèches tordues
Je m'enivre ardemment des senteurs confondues
De l'huile de coco, du musc et du goudron.

Longtemps! toujours! ma main dans ta crinière lourde
Sèmera le rubis, la perle et le saphir,
Afin qu'à mon désir tu ne sois jamais sourde!
N'es-tu pas l'oasis où je rêve, et la gourde
Où je hume à longs traits le vin du souvenir?

It is the scent and wavy texture of her hair that evokes distant worlds and functions as a sea on which to voyage. The erotic fetishization is clear, but it is worth noting the materiality of the vision evoked: the detailed luxury of the port whose waters are like gold and moiré, its full sensuality – perfume, sound, and color –, its products that he detects in her scent: "huile de coco, du musc et du goudron." Fluid, her tresses are the port; in their scents, they carry the traces of exotic imports. When the poetic voice exclaims that his hand "Sèmera le rubis, la perle et le saphir,/Afin qu'à mon désir tu ne sois jamais sourde!" this proferred treasure is less an exchange than a gift that marks the almost inevitable enrichment that this imaginary voyage has entailed. It is, of course, another triad, like the perfume, sound, and color, and coconut oil, musk, and tar, a pattern set at the start with the opening three "Os": "Ô toison, moutonnant jusque sur l'encolure!/Ô boucles! Ô parfum chargé de nonchaloir!" with the assonance of "ou" – suggestive of "poufs" of wind. It is, all told, a striving after riches whose value lie in their ability to conjure something else, which in turn is valued for evoking desire and memory. Synecdoche dominates the figurative language of this poem and serves as the trope for commodity's value.

Returning to Rancière's claim that language makes visible the traits of the historical and social world in a romantic or post-romantic age, we find in this and many other instances that this world emerges in Baudelaire across experiences of the body of his lover, as desire for her materializes as desire for goods to be enjoyed and consumed. Her body serves as a microcosm of and passage to an imagined world of goods, as in "L'Invitation au Voyage":

> Des meubles luisants,
> Polis par les ans,
> Décoreraient notre chambre;
> Les plus rares fleurs
> Mêlant leurs odeurs
> Aux vagues senteurs de l'ambre,
> Les riches plafonds,
> Les miroirs profonds,
> La splendeur orientale,
> Tout y parlerait
> À l'âme en secret
> Sa douce langue natale.

And since "Là, tout n'est qu'ordre et beauté,/Luxe, calme et volupté," we find, too, the dream of order and harmony, the proferred ideal social system of "Au Bourgeois" that represents the exchange of art for bourgeois industry and financial support. It is, of course, a desire for a fair and harmonious society that would mirror an aesthetic harmony, or that is informed by the aesthetic. It is a harmony made real through the things of the imagined room: they embody and represent an ideal, which here is available through an erotic escape. But in "L'Invitation au Voyage," as in many of *Les Fleurs du mal*, such harmony exists only in the imaginary.

MacKay, after allying Baudelaire's "poetics of the dandy" with a "thoroughgoing rejection of the useful – of social effectivity in general" argues nonetheless "that the profusion of artificial detail in Baudelaire's verse – furniture, perfumes, cordials, boudoir bric-a-brac of all sorts, and the city itself – betrays a deep fascination with the productive powers of the modern, with creation untrammeled by natural restriction" (105). I have argued that Baudelaire admits the useful, not only in writing like the 1851 essay on Dupont, with its seemingly aberrant support of poetry with a social message, but more broadly, if subtly, in his aesthetic theories, as in his 1855 conceptualization of the exotic object according to its contextual use, or even the sneer in "Avec ses vêtements ondoyants et nacrés" at the woman whose beauty is like a "useless star." The linkage of artificial things in Baudelaire to "the productive powers of the modern" is likewise multivalent in that his fascination with desired objects emphasizes their creation through imagination, not the powers of mass production. That is not to deny the immediate and constant exposure to such goods through exhibitions, in shop windows, and in advertising in Baudelaire's Paris. But the "meubles luisants" of "L'Invitation au Voyage" are polished by the years: they are not the products of new manufacturing processes; their allure is created by their age. The furniture is not new; the scene is "oriental," not western. These aspects of the luxury goods are key to their appeal through the synecdochal promise of transport away from the present time and place. As we saw in chapter two, the new goods also carried such associations through the imitation of past styles and of foreign motifs and products. So Baudelaire's desires are not so different from everyman's and everywoman's in a postromantic age, that is, whose sensibilities were formed by Romanticism. Of course, these goods are commodity fetishes in Marx's sense: the worker is forgotten as the beholder enters into a relationship with the object. But they are also made by the poet in that these things are explicitly creations of the imagination through the sensual prompts of his mistress's features. In other words, in a state of indolent creativity, reliant on his lover's body, the speaker/ poet (re)creates this décor and its objects. These imagined goods would speak to the soul in its sweet native language: in other words, things talk.

The depressing double of his lover's body as cupboard and vessel of luxury goods is, of course, the poet's own "cerveau" overstuffed with memories:

> Un gros meuble à tiroirs encombré de bilans,
> De vers, de billets doux, de procès, de romances,
> Avec de lourds cheveux roulés dans des quittances,
> Cache moins de secrets que mon triste cerveau.
> ("Spleen")

The room of his desire has faded into a boudoir supercharged with decrepitude:

> Je suis un vieux boudoir plein de roses fanées,
> Où gît tout un fouillis de modes surannées,
> Où les pastels plaintifs et les pâles Boucher
> Seuls, respirent l'odeur d'un flacon débouché.

About this poem, Benjamin writes: "Hardly any poet before Baudelaire wrote a verse that is anything like 'Je suis un vieux boudoir plein de roses fanées' . . . The poem is entirely based on empathy with material that is dead in a dual sense. It is inorganic matter, matter that has been eliminated from the circulation process. . . The image of the Sphinx which concludes the poem has the gloomy beauty of unsaleable articles such as may still be found in arcades" (*Charles Baudelaire* 55-56). It is, of course, only saleable items that have monetary value as commodities; ironically bereft of that value, these outdated things retain a power: to evoke memory, to persist.

It would be wrong to deny the misogyny of Baudelaire's trajectory – across the feminine body to rich cargoes, luxurious chambers, and cabinets full of high-end intoxicants. But if we look at this trajectory in contrast with the dead-end of ideal beauty, as in fact, a way to all the beauty and sensuality promised by art as well as eros, we see something of the purpose and subversiveness of this aesthetic not only contra conventional sexual mores, but also contra an ascetic aestheticism, the *noli me tangere* of Kantian or Cousinian disinterest. If we also consider how early in his career Baudelaire taught the efficacy of socio-aesthetic harmony, it is telling to see where the desire for harmony takes him – out of this world, yes, but also into an imaginary world of goods. It would also be wrong to read this trajectory as some sort of reverse prostitution: she pays him with goods, or to see the association of luxury items and eros itself as suggestive of prostitution. It is too much at the center of desire – for beauty, order, reciprocity – for such equivalents to take on the meaning of mere sexual paid labor, for all that the prostitute has been seen as an emblem of nineteenth-century culture in Baudelaire. The allegory is more complicated. It has to do with the task of poetry to (re)create the sensate, the things of this world, and their meanings. These things *can* be read – unlike the eyes of the adored woman. But that task entails, too, a subject/object dialectic in which the *moi*, drawn by memory and desire, may merge with these very things.

VI

A Subjectivity of Things:
Le Spleen de Paris

Depuis longtemps déjà [Victor Hugo] avait montré, non pas seulement dans ses livres, mais aussi dans la parure de son existence personnelle, un grand goût pour les monuments du passé, pour les meubles pittoresques, les porcelaines, les gravures, et pour tout le mystérieux et brillant décor de la vie ancienne. Le critique dont l'œil négligerait ce détail, ne serait pas un vrai critique ; car non-seulement ce goût du beau et même du bizarre, exprimé par la plastique, confirme le caractère littéraire de Victor Hugo ; non-seulement il confirmait sa doctrine littéraire révolutionnaire, ou plutôt rénovatrice, mais encore il apparaissait comme complément indispensable d'un caractère poétique universel. Que Pascal, enflammé par l'ascétisme, s'obstine désormais à vivre entre quatre murs nus avec des chaises de paille ; qu'un curé de Saint-Roch (je ne me rappelle plus lequel) envoie, au grand scandale des prélats amoureux du *comfort*, tout son mobilier à l'hôtel des ventes, c'est bien, c'est beau et grand. Mais si je vois un homme de lettres, non opprimé par la misère, négliger ce qui fait la joie des yeux et l'amusement de l'imagination, je suis tenté de croire que c'est un homme de lettres fort incomplet, pour ne pas dire pis.
– Baudelaire, "Victor Hugo" (1861)

In the sentences of the significant prose poem "Les Foules" there speaks, with other words, the fetish itself with which Baudelaire's sensitive nature resonated so powerfully; that empathy with inorganic things which was one of his sources of inspiration.
– Benjamin, *Charles Baudelaire: A Lyric Poet in the Era of High Capitalism*

In Baudelaire's last great poetic work*, Le Spleen de Paris*, the dialectic between the sensate and the immaterial, between the prose of the world and the shaping desires of creative subject literally takes another form. This collection of prose poems is the first widely read and influential work in a new genre, the herald and exemplum of a "prosaic" world, an attempt, in his own words, to apply "à la description de la vie moderne, ou plutôt d'*une* vie moderne et plus abstraite, le procédé" that Aloysius Bertrand applied to the painting of "la vie ancienne" in his *Gaspard de la Nuit*. Thus Baudelaire's ambition to capture an "abstract" modernity through glimpses of "modern life" and snatches of overheard conversations that intimate urban modernity.

With this aim, Baudelaire takes up and reworks themes and problems that obsessed him throughout his career: the idea and burden of Beauty; the interrogation of subjectivity and its mercurial qualities; the relationship between this ever-being-formed subjectivity and the phenomenal world, such as it exists outside that self; the desire to immerse the self in the phenomenal world, lose the self, as a way of becoming more "real" through sensation; the voyage as trope for this desire for sensate experience in leaving the self; the material as springboard for the imagination; and, finally, the dark side of the glance: modern blindness to modern social ills.

The focus of this chapter is double, just as Baudelaire's own interrogation of the *moi/non-moi* relationship is twofold: directed at the question of the relationship between the human and the inorganic, between people and things, and questions of social relationships, that is, between the subject and the other, or among people. If we consider for a moment the fate of the utopian equivalences or exchanges outlined in "Au Bourgeois," we can see to what extent that vision of social communion has darkened, through scenarios of dysfunctional or unequal exchange and social disequilibrium. Indeed, the poor's lack of pleasure-producing things compounded by the insensitivity of the wealthy or middle-class to this deprivation is the ethical nucleus of many of these prose poems. There is, however, no condemnation of luxury as such: the promise and lure of the sensate remains, albeit deferred to imagined experiences or a relationship of creative productivity with things. For Baudelaire, as for Hugo in Baudelaire's words, the creative calls for the sensate realm of things "qui fait la joie des yeux et l'amusement de l'imagination."

> toutes ces choses pensent par moi ("Le *Confiteor* de l'artiste")

Bill Brown, in "Thing Theory," draws our attention to the preoccupation with and longing for "things" of the last century in fiction, poetry, philosophy, art, anthropology, sociology, and history, of which the emergence of new fields such as material culture studies is symptomatic. In problematizing the idea of the "thing," or rather in tracing how this idea has been problematized, Brown brings up the importance of the relationship between "things" and the human for modernity and modernism: He cites Bruno Latour's argument that the "ontological distinction" between the two is an artificial construction of modernity and Walter Benjamin's work on the avant-garde showing how modernism resisted modernity by denying this distinction (12).

The study of material culture overall owes a great debt to Benjamin, so it is not surprising that we find in Baudelaire, the subject and point of reference for so much of Benjamin's own theory of modernity, a preoccupation with and longing for "things" *avant la lettre,* that is, before the century marked by Brown, and at the emergence of a consciousness of the "modernity" to which modernism reacts. As W. J. T. Mitchell reminds us in his contribution to the volume, "things" were already being rethought in Romanticism and the revolution in historical consciousness, in part wrought by the circulation of new ideas and locutions about the fossil record and meaning of totems. Mitchell argues that the romantic image is composed of both fossil and totem: "If totemism adumbrates the romantic longing for a reunification with nature, ... fossilism expresses the ironic and catastrophic consciousness of modernity and revolution" as evidence of lost forms of life (242). Rancière, too, points to the new speech of things in delineating a context for the "muteness" of words in nineteenth-century literature:

> Now, in the age of archeology, paleontology and philology, which was also the time of German Romanticism, everybody knew that pebbles, too, spoke in their own way. They had no voice. But they wore on their very bodies the testimony of their own history. And that testimony was much more faithful than any discourse. It was the unfalsified truth of things, opposed to the lies and chatter of orators. Such was the language of literature, its system of meaning. Meaning was no longer a relationship between one will and another. It turned out to be a relationship between signs and other signs. The words of literature had to display and decipher the signs and symptoms written in a 'mute writing' on the body of things and in the fabric of language." ("Politics of Literature" 17)

As discussed in chapter two, this deciphering of "things" extended to the manufactured as well as the natural; the industrial exhibitions and, later, the universal exhibitions were popular public events whose coverage had a hermeneutic side, the deciphering of the language of "produits" in a range of registers. Even in these most public showcases of technological modernity, things "spoke" to the crowds in a range of voices.

As a genre, the prose poem has had a special relationship with "things," through naming, through the presentation of phenomena as a frequent aim, and through self-description of its own "thing-like" nature. Francis Ponge's *Le parti pris des choses* is perhaps the most explicit articulation of this relationship. This association with "things" has a prototype in Baudelaire's description of his book as a kind of chopped-up snake in his dedication to Arsène Houssaye: "Hachez-la en nombreux fragments, et vous verrez que chacun peut exister à part" (275). That is, each prose poem may exist as a *thing* apart from the others; the block-like appearance on the page reinforces this sense. The implication that the prose poem is *prosaic* as opposed to *lyric* poetry adds another aspect to this relationship with things as opposed to the immaterial, the spiritual, or metaphysical; such oppositions are repeatedly posed, and just as often undermined in Baudelaire's works and aesthetic. In *Le Spleen de Paris*, those prose poems with a more lyrical affect as opposed to the flat prose of the streets, such as "Un Hémisphère dans une chevelure" or "L'Invitation au voyage," often, perhaps ironically, convey the desire for lost or elusive things. As Brown points out, "[f]or even the most coarse and commonsensical things, mere things, perpetually pose a problem because of the specific unspecificity that things denote" (3).[1] Of course, it is not merely a matter of "mere things," but of things with an affective charge, and so it is important to note both the semantic fields attached to these "things" and the extent to which the text proposes them as "mere." ("Mereness" itself functions as a litote.)

Baudelaire's examination of the dynamic relationship between self and things, between *le moi* and *le non-moi*, in several of these prose poems may well be an expansion of the idea of transformation through contemplation of the exotic object that marks the cosmopolitan critic of *The Universal Exhibition of 1855*. But, a late Romantic,

---

[1] Brown distinguishes "things" from "objects" here; noting that "although the object was what was asked to join the dance in philosophy, things may still lurk in the shadows of the ballroom and continue to lurk there after the subject and object have done their thing, long after the party is over" (3). Baudelaire's interest in the phenomenal realm always depends on a subject/object relationship, and, indeed, is often an interrogation of the nature of that relationship, so this distinction is not crucial to my discussion of things in *Le Spleen de Paris*.

he also invokes the language of things in the natural realm ("Le langage des fleurs et des choses muettes" of "Élévation" 1: 10) and makes decipherment of this language central to his theory of correspondences, a means of comprehending the "confuses paroles" of Nature ("Correspondances" 1: 11). For all that Baudelaire's stature as the first modern poet rests in part on his repudiation of nature in seizing upon the artificial as his preferred aesthetic and the urban as his preferred stage, even in *Le Spleen de Paris* nature appears as a gorgeous and daunting object, an episode in his *agon* with things. It plays a part in his ongoing interrogation of the function and nature of beauty, and represents *le non-moi*, threatening to transform the subject so completely as to render the subject insubstantial.

Phenomenal Confrontations

If we were to construct the "story" of this romance and *agon* with "things" in *Le Spleen de Paris*, "Le *Confiteor* de l'Artiste" would be a good place to start as a prayer of the artist before the "insensibility" of the natural world:

> Que les fins de journées d'automne sont pénétrantes! Ah! pénétrantes jusqu'à la douleur! car il est de certaines sensations délicieuses dont le vague n'exclut pas l'intensité; et il n'est pas de pointe plus acérée que celle de l'Infini.
>
> Grand délice que celui de noyer son regard dans l'immensité du ciel et de la mer! Solitude, silence, incomparable chasteté de l'azur! une petite voile frissonnante à l'horizon, et qui par sa petitesse et son isolement imite mon irrémédiable existence, mélodie monotone de la houle, toutes ces choses pensent par moi, ou je pense par elles (car dans la grandeur de la rêverie, le *moi* se perd vite!); elles pensent, dis-je, mais musicalement et pittoresquement, sans arguties, sans syllogismes, sans déductions.
>
> Toutefois, ces pensées, qu'elles sortent de moi ou s'élancent des choses, deviennent bientôt trop intenses. L'énergie dans la volupté crée un malaise et une souffrance positive. Mes nerfs trop tendus ne donnent plus que des vibrations criardes et douloureuses.
>
> Et maintenant la profondeur du ciel me consterne; sa limpidité m'exaspère. L'insensibilité de la mer, l'immuabilité du spectacle, me révoltent... Ah! faut-il éternellement souffrir, ou fuir éternellement le beau? Nature, enchanteresse sans pitié, rivale toujours victorieuse, laisse-moi! Cesse de tenter mes désirs et mon orgueil! L'étude du beau est un duel où l'artiste crie de frayeur avant d'être vaincu. (1: 278-79)

Whose prayer or confession is this? Who is "l'artiste"? Is this speaker the poet, Baudelaire's alter ego, or one of the artists derided in *Le*

Peintre de la vie moderne as "des brutes très adroites, de purs ma-
nœuvres, des intelligences de village, des cervelles de hameau" (2:
689) ?[2] Certainly not the latter, since such artists serve as contrast for
Guys "un *homme du monde*," a cosmopolitan painter, and since
Baudelaire approvingly describes Guys as "un kaléidoscope doué de
conscience," "un moi insatiable du non-moi, qui, à chaque instant, le
rend et l'exprime en images plus vivantes que la vie elle-même
toujours instable et fugitive" (2: 692). This prose poem, too, recounts
an emptying of the self, but before the spectacle of natural beauty as
opposed to the urban crowd. And from this difference unfolds a more
crucial contrast: the painful sublime of the artist emptied of self into
the natural scene – "L'énergie dans la volupté crée un malaise et une
souffrance positive" – as opposed to the amorous immersion in the
crowd of *Le Peintre de la vie moderne* and the prose poem "Les Foules." Vanquished by beauty in a duel,[3] this artist carries on the conflict
of the beaten poets of "La Beauté" with "l'azur" as the emblem of
chaste and silent beauty with which he nonetheless enters into ego-
dissolving communion, having drowned his gaze "dans l'immensité
du ciel et de la mer."

It is significant that the "choses" think without the mechanisms of
academic reasoning: "sans arguties, sans syllogismes, sans déduc-
tions." In other words, this experience is aesthetic – musical, picturesque – but also involves a kind of all-enveloping cognition that he insists is distinct from overly-subtle academic reasoning. This contrast is
reminiscent of Baudelaire's strategy when defining his aesthetic of the
bizarre against the strawman of the contemporary neoclassicist in
l'Exposition Universelle de 1855. Both experiences – that of the cosmopolitan critic and this melding of sensation and cognition before a

---

[2] J.A. Hiddleston sees the poet-narrator's position as an instance of a "typical thematic
oscillation between solitude and 'sainte prostitution', between concentration upon self
and dispersion into the outside world of objects or people," between two states of
mind that are "complementary" not "contradictory"; he reads the ending of the prose
poem, however, as a defeat of the artist due to his own inadequacy (26-28). Sonya
Stephens finds an "oscillation between a lyrical 'je' ... and a universal and impersonal
'énonciateur' which means that the subjective identity (that of 'l'artiste') can be
assumed by another," hence the loss of the self through lyrical openness and because
it is "generalizable" (48-49). She argues that such "figuring and fictionalizing other
selves" is ultimately aesthetically productive (50).
[3] Concerning this image of the dueling artist who screams in terror, Benjamin writes:
"Thus Baudelaire placed the shock experience at the very center of his artistic work"
(*Illuminations* 163).

natural scene – involve a revolution in the self: transformation or evacuation. This prolonged contemplation, of course, entails the artistic ego: whereas in the first case, the spectator is the critic, in the prose poem, he is the artist, whose suffering verges on parody. (Interrogation of the artist's special relationship with the beauty of things continues to preoccupy Baudelaire.) On one level, it is the pressure to create, and to create something beautiful, to measure up to nature, that crushes the artist. His abjection is so complete as to insinuate irony – that the artist ought to give up on this old pursuit of imitating nature, who is figured as an indifferent lover. But beyond its genre as poetic complaint, "Le *Confiteor* de l'Artiste" gives a sense of the extent to which the speaker in the poem is drawn to a phenomenal world that ultimately refuses reciprocity: "L'insensibilité de la mer, l'immuabilité du spectacle, me révoltent." This prose poem is the story of that desire and its frustration. But he experiences the extreme sensations he desires: delicious but ultimately unbearable pain, a sublime in which the balance between pain and pleasure shifts.

Looking in more detail at the narrative of the loss of the *moi* in the prose poem, we find that "l'Infini" is first a "sensation" that is both delicious and sharp, not a concept or thought. Once the speaker "drowns" his gaze in the "immensity" of sky and sea, he sees "une petite voile frissonnante à l'horizon" that "par sa petitesse et son isolement imite mon irrémédiable existence" in obvious contrast with its limitless backdrop, yet "toutes ces choses pensent par moi" – *all* these things think through me: the immense and the small, the full to infinity and the isolated, and the chaste and the irredeemable. In other words, thinking through things, here a visual spectacle, involves both identifying with those things and losing oneself in things that are diametrically opposed to one's sense of self. "Thinking" through visual identification with both the shivering sail and the vastness of sea and sky becomes too "intense," although it is the indices of infinity that finally get the blame. But what is perhaps most significant is that this "thought" refuses any sort of mental processing or cognition, but insists on dwelling in the realm of perception and sensation mixed with a feeble projection of self onto the viewed scene. Things and the self "think" in the same mode, that is, are imbued with the same level of consciousness, although finally his frustration is that of a lover defeated by the Other's "insensibility" and remoteness.

One solution for the artist or poet defeated before the project of communication with, or in more Baudelairean terms, a correspondence with nature is to turn to the urban scene and take on the crowd as desired Other. In "Les Foules," the narrator's experience matches Baudelaire's description of Constantin Guys in *Le Peintre de la vie moderne*, implying that the aesthetic of surprise and the *insolite* are more fecund for the modern poet than that of natural beauty or sublimity. The difference between the position and experience of the *moi* in this prose poem from that of "Le *Confiteor* de l'Artiste" helps us see both the contours of this new urban aesthetic as opposed to a more conventional marker of beauty and sublimity (sea and sky) and how the relationship between the viewer and the viewed alters accordingly.

Les Foules

Il n'est pas donné à chacun de prendre un bain de multitude: jouir de la foule est un art; et celui-là seul peut faire, aux dépens du genre humain, une ribote de vitalité, à qui une fée a insufflé dans son berceau le goût du travestissement et du masque, la haine du domicile et la passion du voyage.

Multitude, solitude: termes égaux et convertibles pour le poète actif et fécond. Qui ne sait pas peupler sa solitude, ne sait pas non plus être seul dans une foule affairée.

Le poète jouit de cet incomparable privilège, qu'il peut à sa guise être lui-même et autrui. Comme ces âmes errantes qui cherchent un corps, il entre, quand il veut, dans le personnage de chacun. Pour lui seul, tout est vacant; et si de certaines places paraissent lui êtres fermées, c'est qu'à ses yeux elles ne valent pas la peine d'être visitées.

Le promeneur solitaire et pensif tire une singulière ivresse de cette universelle communion. Celui-là qui épouse facilement la foule connaît des jouissances fiévreuses, dont seront éternellement privé l'égoïste, fermé comme un coffre, et le paresseux, interné comme un mollusque. Il adopte comme siennes toutes les professions, toutes les joies et toutes les misères que la circonstance lui présente.

Ce que les hommes nomment amour est bien petit, bien restreint et bien faible, comparé à cette ineffable orgie, à cette sainte prostitution de l'âme qui se donne tout entière, poésie et charité, à l'imprévu qui se montre, à l'inconnu qui passe.

Il est bon d'apprendre quelquefois aux heureux de ce monde, ne fût-ce que pour humilier un instant leur sot orgueil, qu'il est des bonheurs supérieurs au leur, plus vastes et plus raffinés. Les fondateurs de colonies, les pasteurs de peuples, les prêtres missionnaires exilés au bout du monde, connaissent sans doute quelque chose de ces mystérieuses ivresses; et, au sein de la vaste famille que leur génie s'est faite, ils doivent rire quelquefois de ceux qui les plaignent pour leur fortune si agitée et pour leur vie si chaste. (1: 291-92)

In this opening up of the self, the poet is not overwhelmed, but utterly in control, picking and choosing his objects, controlling his gaze. As Stephens remarks, here the self is not denied, but rather doubled "since the poet-narrator retains his identity as such, as well as adopting a series of roles through observation" and "appropriation" (54). It is a "universelle communion," indeed, a "sainte prostitution de l'âme" but here there is much more pleasure than pain. Of course, this communion is not presented as a battle with beauty, as in "Le *Confiteor* de l'Artiste," but a new sense of beauty is at stake, since this poet is likened to travelers in foreign cultures, like the critic of *L'Exposition Universelle de 1855*, who experience the "bizarre". The expansion of self, the will of the poet exerted in selecting objects worthy of communion, is celebrated, however, unlike the fate of the artist's self in "Le *Confiteor*," lost and flattened before the spectacle of natural beauty. There is also some protection of the self in mask and cross-dressing, in contrast to what feels like the mental nakedness of the artist before nature.

Of course, the poet here is opening himself up to the crowd – anonymous people – not individuals recognized as such. It is striking that the poet experiences "jouissance" in the actual experience of the crowd, of a mass of people while freighted words like "fraternity" are repeatedly shown to be empty abstractions at best, or by-words for a more essential human savagery at worst. (See "Le Gateau," for instance, with the brutal fight between the equally destitute "brothers.") It is as if he wants his encounters to be vivid, raw, and spontaneous, not prescribed or shaped by now discredited revolutionary ideals.

Furnishing Dreams

> The confrontation with furniture in Poe. Struggle to awake from the collective dream.
> – Benjamin, *The Arcades Project*

If these two prose poems directly take up the problem of the relationship between the artist's self and the phenomenal world with possibilities for both "jouissance" and suffering, other prose poems explore a phenomenal realm composed of desirable "things" as they are commonly understood. Bill Brown in *A Sense of Things* would ask questions about "things" that studies focusing on consumer practices as the encoding of value within specific social formations seem to miss: how had things become "recognizable, representable, and exchangeable to begin with"? For answers, Brown turns to literary texts "that seemed to pose those questions, whether or not they meant to" (4). As Baudelaire draws his readers into an imaginary furnished with luxury goods, we might ask the same question.

Besides the tradition of industrial exhibitions representing the applied arts as a sort of counterpart to the Salons as indices of the state of the fine arts, thus putting art and luxury goods in comparable categories, judged according to overlapping standards (see chapter two), Baudelaire had an even clearer authority in Poe's "The Philosophy of Furniture" which he translated. Poe is quite explicit about the comparability of fine art and furnishings: "We speak of the keeping of a room as we would of the keeping of a picture – for both the picture and the room are amenable to those undeviating principles which regulate all varieties of art, and very nearly the same laws by which we decide on the higher merits of a painting, suffice for decision on the adjustment of a chamber" (383). Both fall under the purview of aesthetics. Poe decries the American confusion of market value and aesthetic value, that nations with an aristocracy, like England, avoid, as the nobility set standards of taste that the rest imitates and this taste is unostentatious in order to distinguish the aristocracy from those whose ability to purchase luxury items derives from wealth alone, and not "blood." Poe has some fairly strict ideas about what constitutes good taste in furnishings, emphasizing the relationship among the various items in a room: for instance, the arrangement of the furniture, and color and form relationships among the carpet, drapes, upholstery, and other furnishings. But as evidence of the aesthetic mistake of valuing cost over aesthetic effect, he particularly denounces the "glare" and "glitter" created by, respectively, gas lighting and a profusion of mirrors and cut glass (in chandeliers, for instance) that he finds in the domiciles of wealthy Americans. In presumed contrast, he describes a "small and not ostentatious chamber" whose furnishings create a sense of "repose" replete with slumbering inhabitant (386-87).

Baudelaire in his "présentation" of this essay seems to delight in the difficulty that "une jeune nation *parvenue*" would have in swallowing Poe's "cruels axiomes" concerning the corruption of American taste by an aristocracy of the dollar and calls his specific ideas about interior décor "assez judicieuses" (2: 290-91). But Baudelaire begins this brief piece with an evocation of "un appartement modèle, un domicile idéal, un *rêvoir*" that seems to be a forerunner of the imagined rooms of prose poems like "La Chambre Double" and "L'Invitation au Voyage." In these prose poems, there is no insinuation that cost dictates taste, albeit the furnishings are costly. To get a sense of the function and meaning of these "things" for Baudelaire, we will look closely at what his ideal interiors share with Poe's model room and at how they differ.

First, it is worth noting the affinities between Poe's and Baudelaire's "philosophies of furniture," as it were. Both imagine rooms that induce and embody rest, repose, sleep and dreams. In Poe's room, "[t]he proprietor lies asleep on a sofa—the weather is cool—the time is near midnight" (386), and the room is dominated by crimson and gold curtains and sofas. Of the paintings in the room, "*[r]epose* speaks in all" (387). The ideal room of Baudelaire's "La Chambre double" ressembles "une rêverie" and the furniture dreams as if "doués d'une vie somnambulique" (1: 280). Similarly the prose poem, "L'Invitation au Voyage," elaborates on the atmosphere of "[l]uxe, calme et volupté" of its famous antecedent poem in verse. Baudelaire also delights in Poe's skewering of pretense, "les plaisanteries violentes sur la frénésie des glaces, du verre taillé, et du gaz dans les appartements aristocratiques américains" (1: 290), décor choices that, according to Poe, signal the lack of aristocracy in the United States, by confusing price with measure of taste, in their ostentation, marking the nation itself as "*parvenue.*" This insight of Poe's into what motivates American consumption of luxury goods anticipates Veblen's much later analysis of "conspicuous consumption."

Clearly Poe is not denouncing consumption and display of luxury goods *tout court*, but has targeted those that he finds in bad taste, and this bad taste may be blamed on its motivation: to signify wealth through the high price of items. This "idea" nonetheless generates fashions, the "rage for *glitter*"(385), for instance, instead of the imitation of "true" aristocrats in England, of which Poe approves as "a thorough diffusion of the proper feeling" (382). Baudelaire himself observes in later editions of his preface:

Cependant nous ne pouvons nous empêcher de sourire en voyant que notre auteur, dominé par son imagination quasi orientale, tombe un peu dans le défaut qu'il reproche à ses concitoyens, et que cette chambre qu'il nous offre comme un idéal de simplicité, pourra paraître à beaucoup de gens un modèle de somptuosité. (2: 1219)

In other words, where does one draw the line between imagination and ostentation, between furnishings cast as art, inspired by a desire to live the exotic "Other" (the Orientalist imaginary) and those inspired by a desire to draw distinctions more mundanely between oneself and one's neighbor, in other words, between the aesthetic and the socio-economic?

In Baudelaire's prose poems, "La Chambre Double" and "L'Invitation au voyage," there is, of course, no skewering of bad taste or parvenu ostentation since these are literally daydream decors, produced by opiates (laudanum in "La Chambre Double") or pure reverie ("d'opium naturel" in "L'Invitation au voyage"), in other words, a temporary transformation of self. The economics of décor obtrudes when the dream is dissipated in "Le Chambre Double" to show the room's real face, a "taudis" whose dusty, chipped furniture, cold and spat-upon chimney, dirty windows, and manuscripts, either incomplete or full of erasures, signify use, neglect, poverty, and its cause, unfinished work. (Indeed, the dream is dissipated by the "coup" that announces economic reality: the bailiff's demands, the prostitute's poverty, the errand-boy's message that the rest of the manuscript is due.) In contrast, the imagined room of the prose poem, "L'Invitation au Voyage," is full of "[l]es trésors du monde" "comme dans la maison d'un homme laborieux et qui a bien mérité du monde entier" (1: 302). Here Baudelaire seems to adopt the reading of fine goods ("comme une magnifique batterie de cuisine, comme une splendide orfèvrerie, comme une bijouterie bariolée") as indices of just deserts, the rewards of hard work, due to the industrious. The poet, too, is a worker: "Pays singulier, supérieur aux autres, comme l'Art l'est à la Nature, où celle-ci est reformée par le rêve, où elle est corrigée, embellie, refondue"(1: 302). This is literally an art of reverie, as the narrator himself declares:

Des rêves ! toujours des rêves! plus l'âme est ambitieuse et délicate, plus les rêves l'éloignent du possible. . . . Vivrons-nous jamais, passerons-nous jamais dans ce tableau qu'a peint mon esprit, ce tableau qui te ressemble ? (1: 303)

Whether reverie leads to self-condemnation for idleness and procrastination[4] as in "La Chambre Double" or is a form of creativity as in "L'Invitation au voyage," the positive light in which these imagined "things" appear in both prose poems suggest a similar hermeneutics. A hint of this hermeneutics is already given in Baudelaire's remark about Poe's own self-deceiving quasi-Oriental imagination. While Poe in "The Philosophy of Furniture" lays down interior design dicta with all the aplomb of a nineteenth-century Martha Stewart, Baudelaire in his preface to the essay observes instead that "temperament" guides the day-dreamer as he mentally furnishes his ideal room. The idea of the room as a reflection of the temperament of the "designer" recalls his ideas about art: that great art is a reflection of the temperament of the artist. This idea is also important to Baudelaire's insistence on beauty as a relative, not absolute, standard. In fact, if we look closely at the semiotics of interior design in these two prose poems, we find a complicated vehicle of meaning, designating not only the desire for luxury and repose, but more crucially, a stabilization of the creative self in the world imagined.

In the ideal room of "La Chambre Double," the speaker's experience is equivocal: "L'âme y prend un bain de paresse, aromatisé par le regret et le désir. – C'est quelque chose de crépusculaire, de bleuâtre et de rosâtre; un rêve de volupté pendant une éclipse" (1: 280). While "l'Idole" appears later in the prose poem as the epitome of the object of desire, the cause of regret is never articulated. The crepuscular atmosphere appears in "L'Invitation au voyage" as well in "[l]es soleils couchants, qui colorant si richement la salle à manger ou le salon" (1: 302). In "La Chambre Double," time in the ideal room becomes eternity, there is a desire to stay a time of transition and beauty, to turn the sunset into eternity ; this impulse is present in both versions of "L'Invitation au Voyage" in the iterations of the desire to live and to die in the dream country.

In the same vein as "L'Éloge au Maquillage," the imagined room of "La Chambre Double" is a celebration of artifice over nature: "Les meubles ont des formes allongées, prostrées, alanguis. Les meubles ont l'air de rêver; on les dirait doués d'une vie somnambulique, com-

---

[4] See Cheryl Leah Krueger for a reading of Le Spleen de Paris as literary hesitation and procrastination through manipulation of narrative and figures of time. She finds in "La Chambre double" multiple readings of the schism between eternity and biographical time with signs of procrastination between which the reader "hesitates" (124-27).

me le végétal et le minéral. Les étoffes parlent une langue muette, comme les fleurs, comme les ciels, comme les soleils couchants" (1: 280). In clear echo and revision of "Élévation" – "les pensers ... comprend sans effort/Le langage des fleurs et des choses muettes" (1: 10) – and "Correspondances," with Nature's "confuses paroles" (1: 11), the furniture takes on the functions of Romanticism's Nature – to dream, to invade dreams, and to speak symbolically. Accordingly, the atmosphere is that of the very definition of artificial nature, the hothouse ("serre chaude"). In the same vein, the imaginary country of "L'Invitation au voyage" is "supérieur aux autres, comme l'Art l'est à la Nature, où celle-ci est reformée par le rêve, où elle est corrigée, embellie, refondue" (1: 302). Art and artifice have replaced Nature as index and vehicle to the infinite; by expecting speech from this creation, the artist is somewhat narcissistically listening to a reflection of his own work. Home furnishings carry a weighty metaphysical load.

Curiously, in "La Chambre double," for all that the room as artifice aspires to the condition of art, the next paragraph specifies that no art hangs on the walls: "Sur les murs nulle abomination artistique. Relativement au rêve pur, à l'impression non analysée, l'art défini, l'art positif est un blasphème. Ici, tout a la suffisante clarté et la délicieuse obscurité de l'harmonie" (1: 280). Such art would inject another word, a blasphemy, a desecration of this sacred space of dream by asking for analysis and by introducing alien speech where there is already a mute language, disrupting its meaning and fragile harmony.

In "L'Invitation au Voyage," the imagined country offers a remedy for a kind of nostalgia:

> Tu connais cette maladie fiévreuse qui s'empare de nous dans les froides misères, cette nostalgie du pays qu'on ignore, cette angoisse de la curiosité ? Il est une contrée qui te ressemble, où tout est beau, riche tranquille et honnête, où la fantaisie a bâti et décore une Chine occidentale, où la vie est douce à respirer, où le bonheur est marié au silence. (1: 302)

How does the décor manage to soothe this nostalgia for that which one never knew, imagined as a Westernized Orient? (Baudelaire is keenly aware of the distortive use of the East by the West in which these daydreams indulge.) I will not pursue the obvious psychoanalytic reading of desiring in the beloved a compensation for the lack, but will ask instead: what can the furnishings offer? First of all, unlike the imagined room in "La Chambre Double," there are paintings: "Sur des panneaux luisants, ou sur des cuirs dorés et d'une richesse sombre, vivent discrètement des peintures béates, calmes et profondes, comme les âmes des artistes qui les créèrent" (1: 302); these remind us of the function of the art on the walls in Poe's ideal room – "repose" – and of Baudelaire's notion that art reflect the temperament, or "soul" of the artist. The spirituality of art is heightened by the frames that resemble halos. The paintings are clearly a counterpart to the prose poem itself, an expression of the poet's "soul", or at least, what the poet aspires to – blissful, calm, profound. As mentioned earlier, the sunset casts the room in a certain light – an overlay of transitory beauty that also changes the aspect of the room (lighting matters!). And, as in "La Chambre Double," the furniture seems to hide a dormant life:

> Les meubles sont vastes, curieux, bizarres, armés de serrures et de secrets comme des âmes raffinées. Les miroirs, les métaux, les étoffes, l'orfèvrerie et la faïence y jouent pour les yeux une symphonie muette et mystérieuse ; et de toutes choses, de tous les coins, des fissures des tiroirs et des plis des étoffes s'échappe un parfum singulier, un *revenez-y* de Sumatra, qui est comme l'âme de l'appartement. (1: 302)

The use of the word "bizarre" reminds us of his 1855 aesthetic, and this is, after all, an occidental China.

So the furniture holds secrets, perhaps of other lives, and of other cultures. The multiple reflections of mirrors, metals, fabrics, silverware and glazed earthenware creates a "symphony" of reflections, in contrast with Poe's dislike of mirrors and glitter. A scent evoking "nostalgie du pays" is the soul of this room (unlike Poe's claim for the carpet). In all, the room seems to answer and parody the desire at the heart of the cosmopolitan aesthetic – to know the other as the exotic, but crucially he envisions a sort of domestication of the exotic in this explicitly occidental China. Yet even if the effect is mock oriental, the room evokes fantasies, the same power that Baudelaire saw in painting: the furniture has stories to tell, and all these "things" ("choses") beckon with a scent that rather than remedying nostalgia, or homesickness, instead heightens it. As the prose poem proceeds, this realization becomes explicit: "Des rêves! Toujours des rêves! Et plus l'âme est ambitieuse et délicate, plus les rêves l'éloignent du possible." He finds his final answer in the lover he addresses: "Ces trésors, ces meubles. Ce luxe, cet ordre, ces parfums, ces fleurs miraculeuses, c'est toi…." (1: 303) freighting the lover with all the baggage of his projected desires and nostalgia for such things.

In "Les Projets," Baudelaire narrates the process of such day-dreaming, the erection of three castles in Spain, stimulated by, first, the view of a "grand parc," which gives rise to a fantasy of his lover as princess on the palace steps, secondly, of an engraving of the tropics, leading to a longing to go there "pour cultiver le rêve de ma vie" (1: 314), and finally the sight of "une auberge proprette, où d'une fenêtre égayée par des rideaux d'indienne bariolée se penchaient deux têtes rieuses" which causes him to instead imagine such a simple abode as "si féconde en voluptés." This prose poem, a sort of moral tale, ends with the thoughts of the dreamer when he comes home: "J'ai eu aujourd'hui, en rêve, trois domiciles où j'ai trouvé un égal plaisir. Pourquoi contraindre mon corps à changer de place, puisque mon âme voyage si lestement? Et à quoi bon exécuter des projets, puisque le projet est en lui-même une jouissance suffisante ?" (1: 315) This more down-to-earth conclusion, the realization of the efficacy of mental voyages, helps answer the quandary between the imagination and the acquiring of riches. Unlike the wealthy man of Smith's moral of the "invisible hand" who desires more than he can enjoy, this solitary promeneur satisfies his desires or attains "jouissance" through purely imaginary possession. But such a commonsensical view, and the ability to distance oneself from one's desiring self and judge those desires – their real "ends" – seems too pat. This stance is a distancing from and a mocking of the desiring and inquiring voice of so many other prose poems, especially those sketching the divide between the rich enjoying food or music in luxurious surroundings and the poor who watch. This view denies the meanings attached to such visions, reducing them to "jouissance" alone. By dint of the intense desire ex-pressed in "L'Invitation au voyage" and in the elation followed by self-humiliation of "La Chambre double," it is clear that these things signify powerfully in other cultural registers – through the equation or conflation of art and luxury goods; through the lure of domestic orientalism, the Western self playing the exotic; through the artist's need for "things" in realizing that very identity, a taste that is the "complément indispensable d'un caractère poétique universel" ("Victor Hugo" 2: 130).

The Lack of Things

Le Spleen de Paris is also remarkable for its representations of poverty and of bourgeois hypocrisy and indifference to the poor. Among the prose poems that depict the Parisian poor are "Les Veuves," "Le Vieux Saltimbanque," "Le Gâteau," "Le Joujou du pauvre" and "Les Yeux des pauvres." In contrast with the social equilibrium that Baudelaire sketched in 1846, where bourgeois gifts to the public in the form of museums and other support for the arts are recompensed by the bourgeois's own *jouissance*, gifts in Le Spleen de Paris often fail: the narrator is kept from giving "quelque argent" to the impoverished "vieux saltimbanque" by the press of the crowd; the offering of bread to the poor child in "Le Gateau" leads to a bloody tussle in which the gift itself is crumbled; "Les dons des fées" do not meet the needs of the recipients; the sacrifice of the widow for her son in "Les Veuves" goes unrecompensed even by the child's companionship, precluded by his egoism; and most egregiously the counterfeit alms of "La fausse monnaie" give new definition to "bad faith," to use Susan Blood's term.[5] In sum, charity and other forms of gifting are false, impeded, or when enacted, fail to support social or even familial relations. Further, Baudelaire parodies notions of equality in interclass exchange in "Assommons les Pauvres!" where a bloody exchange of blows evens the ground between the aspiring socialist narrator and the beggar he attacks.

The case of the widow is especially interesting in light of Dupuit's notion of marginal utility that accounts for consumer desire or decision-making. Among the widows observed by the narrator, one in particular seems out of place given her demeanor that would signify a higher class. She is among the "foule de parias qui se présent autour de l'enceinte d'un concert public." After describing the joyous music and the obvious wealth inside the hall – "rien qui ne respire et n'inspire l'insouciance et le plaisir de se laisser vivre" – the narrator notes "à travers ce peuple vêtu de blouses et d'indienne, j'aperçus un être dont la noblesse faisait un éclatant contraste avec toute la trivialité environnante." She watches "le monde lumineux avec un œil profond" and listens, swaying her head in time with the music. The narrator is puzzled:

---

[5] See, too, Jacques Derrida's *Given Time: I. Counterfeit Money* in which Baudelaire's prose poem is central to Derrida's exploration of the question of the gift.

Singulière vision! "A coup sûr, me dis-je, cette pauvreté-là, si pauvreté il y a, ne doit pas admettre l'économie sordide; un si noble visage m'en répond. Pourquoi donc reste-t-elle volontairement dans un milieu où elle fait une tache si éclatante?"

Mais en passant curieusement auprès d'elle, je crus en deviner la raison. La grande veuve tenait par la main un enfant comme elle vêtu de noir; si modique que fut le prix d'entrée, ce prix suffisait peut-être pour payer un des besoins du petit être, mieux encore, une superfluité, un jouet. (1: 293-94)

In other words, the narrator imagines her decision-making as a consumer, her weighing the sacrifice of not attending the concert against sacrificing the needs or wants of her child. It is noteworthy here that the distinction between "besoins" and a "superfluité" suggests a priority of needs that the narrator's "mieux encore" immediately reverses just as the lumping of needs and desires into the definition of "utility" in a marginalist political economy eliminates such priority. Other texts by Baudelaire cast light on the preference for a toy, as I will soon discuss. Baudelaire also emphasizes how alone she is in these choices; the child is incapable of real gratitude or even companionship. This points, too, to the subjectivity of choice in Dupuit's model, the plight of the lone consumer.

Her gazing at the rich concert-goers, the physical barriers between her group, the poor, and those inside, constitutes a pattern of lack of interaction between rich and poor repeated in a café setting in another prose poem, "Les Yeux des pauvres." Even starker than failed gifts are failures to even recognize the needs of others, or to interact with the poor. Among Baudelaire's many poems and prose poems about viewing in the city, "Les Yeux des pauvres" takes up the motif of reading the other's thoughts through the look in the eye most directly. The prose poem is addressed to the speaker's beloved, and their interaction depends on the notion of the eyes as windows to the soul, and love as a unity of thoughts: "Nous nous étions bien promis que toutes nos pensées nous seraient communes à l'un et à l'autre, et que nos deux âmes désormais n'en feraient plus qu'une; – un rêve qui n'a rien d'original, après tout, si ce n'est que, rêvé par tous les hommes, il n'a été réalisé par aucun" (1: 318). The speaker and his beloved sit at a new café in a new boulevard, and a poor family – a father and two children – stand in front of the café. The speaker reads their regards, their gazes, feels pity and is even a little ashamed "de nos verres et de nos carafes, plus grands que notre soif." He looks to his beloved's eyes for the same sentiment – "pour y lire *ma* pensée; je plongeais dans vos yeux verts, habités par le Caprice et inspirés par la Lune" but her remark reveals that her thoughts are the reverse of his own: "Ces gens-là me sont insupportables avec leurs yeux ouverts comme des portes cochères ! Ne pourriez-vous pas prier le maître du café de les éloigner d'ici ?" (1: 319) Thus this reading of eyes fails as the beauty and softness of her eyes give no glimmer of the harshness of her thoughts.

It's worth noting that the speaker does not exchange glances with the poor family, but instead reads their gaze and is "attendri par cette famille d'yeux" (1: 319). In their eyes, he sees not a request for food or drink, but instead bedazzlement before the splendors of the new café:

> Les yeux du père disaient: "Que c'est beau! que c'est beau! on dirait que tout l'or du pauvre monde est venu se porter sur ces murs." –Les yeux du petit garçon : "Que c'est beau ! que c'est beau ! mais c'est une maison où peuvent seuls entrer les gens qui ne sont pas comme nous." – Quant aux yeux du plus petit, ils étaient trop fascinés pour exprimer autre chose qu'une joie stupide et profonde. (1: 318)

For all that the speaker shows himself to be a poor reader of his lover's eyes, there is no similar recognition of misreading the eyes of the poor on his part. It is, of course, a reading, a projection of his discomfort in enjoying all the gold of the *poor* world (certainly two meanings of "pauvre" are implied here – poor world! and the world of the poor) seated in the gaudy café, and that the little boy *sees* the class barriers (which are realized in the grilled fence separating the rich from poor child in "Le Joujou du pauvre"). But what are they looking at? The café that the speaker has viewed and described, although at this moment his view is necessarily turned towards them. (The direction of his gaze is made explicit when he turns to look into his lover's eyes.)

The status of the café itself is equivocal: it is new and is situated on the corner of a new boulevard "encore tout plein de gravois et montrant déjà glorieusement ses splendeurs inachevées." In other words, this is Paris under Haussmannization, and the scene betrays the incompleteness of this urban project, like the lithographs by Martial, for instance, showing the rubble from the destruction of old Paris next to the splendors of new Paris, the Opera House and new, wide boulevards. He describes the café itself as illuminated with gaslight (it is "le soir"), and effectively dazzling, even blinding:

> Le café étincelait. Le gaz lui-même y déployait toute l'ardeur d'un début, et éclairait de toutes ses forces les murs aveuglants de blancheur, les nappes éblouissantes des miroirs, les ors des baguettes et des corniches, les pages aux joues rebondies traînés par les chiens en laisse, les dames riant au faucon perché sur leur poing, les nymphes et les déesses portant sur leur tête des fruits, des pâtés et du gibier, les Hébés et les Ganymèdes présentant à bras tendu la petite amphore à bavaroises où l'obélisque bicolore des glaces panachées ; toute l'histoire et toute la mythologie mises au service de la goinfrerie. (1: 318)

The strength of the gas light transforms the scene: The white walls blind, the mirrors gleam like liquid sheets of light. But as the speaker continues detailing the scene, his eye moves from these dazzling surfaces and the attraction of the gold-painted moldings and cornices, to particular characters: medieval pages with their dogs, ladies with their pet falcons, and figures from mythology serving as porters of food. The scene is not only dazzling but deceptive, the elevated subject matter of history painting used to make the food tempting, all devoted to the crass servicing of that medieval sin, gluttony. The irony here is obvious; but the ambiguity – what does he see – is more disconcerting.

So what would his lover deny the poor family? To feast their eyes on gold, history, and myth, as well as food and drink. In the new democracy of Haussmann's sidewalks, she would turn them away from the spectacle, reinstating class barriers quite literally. She does not want to meet their eyes, which she ridicules as "carriage entrances" – openings into an interior (the courtyard) that is still outside. (Does the association with carriages also suggest that they are on the move, like Dicken's homeless boy Jo in *Bleak House*, repeatedly told to "move on"?) Her remark is dehumanizing, by making their eyes into things, but as a metaphor reveals something of the plight of the poor beyond even what he sees. Of course, they cannot afford to eat and drink there, but the sidewalk spectacle is available in this new modernity.[6] The irony of this spectacular new urban scene

---

[6] Geraldine Friedman finds a discrediting of the specular as ideology in this prose poem, a process begun with the speaker's misreading of his lover's eyes that ends in his hypocritical disappointment with her insensitivity. The hypocrisy resides in his further misreading of aesthetic appreciation in the eyes of the hungry poor, a misreading that reifies the categories of the economic and aesthetic (323). As brilliant

and these networks of gazing is that the furnishings of the café as history and mythology cry out to be read while the narrator's reading of his lover's eyes fails utterly.

Another prose poem offers a happier scenario, where a desired object connects rich with poor for a utopian moment, albeit laced with a heavy dose of irony. "Le Joujou du Pauvre" follows "L'Invitation au voyage" in the collection and thus may serve as an ironic comment on desire for things and the class boundaries elided in the dream-like piece. But unlike "L'Invitation au voyage," in which Baudelaire re-writes a "fleur du mal," "Le Joujou du pauvre" has its pre-text in a short essay, "Morale du joujou" (1853) which makes clear the special role of toys as objects.

In "Morale du joujou," Baudelaire explores at much greater length the child's desire for the toy and in so doing, not only illumi-nates adult possessive desires as a continuation, in a minor key, of childhood anticipation and *jouissance*, but also casts toys and child's play as prefigures for art and artistic creativity. The essay gives us a sense of how the creative and aesthetic questions that Baudelaire turned to again and again inform the prose poem while the *economy* of the prose poem, its verbal parsimony, gives these concerns a different inflection as economic deprivation and hollow political rhetoric loom larger.

"Morale du joujou" begins with a childhood memory. The speaker recalls visiting Madame Panckoucke, who made him a present in the following way:

> Je me rappelle très distinctement que cette dame était habillée de velours et de fourrure. Au bout de quelque temps, elle dit : "Voici un petit garçon à qui je veux donner quelque chose, afin qu'il se souvienne de moi." Elle me prit par la main, et nous traversâmes plusieurs pièces; puis elle ouvrit la porte d'une cham-bre où s'offrait un spectacle extraordinaire et vraiment féerique. Les murs ne se voyaient pas, tellement ils étaient revêtus de joujoux. Le plafond disparaissait

---

as this reading is, and certainly the prose poem is all about representation and referentiality as ideology (317), the speaker's description of the bedazzled eyes of the poor is bolstered by his description of the dazzling surfaces of the new café, so to ascribe mere hunger to their stares is to undercut Baudelaire's depiction of their reception of this new urban spectacle, that it is available even to the poor, albeit obliquely, in glimpses. This is not to deny Friedman's and Sanyal's point that "[t]he principle of *correspondances* is deployed both in its poetic and social form to unveil a structural inequity before which poetic empathy and bourgeois humanism are woefully inadequate" (Sanyal 81).

Material Figures

sous une floraison de joujoux qui pendaient comme des stalactites merveilleuses.
Le plancher offrait à peine un étroit sentier où poser les pieds. Il y avait là un
monde de jouets de toute espèce, depuis les plus chers jusqu'aux plus modestes,
depuis les plus simples jusqu'aux plus compliqués.

"Voici, dit-elle, le trésor des enfants. J'ai un petit budget qui leur est
consacré, et quand un gentil petit garçon vient me voir, je l'amène ici, afin qu'il
emporte un souvenir de moi. Choisissez."

Avec cette admirable et lumineuse promptitude qui caractérise les enfants,
chez qui le désir, la délibération et l'action ne font, pour ainsi dire, qu'une seule
faculté, par laquelle ils se distinguent des hommes dégénérés, en qui, au contraire, la délibération mange presque tout le temps, — je m'emparai immédiatement
du plus beau, du plus cher, du plus voyant, du plus frais, du plus bizarre des
joujoux. Ma mère se récria sur mon indiscrétion et s'opposa obstinément à ce
que je l'emportasse. Elle voulait que je me contentasse d'un objet infiniment
médiocre. Mais je ne pouvais y consentir, et, pour tout accorder, je me résignai à
un *juste-milieu*....

Cette aventure est cause que je ne puis m'arrêter devant un magasin de
jouets et promener mes yeux dans l'inextricable fouillis de leurs formes bizarres
et de leurs couleurs disparates, sans penser à la dame habillée de velours et de
fourrure, qui m'apparait comme la Fée du joujou. (1: 581-82)

First of all, Baudelaire clearly wants to associate this gift of a toy with
his impression of this lady in velvet and furs, implying that his desire
for the toys is compounded by proto-erotic desire. But we would miss
the broader implications of his analysis if we were to settle for a
reading of toy as merely fetish or erotic substitute. Of course,
according to his story, she wants the toy to become a *souvenir*; that is,
she wants him to take away a memory of her, for which the toy would
serve as prompt and embodiment. In enduring as memory, she is
successful. In this memory, she appears "comme la Fée du joujou,"
bringing in associations of toys, play, and imaginary worlds. When he
enters her room full of toys, he witnesses a "spectacle" that was
"vraiment féerique." The walls, ceiling, and floor nearly disappear
behind the profusion of toys. Like so many princes, or children in
magical lands, he is given a choice. Having grabbed the most beautiful, expensive, gaudy, new, and bizarre toy, he is rebuked by his
mother and ultimately settles for something between what he wants
and what his mother thinks he should take, "un *juste-milieu*," a
compromise typical of the dominant political philosophy of the July
Monarchy and its philosophical counterpart in Cousin's eclecticism.
That Baudelaire the child prefers the most beautiful and bizarre
replays this aesthetic debate in miniature, as it were.

Thus he remembers her as magical and associates her with velvet and fur, that is, with sensual pleasure. His visual pleasure at the sight of the toys is also stressed, and so the scene repeats itself in his adult life each time he stops in front of a toy store and enters: the visual promise of the window, "l'inextricable fouillis de leurs formes bizarres et de leurs couleurs disparates," is borne out in the store itself: "Il y a dans un grand magasin de joujoux une gaieté extraordinaire qui le rend préférable à un bel appartement bourgeois.[7] Toute la vie en miniature ne s'y trouve-t-elle pas, et beaucoup plus colorée, nettoyée et luisante que la vie réelle ?" (1: 582) Again, drawn by the spectacle, he enters an alternative, fairylike world, but this time, it is a shop. If we return, for a moment, to his description of how children make decisions, we see this sequence repeated: children desire, deliberate, and act all at once; as a child he saw and immediately acted, and likewise as an adult, he acts visually – "promener mes yeux" – and enters the miniature world of the toy store. In this, he is unlike most adults, for whom "la délibération mange presque tout le temps." Later in the essay, we learn that, like Mme Panckoucke, he buys toys to distribute to children, for his own pleasure. He is now himself the magical figure, the toy fairy, but also a consumer, the toy store's customer.

At one level, this seems to be a story about impulse buying, an immediate reaction to the stimulus of visual display of goods, a behavior learned in childhood through an experience of impulsive choice when offered a gift. This suggests both the replay of childish delight in the impulsive purchase and a paying-back the "gift-fairies" in life by becoming one himself. This economic activity is telling in its mixture of buying and giving, of shopping and imaginative flights: can impulse buying be redeemed by generosity? Can we relish the display and desire the most beautiful and bizarre things without guilt, like children? The market, or economic exigency, is like his mother, forcing the compromise choice. Ideally for the desiring self, the world of the shop (the market) would function like Madame Panckoucke's

---

[7] By putting the fantastical shop display in competition, as it were, with the décor of a bourgeois apartment, Baudelaire casts the bourgeois space as similarly fantastical, a place of willed illusions. The theme of the bourgeois interior as an expression of personal fantasies, of course, central to Benjamin's analysis: "The private individual, who in the office has to deal with realities, needs the domestic interior to sustain him in his illusions" (*Arcades Project* 19).

spectacular and fairy-like room for which it substitutes: he could choose without regard for price.

Baudelaire explores an additional dimension of these spectacles and entrances into magical spaces beyond the enchantment and emotional gratification of shopping: once possessed, what are toys good for? What happens to desire? Toys as playthings are literally good for nothing; they are superfluous. If we recall Gautier's claim in the preface to *Mademoiselle de Maupin*, "je suis de ceux pour qui le superflu est le nécessaire" (193), we find here a similar paradox: the valuing of toys and play as aesthetic objects and aesthetic productivity, as the most superfluous and the most valuable of things and actions.

According to Baudelaire, what do children do with their toys?

> Tous les enfants parlent à leurs joujoux; les joujoux deviennent acteurs dans le grand drame de la vie, réduit par la chambre noire de leur petit cerveau. Les enfants témoignent par leurs jeux de leur grande faculté d'abstraction et de leur haute puissance imaginative. Ils jouent sans joujoux. (1: 582-83)

What is surprising here is Baudelaire's ascribing to children the power of abstraction along with their powerful imaginations. As an example of abstraction, Baudelaire speaks of the admirable simplicity of a child's "mise-en-scene" in the game of "diligence"[8] as opposed to adult audiences that demand "une perfection physique et mécanique" because of the weakness of their imaginations (1: 583). For children, toys may not even be necessary for play, given the strength of their imaginations. And yet they bring a material realization to imaginative play like that of the work of art (play, painting, or poem) as a translation of the *spirituel:*

> Cette facilité à contenter son imagination témoigne de la spiritualité de l'enfance dans ses conceptions artistiques. Le joujou est la première initiation de l'enfant à l'art, ou plutôt c'en est pour lui la première réalisation, et, l'âge mûr venu, les réalisations perfectionnées ne donneront pas à son esprit les mêmes chaleurs, ni les mêmes enthousiasmes, ni la même croyance. (1: 583).

---

[8] Cynthia Chase points out that the name of this game functions as a "dual sign" as the name, too, of devotion to work that recalls another "abusive" dual sign in Rousseau's Neuvième Promenade in *Rêveries du promeneur solitaire* (44).

But Baudelaire is careful not to praise childish play that is merely imitative, "les pauvres petites" who imitate "leur mamans." The child at play is an artist in embryo, her mind and imagination engaged, but, like artists, she should avoid mere imitation.

In fact, Baudelaire finds many of the same features in toys that he values in art. He delights in how the toy store display exceeds imitation of "life": "Toute la vie en miniature ne s'y trouve-t-elle pas, et beaucoup plus colorée, nettoyée et luisante que la vie réelle?" And the toy is meant to evoke memories – of the benevolent donor but also of the magical moment of choosing – just as for Baudelaire, the best art draws on memory. Finally he praises the new "scientific toys," describing the stereoscope and phenakistiscope, which create optical illusions, like the adept use of color in "De la couleur" of the *Salon de 1846* which he compares in its effect to a spinning top. These toys affect the children's brains and create tastes: "ils peuvent amuser long-temps, et développer dans le cerveau de l'enfant le goût des effets merveilleux et surprenants" (1: 585).

In sum, toys initiate the child in the making of art, through stimulation of the imagination, through playing as a refashioning of "life" (abstraction and exaggeration), and through realizing the "spiri-tual" in the material. The bright and bizarre beauty of some toys and the "marvelous and surprising effects" created by the new optical toys also train the child's eye. The problem of incorporating the spiritual in art, of making tangible the *surnaturel*, affects toys, too. Children want to see the soul of the toy:

> La plupart des marmots veulent surtout *voir l'âme*, les uns au bout de quelque temps d'exercice, les autres *tout de suite*. C'est la plus ou moins rapide invasion de ce désir qui fait la plus ou moins grande longévité du joujou. Je ne me sens pas le courage de blâmer cette manie enfantine : c'est une première tendance métaphysique. Quand ce désir s'est fiche dans la moelle cérébrale de l'enfant, il remplit ses doigts et ses ongles d'une agilité et d'une force singulières. L'enfant tourne, retourne son joujou, il le gratte, il le secoue, le cogne contre les murs, le jette par terre. De temps en temps il lui fait recommencer ses mouvements mécaniques, quelquefois en sens inverse. La vie merveilleuse s'arrête. L'enfant, comme le peuple qui assiège les Tuileries, fait un suprême effort ; enfin il l'entrouvre, il est le plus fort. Mais *où est l'âme ?* C'est ici que commencent l'hébétement et la tristesse. (1: 587)

Dazed and sad, the child and the people cannot get at the heart/soul of the thing, and destroy the very thing they desire. The power of the

Tuileries is not in the building; the power of the toy is not in the thing itself, but in the interaction of child and toy, in play.

Among these reflections on toys and play in general, Baudelaire describes two scenarios having to do with poor children, one framed as advice for amusing oneself through distributing cheap toys to street children, and the other, a encounter between a rich and poor child observed by the narrator. Both appear in "Le Joujou du pauvre":

> Je veux donner l'idée d'un divertissement innocent. Il y a si peu d'amusements qui ne soient pas coupables!
>
> Quand vous sortirez le matin avec l'intention décidée de flâner sur les grandes routes, remplissez vos poches de petites inventions à un sol, – telles que le polichinelle plat mû par un seul fil, les forgerons qui battent l'enclume, le cavalier et son cheval dont la queue est un sifflet, – et le long des cabarets, au pied des arbres, faites-en hommage aux enfants inconnus et pauvres que vous rencontrerez. Vous verrez leurs yeux s'agrandir démesurément. D'abord ils n'oseront pas prendre; ils douteront de leur bonheur. Puis leurs mains agripperont vivement le cadeau, et ils s'enfuiront comme font les chats qui vont manger loin de vous le morceau que vous leur avez donné, ayant appris à se défier de l'homme.
>
> Sur une route, derrière la grille d'un vaste jardin, au bout duquel apparaissait la blancheur d'un joli château frappé par le soleil, se tenait un enfant beau et frais, habillé de ces vêtements de campagne si pleins de coquetterie.
>
> Le luxe, l'insouciance et le spectacle habituel de la richesse, rendent ces enfants-là si jolis, qu'on les croirait faits d'une autre pâte que les enfants de la médiocrité ou de la pauvreté.
>
> À côté de lui, gisait sur l'herbe un joujou splendide, aussi frais que son maître, verni, doré, vêtu d'une robe pourpre, et couvert de plumets et de verroteries. Mais l'enfant ne s'occupait pas de son joujou préféré, et voici ce qu'il regardait:
>
> De l'autre côté de la grille, sur la route, entre les chardons et les orties, il y avait un autre enfant, sale, chétif, fuligineux, un de ces marmots-parias dont un œil impartial découvrirait la beauté, si, comme l'œil du connaisseur devine une peinture idéale sous un vernis de carrossier, il le nettoyait de la répugnante patine de la misère.
>
> À travers ces barreaux symboliques séparant deux mondes, la grande route et le château, l'enfant pauvre montrait à l'enfant riche son propre joujou, que celui-ci examinait avidement comme un objet rare et inconnu. Or, ce joujou, que le petit souillon agaçait, agitait et secouait dans une boîte grillée, c'était un rat vivant! Les parents, par économie sans doute, avaient tiré le joujou de la vie elle-même.
>
> Et les deux enfants se riaient l'un à l'autre fraternellement, avec des dents d'une égale blancheur. (1: 304-305)

The two most striking changes between the paragraphs in the original essay and the prose poem appear in the description of the poor child and the addition of the last sentence. In the essay, the child is described as "sale, assez chétif, un de ces marmots sur lesquels la morve se fraye lentement un chemin dans la crasse et la poussière" (1: 585). In the prose poem, the child becomes a soiled work of art, poorly varnished, a test for the discerning eye of the flâneur/critic, as opposed to the emphasis on disgust in describing the "path" of snot on his dirty face. On rewriting, Baudelaire chose to emphasize the "equal" beauty, as it were, of the children, which heightens the sense of inequity in the difference of their appearances, environments, and belongings. The echoes of the ideal of "Liberté, Egalité, et Fraternité" in the final line add resonance to the sense of injustice in this confrontation of unequal equals.[9] The irony of the rich child's preference for the disgusting, albeit live toy of the poor child is obvious, but it is also worth noting that this encounter of "fraternité" is the only instance of toys stimulating communication between children in the essay, a sort of mini-utopia.[10] It is a curious anecdote in an essay that begins with the memory of desiring and grabbing the best, most beautiful toy which remains, for the adult, a remembrance of a benefactress and a hallowed object. This anecdote implies, instead, that the child sated with beautiful things will desire what the other has and will enjoy his enjoyment, like a Humean sympathetic observer. (Of course, there is also the implication that children delight in what is disgusting, like Baudelaire himself!) In other words, admiration of the "thing" has brought them together.

In both the essay and prose poem, the "economy" of the poor child's parents is mentioned. In the essay, this is one of several remarks about the price of toys. As we have seen, Mme Panckoucke has a "small budget" out of which to buy her "treasure" of toys, and, likewise, the narrator suggests filling one's pockets with cheap toys to

---

[9] As Sanyal observes about the employment of revolutionary slogans in Baudelaire's prose poems in general, "*Le Spleen de Paris* unsteadily grounds itself in the commonplaces, or *lieux communs*, of the postrevolutionary historical imagination and its field of cultural production. The inscription of such commonplaces presses into visibility the interwoven violences of the social fabric" (64-65).

[10] In her reading of the encounter in the prose poem, Stephens notes that the poor child's shaking of the cage reproduces the class oppression that divides the children in the first place as the cage reproduces the chateau walls that confine and protect the rich child (103). She is taking issue with Jonathan Monroe's comment that the agitation of the rat suggests "the energy that might be released by the proletariat in class struggle" (109).

give out in the streets. But cheap does not imply valueless, for in the essay, it is emphasized that a simple toy, made as cheaply as possible, with "une image aussi approximative que possible avec des éléments aussi simples" is as stimulating to the child's imagination as richly realized toys, and perhaps more so: "Croyez-vous que ces images simples créent une moindre réalité dans l'esprit de l'enfant que ces merveilles du jour de l'an, qui sont plutôt un hommage de la servilité parasitique à la richesse des parents qu'un cadeau à la poésie enfantine?" (1: 584) The cheapness of these most effective toys undermines the assumption that price and value are equivalent. As with art, price does not indicate value; we might recall, for instance, Baudelaire's criticism of Horace Vernet for detailing every button, the wear on gaiters and boots, and even the verdigris marks made by weapons rubbing against the straps and belts of uniforms in his military paintings (*Salon de 1846* 2:470). In light of the parallel between art and toys, another conclusion may be drawn: just as the simplest image or even a rat may constitute an attractive toy, so art may be made of many things – a prose poem may be made from the fragments of an essay, or a lyric poem may be inspired by the beauties of a rotting corpse.[11]

* * *

C'est en feuilletant, pour la vingtième fois au moins, le fameux *Gaspard de la Nuit*, d'Aloysius Bertrand (un livre connu de vous, de moi et de quelques-uns de nos amis, n'a-t-il pas tous les droits à être appelé *fameux*?) que l'idée m'est venue de tenter quelque chose d'analogue, et d'appliquer à la description de la vie moderne, ou plutôt d'*une* vie moderne et plus abstraite, le procédé qu'il avait appliqué à la peinture de la vie ancienne, si étrangement pittoresque. (1: 275)

To return to the passage from Baudelaire's dedication of *Le Spleen de Paris* to Arsène Houssaye, quoted more fully, we might question again what is meant by a modern and more abstract life, as

---

[11] Monroe reads the difference between the two toys symbolically: if the toy initiates the child to art, "then the literary art to which the poor child receives initiation would certainly be unadorned prose, that of the rich child the aristocratic art of classical French poetry with its intricate rhyme schemes and other aesthetic devices and adornments" (107). But Baudelaire's discussion of play in the essay, "Morale du joujou," complicates this symbolism since the intricacy and richness of finish of the toy may be inversely proportional to its art-inducing capacity. Of course, Monroe is also implying that the rat **is** the preferred artwork/toy as prose in a work of prose.

opposed to the ancient and picturesque life depicted by Bertrand. It is "abstract" that surprises us; it is set up in contrast with "picturesque," yet implies a distancing from the phenomenal that seems opposed to Baudelaire's seeking and rendering of the sensual in these prose poems and elsewhere. But we may understand his correction (not "la vie moderne," but "*une* vie moderne et plus abstraite") as a critical comment on the nature of modern life – that in modernity the subject knows only his life (*une* vie modern) from which he is distanced (plus abstraite).

Nonetheless, desire drives this subject towards things, by which this very subjectivity is formed and threatened. In the sensory experience the *moi* may feel both delight and pain: "L'énergie dans la volupté crée une malaise et une souffrance positive" ("Le *Confiteor* de l'Artiste") – an experience of the sublime. More frequently, the sensorium is imagined, informed by a "nostalgie du pays qu'on ignore" ("L'Invitation au voyage"); it takes the form of luxurious furnishings and goods and gives form to his desire for his lover, and a means of configuring her otherness, making her as readable through such transformation into things. Baudelaire protests the denial of the sensorium to the poor, a denial that is often partial in the new spectacle-filled public space (the poor can see the glittering café; the widow catches strains of music outside the concert walls).

Creativity and play offer a solution to such deprivation and class division as Baudelaire's several prose poems about children and toys suggest. Only in the case of toys is gift-giving efficacious, leading to good results and the bridging of social class. And, if the child is the ideal recipient of gifts, so, too, is the child the ideal artist, lacking the consciousness of inadequacy that the adult finds so disabling in "Le *Confiteor* de l'Artiste." Imagination and creativity bridge the divide between subject and thing as the subject invests himself in the thing through play and the making. But the thing nonetheless puzzles: its phenomenality informed by so many meanings still seems to hide a soul that remains elusive. The drama of desire and projection of meaning continues: in shops, in studios, in galleries and museums, alongside Baudelaire's sharp social criticism of bourgeois monopolization of such things and their enjoyment.

Afterword

What does it mean to consider Baudelaire the poet of high capitalism? Sanyal, in the "Afterword" of her study of Baudelaire's assault on and engagement with the violence of modernity through irony, sums up the economic catalyst to this violence as follows:

> As Walter Benjamin famously observed, Baudelaire is the poet of high capitalism. The self-conscious production of violence in his poetry invites an ever-actual inquiry into the hidden structures of sacrifice in capitalist, imperial modernity. In a prescient diagnosis of commerce as an order of terror, maintained by methods that would make humanity shudder ("par des moyens qui feraient frissonner notre humanité actuelle"), Baudelaire attests to nascent structures of domination in a life-world governed by commercial investments and the quest for new markets. His poems offer a fractured but legible genealogy of reification. They perform the logic of commodification in shifting arenas, moving from the private spaces of the bourgeois interior into the urban and even global display of commodities. (203)

This general depiction of the ravages of industrial modernity and its products on everyday life is part of a tradition in cultural criticism as Sanyal's homage to Benjamin implies. But this picture presents a partial truth, for it does not account for the part played by aesthetics that drove Baudelaire's own material desires, themselves bound up with the art he admired and wrote about and his own creative work. These desires are reflected in his works, full of material objects that serve as sources of stimulation and comfort, and informed by an aesthetics that would deploy a full sensorium.

There is also a different story unfolding among some historians concerning the birth of the modern consumer. The formation of patterns of consumption that was in place through the mid-nineteenth century may well predate the Industrial Revolution. Jan de Vries has coined the term "industrious revolution" to describe these shifts in the relationship between individuals and households and their material belongings that began in Holland as early as the seventeenth century. During the course of the long eighteenth century, households themselves underwent some division of labor, diverting more labor into market-oriented activities, motivated by new consumer aspirations

(122). Recent studies of probate inventories shed some light on these new patterns. For instance, in the early seventeenth century, individuals in every social class lived among material goods that they had inherited and that would survive them (144). But in the long eighteenth century (after 1650), "consumer priorities shifted from the standard of the material – the metal, the wood – to the standard of the workmanship. That is, the appeal of an object was located less in its intrinsic value – the scrap value of the material – than in the appearance given to it in the processes of fabrication" (146). These new goods were often more breakable – glass goblets instead of pewter, for instance, – requiring more frequent replacement, but the new materials were also more functional on the whole. Clearly they could also reflect fashion, adding novelty, taste, and stylishness to the calculus of their value. What the probate inventories have shown is that this changing world of goods was available to a broadening range of social classes even before the Industrial Revolution. According to one study of pauper inventories, the poor of the late eighteenth century "were materially better provided than the wealthier husbandmen of a century earlier" (151). Consumption patterns also showed clustering, or "consumption bundles"; the taste for coffee, tea, and sugar would be accompanied by the acquisition of coffee or tea pots, spoons, and other accoutrements, creating aspects of a "habitus" in Bourdieu's sense. But, as De Vries stresses, such consumer choice, creating "distinctions," was available to a broader range of society than just the wealthy. Yet for the poorer classes there was a significant cost: the diversion of labor outside the household, the stepped-up participation of women and children in the labor force. Critics observed a trend that they deemed detrimental to the family as individual incomes supported individuated tastes, and sociability moved outside the home (178). But that is a topic beyond the scope of this book.

Such economic history does shed light on consumer desire in Baudelaire's Paris. The crowds who thronged the industrial exhibitions were already schooled in the estimate of the value of things through their appearance (which the display would only reinforce). Things carried with them reference to a life style, functioning as synecdoches for a habitus to which the viewer aspired, a material imaginary. In other words, as a sort of fetish.

Bill Brown in "The Tyranny of Things (Trivia in Karl Marx and Mark Twain)" points out the difference between Marx's commodity fetish and Walter Benjamin's appropriation of Marx's fetish. The commodity serves as a starting point for *Capital*, as Brown quips, "*in media res*, in the midst of *things*" (450). But Marx's fetish as defined, despite the surreal image of a table that "stands on its head, and evolves out of its wooden brain grotesque ideas," has nothing to do with the consumer desire that "fetish" seems to invoke for any reader after Freud:

> This mystery story – predicated on the difference between the commodity's apparent and actual source of value and requiring Marx to write the vast and complex history of social relations that the commodity as such obscures – never begins to address the mystery of consumer desire, without which capitalism (in any of its stages) cannot be sustained. (451)

In Benjamin's use of Marx's fetish, Brown sees a mistake, which he diagnoses as a "compensation for having abandoned the theoretical foundation of *Capital*'s first chapter while preserving its dominant trope" (453):

> When he [Benjamin] writes that "world exhibitions are places of pilgrimage to the commodity fetish," he confuses (or conflates) commodity fetishism with a scene of seeing, returning, the question of value to the aesthetics of the every-day, to a materialist phenomenology, and thus making a muck of Marx: "'Europe is off to *view* the merchandise.'" [Brown's emphasis] (452)

And so, in Brown's reading, Benjamin understands the institution of the exhibition and its display strategies as distorting the value of the object, not exchange itself, the Marxian view.

The Arcades Project itself is evidence of the extent to which the study of the everyday practices of nineteenth-century life, especially in Paris, occupied and fascinated Benjamin. Clearly he recognized the ways and new urban venues in which commodities drew consumers, something perhaps that Marx would forget in emphasizing the asocial nature of the commodity as perceived, a fetish in that the social relations that are embedded in it are forgotten and hidden by its exchange value. There is an aspect of Marx's fetish, however, that intimates his recognition of its power to fascinate, beyond the image of the acrobatic chair: the fetish refers to religious beliefs:

> In order, therefore, to find an analogy, we must have recourse to the mist-enveloped regions of the religious world. In that world the productions of the human brain appear as independent beings endowed with life, and entering into

relation both with one another and the human race. So it is in the world of commodities with the products of men's hands. This I call the Fetishism which attaches itself to the products of labour, so soon as they are produced as commodities, and which is therefore inseparable from the production of commodities. (72)

In this sense, commodities are an imaginary form of the product in the "bourgeois economy" like gods who are embodied ideas. That is, objects embody and hide social relations, and have relationships with other objects and with people. Marx's fetish implies both a misled imagination and the animation of objects as concealers of real social relations and something that, even in concealment, enters into social relations. The power of the commodity to fascinate and to speak to the consumer is thus implied, and so Marx's fetish, too, is shaped by the notion of display or apparition, common to religious ritual and the market. This passage in Marx indicates not only his awareness of the power of consumer desire, but that it may be shaped by pre-existing cultural practices, here those surrounding religious adoration.

Brown's point resonates with a familiar criticism of Benjamin, that he lets the Marxian view of the economy slip away before the pull of material culture. But, in light of his characterization of the commodity as comparable to a religious fetish, does Marx himself open the door to a more cultural understanding of commodities? Regardless, when things assume commodity status, they are by definition appraised or assigned value, but that exchange value by no means exhausts their cultural status or resonance. It is a mistake to see what may be an increased commodification of everyday life, or at least a proliferation of commodities as a simple flattening out of meaning in material culture. Both display practices and literally putting things up for sale work to draw cultural evaluation and signification, as shown in the reviews of the industrial exhibitions. Further, one effect of display is to heighten the everyday realm of visual sensation, whetting the appetite for touch, feel, taste, the constant assault of new things on the sensorium. Finally, the experience of visiting the exhibitions brought to the forefront the difference between seeing and owning. Such tensions form or discipline the viewing subject and reflect class divisions; they also translate philosophically into age-old conflicts between the eye and the hand, or of the hierarchy of the senses, as the public seeks to make sense of a new culture of spectacle. How does the nineteenth-century subject respond? Baudelaire's poetry in which he strives to incorporate more and more of the sensorium gives us a window into the exhilaration and exhaustion of the subject in this process.

It is, of course, not just the appearance of things, but the discourse that frames them that creates their cultural worth and significance. I have substituted "economic" for "political" in the following passage by Rancière on the literally productive power of discourse:

> [Economic] statements and literary locutions produce effects in reality. They define models of speech or action but also regimes of sensible intensity. They draft maps of the visible, trajectories between the visible and the sayable, relationships between modes of being, modes of saying, and modes of doing and making. They define variations of sensible intensities, perceptions, and the abilities of bodies. (*Politics of Aesthetics* 39)

This study has considered economic statements to be as potent as literary ones in shaping sensibilities – of order, of equity and equivalence, of value. When the order seems a sham and a lie to the subject experiencing those economic forces, other discourses arise out of the same logic and vocabulary to counter the former: dissonance of form, social disequilibrium. We see this in the temporality that disturbs economic equilibrium as economic subjects may starve before the market finds its balance. We see this in the trajectory of Baudelaire's writing, not only in shifts from the "Ideal" to the miasma of personal spleen and ennui, but in the adjustment of an aesthetic based in the complicated harmonies of the correspondences that redefines beauty as the bizarre, and seeks it through an exotic other and utterly transformed self, and in the jerky tempos of modernity and the real of an overwrought human artifice, the made-up beauty of Parisian streets. He shows us the possibility of *jouissance*, of delectation without possession, and its frustrations, when poverty affords only a partial view, a fleeting glimpse, a distant snatch of music.

Works Cited

Allen, Mary B. "P.J. Proudhon in the Revolution of 1848." *Journal of Modern History* 42.1 (1952): 1-14.

Andrews, Naomi J. "Utopian Androgyny: Romantic Socialists Confront Individualism in July Monarchy France." *French Historical Studies* 26.3 (2003): 437-57.

Bastiat, Frédéric. *Economic Harmonies*. Trans. H. Hayden Boyers. Princeton, NJ: Van Nostrand, 1964.

Baudelaire, Charles. *Œuvres Complètes*. Ed. Claude Pichois. 2 vols. Paris: Pléiade-Gallimard, 1975-76.

Baudrillard, Jean. *Seduction*. Trans. Brian Singer. New York: St. Martin's, 1990.

Beecher, Jonathan. *Charles Fourier: The Visionary and His World*. Berkeley: U of California P, 1986.

Bell-Villada, Gene H. *Art for Art's Sake & Literary Life: How Politics and Markets Helped Shape the Ideology & Culture of Aestheticism 1790-1990*. Lincoln: U of Nebraska P, 1996.

Benjamin, Walter. *The Arcades Project*. Ed. Rolf Tiedemann. Trans. Howard Eiland and Kevin McLaughlin. Cambridge, MA: Harvard UP, 1999.

——.*Charles Baudelaire: A Lyric Poet in the Era of High Capitalism*. Trans. Harry Zohn. London: NLB, 1973.

——. *Illuminations*. Trans. Harry Zohn. New York: Schocken, 1968.

Bigelow, Gordon. *Fiction, Famine, and the Rise of Economics in Victorian Britain and Ireland*. Cambridge: Cambridge UP, 2003.

Black, R. D. Collison. "Utility" in *The New Palgrave: Utility and Probability*. Ed. John Eatwell, Murray Milgate, and Peter Newman. New York: Norton, 1987. 295-302.

Blaug, Mark. *Economic theory in retrospect*. 5th ed. Cambridge: Cambridge UP, 1997.

Bonner, John. *Economic efficiency and social justice: the development of utilitarian ideas in economics from Bentham to Edgeworth*. Aldershot, Hants, England: Elgar, 1995.

Bourdieu, Pierre. "The Market of Symbolic Goods." Trans. R. Swyer. *The Field of Cultural Production: Essays on Art and Literature.* Ed. Randal Johnson. New York: Columbia UP, 1993. 112-41.

——. "The link between literary and artistic struggles." *Artistic Relations: Literature and the Visual Arts in Nineteenth-Century France.* Eds. Peter Collier and Robert Lethbridge. New Haven: Yale UP, 1994. 30-39.

——. *The Rules of Art : Genesis and Structure of the Literary Field.* Trans. Susan Emanuel. Stanford, CA : Stanford UP, 1996. Trans. of *Les Règles de l'Art : Genèse et structures du champ littéraire.* 1992.

"La Bourgeoisie n'est plus qu'un vieux mot." *Le Corsaire-Satan* 4 November 1844: 1.

Boym, Svetlana. *The Future of Nostalgia.* New York: Basic, 2001.

Brantlinger, Patrick. *Fictions of State: Culture and Credit in Britain, 1694-1994.* Ithaca: Cornell UP, 1996.

Brennan, Timothy. "Cosmo-Theory." *South Atlantic Quarterly* 100.3 (2001): 659-91.

Brix, Michel. "Modern Beauty versus Platonist Beauty." Trans. Tony Campbell. *Baudelaire and the Poetics of Modernity.* Ed. Patricia A. Ward and James S. Patty. Nashville: Vanderbilt UP, 2001. 1-14.

Brombert, Victor. "The Will to Ecstasy: The Example of Baudelaire's 'La Chevelure.'" *Yale French Studies* 50 (1974): 55-63.

Brown, Bill. "Reification, Reanimation, and the American Uncanny." *Critical Inquiry* 32.2 (2006): 175-207.

——. *A Sense of Things: The Object Matter of American Literature.* Chicago: U of Chicago P, 2003.

——. "Thing Theory." *Critical Inquiry* 28.1 (2001): 1-21.

——. "The Tyranny of Things (Trivia in Karl Marx and Mark Twain)." *Critical Inquiry* 28.2 (2002): 442-69.

Buck-Morss, Susan. "Envisioning Capital: Political Economy on Display." *Critical Inquiry* 21.2 (1995): 434-67.

Burton, Richard D. E. *Baudelaire and the Second Republic: Writing and Revolution.* New York: Clarendon-Oxford UP, 1991.

Campbell, Colin. *The Romantic Ethic and the Spirit of Modern Consumerism.* Oxford: Blackwell, 1987.

Canard, Nicolas-François. *Principes d'économie politique.* Paris : Buisson, 1801; reprint, Rome: Bizzarri, 1969.

Caygill, Howard. *Art of Judgement*. Oxford : Blackwell, 1989.

Chambers, Ross. "Baudelaire's Dedicatory Practice." *SubStance* 56 (1988): 5-17.

Chase, Cynthia. "Paragon, Parergon: Baudelaire translates Rousseau." *Diacritics* 11.2 (1981): 42-51.

Commission impériale. *Rapport sur l'exposition universelle de 1855 présenté à l'Empereur par S.A.I le Prince Napoléon*. Paris: Imprimerie impériale, 1857.

Compagnon, Antoine. *The Five Paradoxes of Modernity*. Trans. Franklin Philip. New York: Columbia UP, 1994.

Connell, Philip. *Romanticism, Economics and the Question of "Culture."* Oxford: Oxford UP, 2001.

Cooper, Brian P., and Margueritte S. Murphy. "The Death of the Author at the Birth of Social Science: The Cases of Harriet Martineau and Adolphe Quetelet." *Studies in History and Philosophy of Science* 31.1 (2000): 1-36.

——. "Object Lessons: How the Humanities and Social Sciences Learn Differently from Things and Why That Matters." *International Journal of the Humanities* 5.9 (2007): 141-50.

Cousin, Victor. *Cours de l'histoire de la philosophie moderne*. Vol. 2. Paris: Ladrange Didier, 1846. 5 vols.

Crary, Jonathan. *Techniques of the Observer: On Vision and Modernity in the Nineteenth Century*. Cambridge, Mass.: MIT P, 1990.

Dallal, Jenine Abboushi. "French Cultural Imperialism and the Aesthetics of Extinction." *Yale Journal of Criticism* 13.2 (2000): 229-65.

"De l'exposition des produits de l'industrie." *L'Artiste* 2nd ser. 2 (1839): 1-4.

de Man, Paul. *Blindness and Insight: Essays in the Rhetoric of Contemporary Criticism*. 2nd ed. Minneapolis: U of Minnesota P, 1983.

de Marchi, Neil "Adam Smith's accommodation of 'altogether endless' desires." *Consumers and luxury: consumer culture in Europe 1650-1850*. Ed. Maxine Berg and Helen Clifford. Manchester: Manchester UP, 1999. 18-36.

Derrida, Jacques. *Given Time: I. Counterfeit Money*. Trans. Peggy Kamuf. Chicago: U of Chicago P, 1992.

Desolme, Charles. "Paris Industriel. Exposition de l'industrie nationale. " *Le Corsaire* 6 May 1844: 1-3.

De Vries, Jan. *The Industrious Revolution : Consumer Behavior and the Household Economy, 1650 to the Present.* Cambridge : Cambridge UP, 2008.

Dickson, W. "Exposition de l'Industrie. Orfèvrerie de M. Odiot." *Le Commerce* 26 June 1844: 3.

"Distribution des récompenses accordées à l'industrie." *Journal du Commerce* 16 July 1834: 2.

Dixon, William, and David Wilson. "'Sympathy', 'character' and economic equilibrium." *Equilibrium in Economics: Scope and Limits.* Ed. Valeria Mosini. London: Routledge, 2007. 77-91.

Dupuit, Jules. *De l'utilité et de sa mesure.* Torino: Riforma Sociale, 1933.

Ekelund, Robert B., and Robert F. Hébert. *Secret Origins of Modern Microeconomics: Dupuit and the Engineers.* Chicago: U of Chicago P, 1999.

"Exposition de l'industrie française." *L'Artiste* 7 (1834): 193-94.

"Exposition de l'industrie française. Les nielles françaises. – La lithographie. Les bronzes." *L'Artiste* 7 (1834): 249-52.

"Exposition des produits de l'industrie nationale." *La Presse* 5 May 1844: 1-2.

F. "Salon de 1844. I." *Le Corsaire* 22 March 1844: 1-3.

——. "Salon de 1844. II." *Le Corsaire* 4 April 1844: 1-2.

"Feuilleton. Du goût dans les arts industriels." *Journal du Commerce* 10 February 1839: 1-2.

"Feuilleton. Exposition des produits de l'industrie." *Journal du Commerce* 4 May 1834: 1-2.

Fix, Théodore. "Exposition des produits de l'industrie." *Journal des Économistes* April 1844: 1-11.

Fontaine, Philippe. "The French Economists and Politics, 1750-1850: The Science and Art of Political Economy." *Canadian Journal of Economics* 29. 2 (1996): 379-93.

Forget, Evelyn L. "J.-B. Say and Adam Smith: An Essay in the Transmission of Ideas." *Canadian Journal of Economics* 26.1 (1993): 121-33.

——. "Jean-Baptiste Say and Spontaneous Order." *History of Political Economy* 33. 2 (2001): 193-218.

——. *The Social Economics of Jean-Baptiste Say: Markets and virtue.* London: Routledge, 1999.

Foucault, Michel. *The Archaeology of Knowledge and the Discourse on Language.* Trans. by A. M. Sheridan of *L'Archaéologie du Savoir* (1969) and *L'ordre du discours* (1971). New York: Pantheon, 1972.

——. *The Order of Things: An Archaeology of the Human Sciences.* 1970. Trans. *Les mots et les choses.* 1966. New York: Vintage-Random, 1973.

Friedman, Geraldine. "Baudelaire's Theory of Practice: Ideology and Difference in 'Les yeux des pauvres.'" *PMLA* 104.3 (1989): 317-28.

Friedman, Susan Stanford. "Periodizing Modernism: Postcolonial Modernities and the Space/Time Borders of Modernist Studies." *Modernism/Modernity* 13.3 (2006): 425-43.

Gagnier, Regenia. *The Insatiability of Human Wants: Economics and Aesthetics in Market Society.* Chicago: U of Chicago P, 2000.

Gallagher, Catherine. *The Body Economic: Life, Death, and Sensation in Political Economy and the Victorian Novel.* Princeton, NJ: Princeton UP, 2006.

Gautier, Théophile. *Les Beaux-Arts en Europe.* Paris: Michel Lévy Frères, 1857.

——. "Exposition des manufactures royales de Sèvres, des Gobelins et de Beauvais." *La Presse* 21 June 1844: 1-3.

——.Préface de *Mademoiselle de Maupin.* Paris: Gallimard, 1973.

Guillory, John. *Cultural Capital: The Problem of Literary Canon Formation.* Chicago: U of Chicago P, 1993

Guyer, Paul. "Beauty and Utility in Eighteenth-Century Aesthetics." *Eighteenth-Century Studies* 35. 3 (2002): 439-53.

Hamon, Philippe. *Expositions : Literature and Architecture in Nineteenth-Century France.* Trans. Katia Sainson-Frank and Lisa Maguire. Berkeley: U of California P, 1992.

Harpham, Geoffrey Galt. "Aesthetics and the Fundamentals of Modernity." *Aesthetics and Ideology.* Ed. George Levine. New Brunswick, NJ: Rutgers UP, 1994. 124-49.

Heck, Francis S. "'La Beauté': Enigma of Irony." *Nineteenth-Century French Studies* 10.1-2 (1981-82): 85-95.

Herbert, Christopher. *Culture and Anomie: Ethnographic Imagination in the Nineteenth Century.* Chicago: U of Chicago P, 1991.

Hiddleston, J.A. *Baudelaire and* Le Spleen de Paris. Oxford: Clarendon, 1987.

Hiner, Susan. "Lust for *Luxe*: 'Cashmere Fever' in Nineteenth-Century France." *Journal for Early Modern Cultural Studies* 5.1 (2005): 76-98.

Houssaye, Arsène. "Salon de 1844, I. - Les Absents." *L'Artiste* 10 March 1844: 145-47.

——. "Salon de 1844, II." *L'Artiste* 17 March 1844: 161-62.

Howells, Bernard. *Individualism, Dandyism and the Philosophy of History*. Oxford: Legenda, 1996.

Hugo, Victor. Préface de *Cromwell. Théâtre complet de Victor Hugo*. Eds. J.-J. Thierry and Josette Mélèze. Vol. 1. Paris: Pléiade-Gallimard, 1963. 409-54.

Hülsmann, Jörg Guido. "Bastiat's Legacy in Economics." *Quarterly Journal of Austrian Economics* 4.4 (2001): 55-70.

Hume, David. *A Treatise of Human Nature*. Ed. David Fate Norton and Mary J. Norton. Oxford: Oxford UP, 2000.

Ingrao, Bruna, and Giorgio Israel. *The Invisible Hand: Economic Equilibrium in the History of Science*. Trans. Ian McGilvray. Cambridge, MA: MIT P, 1990.

J.B. "Feuilleton. Exposition des produits de l'industrie. (1er article.) Des expositions des produits de l'industrie en général." *Journal du Commerce* 1 May 1834 : 1-2.

——. "Feuilleton. Exposition des produits de l'industrie. Salle des tissus. -- (1er article.) – Des laines." *Journal du Commerce* 12 May 1834 : 1-2.

Jameson, Fredric. *A Singular Modernity: Essay on the Ontology of the Present*. London: Verso, 2002.

Janin, Jules. "Exposition des produits de l'industrie. (Premier Article.)" *L'Artiste* 2nd ser. 3 (1839) : 17-23.

Jasenas, Eliane. "Stendhal et Baudelaire: La dédicace 'Aux Bourgeois.' La problématique d'un texte." *Nineteenth-Century French Studies* 9.3-4 (1981): 192-203.

Johnson, Barbara. *Mother Tongues : Sexuality, Trials, Motherhood, Translation*. Cambridge, MA and London : Harvard UP, 2003.

Kant, Immanuel. *The Critique of Judgement*. Trans. James Creed Meredith. Oxford: Clarendon-Oxford UP, 1952.

Kelley, D. J. "Deux aspects du *Salon de 1846* de Baudelaire: la dédicace Aux Bourgeois et la Couleur." *Forum for Modern Language Studies* 5.4 (1969): 331-46.

Krueger, Cheryl Leah. *The Art of Procrastination: Baudelaire's Poetry in Prose.* Newark: U of Delaware P, 2007.

Lapaire, Pierre J. "L'Esthétique binaire de Baudelaire : 'À une passante' et la beauté fugitive." *Romance notes* 35.3 (1995): 281-91.

Laviron, Gabriel. "Exposition des produits de l'industrie." *L'Artiste* 28 April 1844: 265-67.

——. "Exposition des produits de l'industrie." *L'Artiste* 3 May 1844 : 11-12.

——. "Exposition des produits de l'industrie. Tissus – meubles – machines." *L'Artiste* 4 August 1844: 217-20.

——. "Exposition des produits de l'industrie." *L'Artiste* 12 May 1844: 29-30.

——. "Salon de 1844. II." *L'Artiste* 17 March 1844: 161-64.

Lemaitre, Henri, ed. *Curiosités esthétiques L'Art romantique et autres Œuvres critiques.* By Charles Baudelaire. Paris: Garnier Frères, 1962.

Littré, Émile. *Dictionnaire de la Langue Française.* Vol. 1. Paris: L. Hachette, 1863.

MacKay, John. *Inscription and Modernity: from Wordsworth to Mandelstam.* Bloomington: Indiana UP, 2006.

Mainardi, Patricia. *Art and Politics of the Second Empire: The Universal Expositions of 1855 and 1867.* New Haven: Yale UP, 1987.

Majluf, Natalia. "'Ce n'est pas Le Pérou,' or, the Failure of Authenticity: Marginal Cosmopolitans at the Paris Universal Exhibition of 1855." *Critical Inquiry* 23.4 (1997): 868-93.

Marder, Elissa. *Dead Time: Temporal Disorders in the Wake of Modernity (Baudelaire and Flaubert).* Stanford, CA: Stanford UP, 2001.

Milgate, Murray. "Equilibrium: development of the concept." *The New Palgrave: The Invisible Hand.* Ed. John Eatwell, Murray Milgate, and Peter Newman. New York: Norton, 1987. 105-13.

Millard, Charles W. "Sculpture and Theory in Nineteenth Century France." *Journal of Aesthetics and Art Criticism* 34.1 (1975): 15-20.

Miller, Paul Allen. "Beauty, Tragedy and the Grotesque: A Dialogical Esthetics in Three Sonnets by Baudelaire." *French Forum* 18.3 (1993): 319-33.

Mitchell, W. J. T. "Romanticism and the Life of Things: Fossils, Totems, and Images." *Critical Inquiry* 28.1 (2001): 167-84.

Mitzman, Arthur. "Michelet and Social Romanticism: Religion, Revolution, Nature." *Journal of the History of Ideas* 57.4 (1996): 659-82.

Monroe, Jonathan. *A Poverty of Objects: The Prose Poem and the Politics of Genre.* Ithaca: Cornell UP, 1987.

Moriarty, Michael. "Structures of cultural production in nineteenth-century France." *Artistic Relations: Literature and the Visual Arts in Nineteenth-Century France.* Eds. Peter Collier and Robert Lethbridge. New Haven: Yale UP, 1994. 15-29.

Osborne, Peter. "Modernisms and Mediations." *Rediscovering Aesthetics: Transdisciplinary Voices from Art History, Philosophy, and Art Practice.* Ed. Francis Halsall, Julia Jansen, and Tony O'Connor. Stanford, CA: Stanford UP, 2009. 163-177.

Phillips, Jennifer. "Relative Color: Baudelaire, Chevreul, and the Reconsideration of Critical Methodology." *Nineteenth-Century French Studies* 33.3-4 (2005): 342-57.

Pichois, Claude. Notes. Baudelaire, Charles. *Œuvres Complètes.* Ed. Claude Pichois. 2 vols. Paris: Pléiade-Gallimard, 1975-76.

Poe, Edgar Allan. "The Philosophy of Furniture." *Poetry and Tales.* New York: Library of America, 1984. 382-87.

Pollock, Sheldon. "Cosmopolitan and Vernacular in History." *Public Culture* 12.3 (2000): 591-625.

Pommier, Jean. *La Mystique de Baudelaire.* 1932. Rpt. Geneva: Slatkine, 1967.

Poovey, Mary. *Genres of the Credit Economy: Mediating Value in Eighteenth- and Nineteenth-Century Britain.* Chicago: U of Chicago P, 2008.

——. *A History of the Modern Fact: Problems of Knowledge in the Sciences of Wealth and Society.* Chicago: U of Chicago P, 1998.

Proudhon, Pierre-Joseph. *System of Economical Contradictions or, the Philosophy of Misery.* Trans. Benjamin R. Tucker. Boston: Benjamin R. Tucker, 1888. Rpt. New York: Arno, 1972.

Rancière, Jacques. "The Aesthetic Dimension: Aesthetics, Politics, Knowledge." *Critical Inquiry* 36.1 (2009): 1-19.

——. *Aesthetics and Its Discontents.* Trans. Steven Corcoran. Cambridge: Polity, 2009.

——. *The Flesh of Words: the Politics of Writing.* Trans. Charlotte Mandell. Stanford, CA: Stanford UP, 2004.

——. *The Philosopher and His Poor.* Trans. John Drury, Corinne Oster, and Andrew Parker. Ed. Andrew Parker. Durham: Duke UP, 2003.

——. *The Politics of Aesthetics: The Distribution of the Sensible. Le Partage du sensible: Esthétique et politique.* 2000. Trans. Gabriel Rockhill. London: Continuum, 2004.

——. "The Politics of Literature." *SubStance* 103.33.1 (2004): 10-24.

Raser, Timothy. *A Poetics of Art Criticism: the Case of Baudelaire.* Chapel Hill: UNC Department of Romance Languages, distributed by U of North Carolina P, 1989.

——. "The Politics of Art Criticism: Baudelaire's *Exposition Universelle.*" *Nineteenth-Century French Studies* 26.3-4 (1998): 336-45.

Ray, William. "Talking About Art: The French Royal Academy Salons and the Formation of the Discursive Citizen." *Eighteenth-Century Studies* 37.4 (2004): 527-52.

Ricardo, David. *Letters 1810-1815.* Vol. 6 of *The Works and Correspondance of David Ricardo.* Ed. Piero Sraffa. 11 vols. Cambridge: Cambridge UP, 1952.

——. *Letters 1819-June 1821.* Vol. 8 of *The Works and Correspondance of David Ricardo.* Ed. Piero Sraffa. 11 vols. Cambridge: Cambridge UP, 1952.

——. *Letters July 1821-1823.* Vol. 9 of *The Works and Correspondance of David Ricardo.* Ed. Piero Sraffa. 11 vols. Cambridge: Cambridge UP, 1952.

——. *On the Principles of Political Economy and Taxation.* Vol. 2 of *The Works and Correspondance of David Ricardo.* Ed. Piero Sraffa. 11 vols. Cambridge: Cambridge UP, 1981.

Richter, Mario. *Baudelaire,* Les Fleurs du Mal*: Lecture intégrale.* Genève: Slatkine, 2001.

Robb, Graham. "Le *Salon de 1846*: Baudelaire s'explique." *Nineteenth-Century French Studies* 15.4 (1987): 415-24.

Rosen, Frederick. *Classical Utilitarianism from Hume to Mill.* London: Routledge, 2003.

Rothschild, Emma. *Economic Sentiments: Adam Smith, Condorcet, and the Enlightenment.* Cambridge, MA: Harvard UP, 2001.

Ryan, Judith. "More Seductive Than Phryne: Baudelaire, Gerome, Rilke, and the Problem of Autonomous Art." *PMLA* 108.5 (1993): 1128-41.

"Salon de 1834. Conclusion." *L'Artiste* 7 (1834): 159-63.

Sanyal, Debarati. *The Violence of Modernity: Baudelaire, Irony, and the Politics of Form.* Baltimore: Johns Hopkins UP, 2006.

Say, Jean-Baptiste. *Traité d'économie politique.* Paris: Calmann-Lévy, 1972.

Schlossman, Beryl. "The Night of the Poet: Baudelaire, Benjamin, and the Woman in the Street." *MLN* 119 (2004): 1013-32.

Sewell, William H. Jr. *Work and revolution in France: The language of labor from the old regime to 1848.* Cambridge: Cambridge UP, 1980.

Shakespeare, William. *A Midsummer Night's Dream. The Riverside Shakespeare.* Ed. G. Blakemore Evans. Boston: Houghton, 1974. 222-249.

Sharp, Lynn. "Metempsychosis and Social Reform: The Individual and the Collective in Romantic Socialism." *French Historical Studies* 27.2 (2004): 349-79.

Smith, Adam. *The Theory of Moral Sentiments.* Oxford: Clarendon, 1976; Indianapolis: Liberty, 1982.

——. *The Wealth of Nations.* New York: Modern Library, 1994.

Spitzer, Alan B. *The French Generation of 1820.* Princeton, NJ: Princeton UP, 1987.

Stanford Friedman, Susan. "Periodizing Modernism: Postcolonial Modernities and the Space/Time Borders of Modernist Studies." *Modernism/Modernity* 13.3 (2006): 425-43.

Stephens, Sonya. *Baudelaire's Prose Poems: The Practice and Politics of Irony.* Oxford: Oxford UP, 1999.

Stewart, Susan. *On Longing: Narratives of the Miniature, the Gigantic, the Souvenir, the Collection.* Baltimore: Johns Hopkins UP, 1984.

Terdiman, Richard. "Deconstructing Memory: On Representing the Past and Theorizing Culture in France since the Revolution." *Diacritics* 15.4 (1985): 13-36.

——. *Discourse/Counter-Discourse: The Theory and Practice of Symbolic Resistance in Nineteenth-Century France.* Ithaca: Cornell UP, 1985.

Le Travail universel: Revue complète des Œuvres de l'art et de l'industrie, exposées à Paris en 1855. Ed. J.-J. Arnoux. Paris: Bureaux de la Patrie, 1856.

Van Slyke, Gretchen. "Les épiciers au musée: Baudelaire et l'artiste bourgeois." *Romantisme: revue de dix-neuvième siècle* 55 (1987): 55-66.

Williams, Raymond. *Keywords: a vocabulary of culture and society.* Rev. ed. New York: Oxford UP, 1983.

Williams, Rosalind H. *Dream Worlds: Mass Consumption in Late Nineteenth-Century France.* Berkeley: U of California P, 1982.

Woodmansee, Martha, and Mark Osteen. "Taking account of the New Economic Criticism: an historical introduction." Introduction. *The New Economic Criticism: Studies at the intersection of literature and economics.* London: Routledge, 1999. 1-50.

Z. "Exposition des produits de l'industrie. Les Meubles. V (1)." *La Presse* 22 June 1844: 1-2.

Žižek, Slavoj. "The Ongoing 'Soft Revolution.'" *Critical Inquiry* 30.2 (2004): 292-323.

——. *The Sublime Object of Ideology.* London: Verso, 1989

Index I

Works by Baudelaire

Index II